FINLAND

SWEDEN

NORWAY

RUSSIA

DENMARK

LITHUANIA

BELARUS

IRELAND

UNITED
KINGDOM

NETHERLANDS

POLAND

GERMANY

BELGIUM

FRANCE

AUSTRIA

HUNGARY

SWITZERLAND

SLOVENIA

CROATIA

ITALY

YUGOSLAVIA

PORTUGAL

SPAIN

TURKEY

EUROPEAN DESIGN ANNUAL 5

A RotoVision Book
Published and Distributed by RotoVision SA
Rue Du Bugnon 7
CH-1299 Crans-Près-Céligny
Switzerland

RotoVision SA,
Sales & Production Office,
Sheridan House,
112-116A Western Road,
Hove, East Sussex,
BN3 1DD,
United Kingdom

Tel: +44 (0) 1273 72 72 68
Fax: +44 (0) 1273 72 72 69
email: sales@rotovision.com
www.rotovision.com

10 9 8 7 6 5 4 3 2 1

ISBN: 2-88046-472-2

Book design by Karen J Robins for Red Design
Tel/ Fax: +44 (0) 1273 321 621
www.delete-me.com

Production and separations in Singapore by
Provision Pte. Ltd.
Tel: +65 334 7720
Fax: +65 334 7721

FOREWORD

The European Design Annual began in 1995 as a joint venture between RotoVision SA and Print Magazine of America. Aiming to bring together the best in contemporary graphic design across Europe, the Annual has steadily grown in size and influence over recent years, and is sister to Print Magazine's own North American Regional Design Annual.

Graphic design work is invited from graphic designers all over Europe every year, and an international jury convenes each Autumn to select the best work from each country for inclusion in the Annual. Work is judged country by country, regardless of category, and this is how you will find the work displayed in the following pages.

This is the fifth European Design Annual featuring almost 400 pieces of winning graphic work from 24 European countries. We hope you make some interesting discoveries amongst them.

A NOTE ON THE COUNTRY FILES

The Country Files pages list a selection of places that may be of interest to designers on their travels around Europe. We are very grateful to Pentagram for allowing us to make use of their book Feedback, and to all those designers who contributed so willingly with their own suggestions.

ACKNOWLEDGEMENTS

A project the size and breadth of the European Design Annual requires help and assistance from many quarters, and RotoVision would like to sincerely thank the following people for helping to make the fifth Annual such a success:

Andy Kner, Carol Stevens, Tim Rich, Dragan Sakan and François Sargologo, the five jury members, for their co-operation and enthusiasm in judging thousands of submissions over two very full days, and for all their help, advice and support throughout the year; Gary French and Nicole Harman at RotoVision for their assistance in putting this book together; Pat and Simon Jameson, Amy Davies and Nick Anderson for helping to make the judging weekend run without a hitch; Simon Hennessey for his contributions on all computer and database matters; the team at Print for their always-cheerful assistance; Navy Blue Design Consultants for taking on the task of designing the 1999 promotional campaign and Karen J Robins at Red Design, Brighton for designing this book.

Finally, we are grateful to the following people, associations and magazines for all their help and input over the years:

Advertising Association of Sweden
Acta Graphica magazine, Croatia
Allianz Deutscher Designer, Germany
Art Directors' Club für Deutschland, Germany
ADG/FAD/Art Directors' Club, Spain
Art Directors' Club Schweiz, Switzerland
Artes bookshop, Poland
Association Design Communication, France
Associação Portuguesa de Designers, Portugal
Barcelona Centre de Disseny, Spain
Beroepsorganisatie Nederlandse Ontwerpers, The Netherlands
British Design & Art Direction, UK
British Design Initiative, UK
Buchhandlung Lia Wolf, Austria
Bureau of European Design Associations, The Netherlands
Bruil & Van der Staaij, The Netherlands
Creative Club, Austria
Centro Português de Design, Portugal
Creative Review magazine, UK
Croatian Designers Society
Design Austria
Design and Applied Arts Index (DAAI), UK
Drustvo Oblikovalcev Slovenije, Slovenia
Etapes Graphiques magazine, France
Föreningen Danske Designere, Denmark
Föreningen "O", Sweden
Föreningen Svenska Tecknare, Sweden
Grafill, Norway
Grafia Ry, Finland
Hungarian Advertising Association
IDEA99, Poland
Index Book, Spain
Institute of Creative Advertising & Design, Ireland
Institute of Practitioners in Advertising, UK
João Mario de Silva, Portugal
Jump magazine, Italy
Kopp Fachbuch und-Medienversand, Germany
LineaGrafica magazine, Italy
Lithuanian Association of Graphic Design
New Moment magazine, Yugoslavia/Slovenia
MM-Marketing magazine, Slovenia
Media & Marketing Polska magazine, Poland
Novum magazine, Germany
Packaging Design Association, France
Page magazine, Germany
Platforml Illustratoren, The Netherlands
Rat für Formgebung, Germany
Slovensko Oglasevalsko Zdruzenje, Slovenia
Society of Typographic Designers, UK
Struktur Design, UK
TegneCenter, Denmark
Vormberichten magazine, The Netherlands

RotoVision SA
Publishers

Introduction by Tim Rich

Why does someone choose to become a designer? It's a question that kept nagging at my brain throughout our European Design Annual 2000 judging sessions. There are, of course, at least as many answers as there are designers, but wading through some of the entries in a competition makes you question people's motives when working. Why use the established graphic language of a particular sector or genre? Why produce an item that looks and feels like almost every other of its kind?

If the answer to such questions was simply "to make money" I would respect the responders' unfashionable but refreshing honesty. But I don't think the people who submit things to design annuals go to work just to earn money. If they did, the client's cheque would be reward enough, and they'd probably prefer to read their bank statements rather than this publication.

No, issues such as a belief in the value of self-expression and a desire to make things better (in all sorts of ways) often inform the decision to enter an item into a competition. And yet, why does so much of the work sent in to design awards have the charisma of an ailing whelk and the inventive flair of a photo-copying machine?

Perhaps because the work entered can't help but reflect a wider malaise. There is something missing from most of the design produced today. The quality of the printing and paper and the professionalism of imagery and layout often mislead viewers into thinking they're experiencing something of substance when the reality is that most items are mere flimflam – the graphic result of a client uttering the words "I suppose we need some marketing" to a designer who doesn't really know why he or she is a designer.

This is a problem, for the client at least. We live in a world where the proliferation of messages and materials has reduced our desire to be communicated to per se while sharpening our appetite for individually excellent communications. This is, some say, an age of post-design, a time when what "we" in the design community are required to do is find or create or inspire real and valuable points of difference between our clients and somebody else's.

I'm not sure this is so very different from what great designers have always done; it's just that the need to do it has become even more urgent. That's why seeing such me-too or mediocre work is so puzzling – a failure to express real difference equals, in the world of communications at least, death.

Of course, trying to create difference is dangerous and difficult, but isn't that what makes being a designer interesting? In fact, apart from money, isn't it what makes designing meaningful? For me, the highlights of the EDA have always been projects that risked something to gain something. Such as one of this year's entries – Thomas Richter Eigenhufe's limited-edition book exploring the micro-world found in a housing community, the Schloss Blankenburg. Here, the designer created the photographs, illustrations, writing, and design. He was closely involved with the printing, too. He probably even thought about trying to make the paper. The project is a fine example of a designer being totally engaged with a subject – there is both immersion and expression. What was the risk? Perhaps that no one would care a jot about the subject or what he'd done or that he wouldn't do his subject justice. I suppose he risked wasting his time. But he didn't waste his time; he created something truly exceptional.

There were memorable entries from many other quarters in this year's awards, but particularly from Sweden. Campaigns for Fisherman's Friend and Fender Guitars (both by Jerlov & Co. of Gothenburg) exemplified the rewards of letting personality shine through, while a brochure by Log (from Stockholm) for an insurance company was the very best of a large group of Swedish print entries displaying fresh and inventive art direction and imagery and a clear desire not to simply do what everyone else is doing.

Last year, I remarked that we received a number of Web entries even though this area wasn't actively promoted for the Annual. This year, the Web entries grew tenfold, and a healthy quantity of CD-ROMs was submitted, too. I say healthy, though I detest CD-ROMs. They have all the worst qualities of print and the Web rolled up in one ugly little object. They are intrinsically pretentious, the pretence being that the viewer is enjoying an experience enhanced by the technology. The truth is that the technology clunks and clonks and gets in the way of every natural interface instinct. Even so, a number of entries managed to escape the horror of the medium and offer something interesting, which is no small feat.

The Web entries reflected the dynamism, confidence, and experimentalism of what's happening on-line. There can be little doubt that the Web is currently the most exciting design medium and an area in which fascinating issues are being raised about the role and value of designers. Certainly, some dull sites were entered to the awards, but the overall creative standard was much higher for the Web than it was for print – an interesting point when you consider that design-for-print can boast decades of history while design-for-the-Web is less than ten years old. I particularly enjoyed experiencing the eccentricities of www.bjoerk.de – an illustrator's site, and one electric with character, intrigue, and craft – while www.mandarinaduck.com and its "Newspaper of the Future" concept was entertaining and a blessed relief from the po-faced propaganda shovelled out by most fashion brands. The Internet is not the place to take yourself too seriously, which is a difficult thing for the fashion set to comprehend.

But perhaps the most fascinating entries this year came from eastern Europe, or New Europe as Dragan Sakan and his colleagues at New Moment magazine call it. The formal influences on design in this area (the aesthetics of the West, local visual traditions and heritage, the Web), together with social, political, and artistic upheaval, ensures that the output of designers here is excitingly unpredictable. It certainly makes for interesting viewing when a magazine is created while its offices are being bombed by NATO, an experience enjoyed by the staff of New Moment, which is based in Belgrade.

I'm no expert in eastern European matters, so I won't prolong my comments. My one hope is that, as more and more businesses there look to marketing to lead their growth, designers do not simply rework what has been done in more affluent areas of Europe and North America. If the most exciting design ideas are to be explored, a degree of resistance will be necessary and a respect for the value of local heritage and ideas must stand firm. Whether it's English visual punning or Carsonogenic typography, I'd hate to see Western approaches run riot. No doubt that's easy for me to say, sitting here in London, but I think New European design will be much more exciting and effective if it uses, rather than discards, its local design heritage.

Wherever you are based and whatever the issues facing you, I hope that you enjoy the collection of work that follows. There are certainly some wonderful examples of designers engaging with their subjects and creating difference. I particularly hope that the best work encourages designers – from across Europe and beyond – to keep asking the question "why am I a designer?" and perhaps even to find some interesting answers along the way.

THE JUDGING

This year's European Design Annual brought in work from 28 countries and territories: Austria, Belarus, Belgium, Croatia, Czech Republic, Denmark, Finland, France, Germany, Greece, Hungary, Ireland, Italy, Lithuania, Netherlands, Northern Ireland, Norway, Poland, Portugal, Russia, Slovakia, Slovenia, Spain, Sweden, Switzerland, Turkey, United Kingdom and Yugoslavia.

As was the case last year, the panel was made up of five people: the three regulars – Andrew Kner, Print's then art director; Carol Stevens, a contributing editor to Print, and me – plus two newcomers, François Sargologo and Dragan Sakan.

The judging was divided into two sessions: Print entries were reviewed over two days in Brighton, England, close to the offices of RotoVision, co-sponsors of the competition; digital entries (i.e. Web sites and CD-ROMs) were viewed and assessed by each individual judge at his or her own office over a period of two weeks.

The method: The judges viewed the entries country by country, with each judge individually voting for an item to be included or not. Securing three votes ensured inclusion; an entry with two votes was discussed, reassessed, and included or rejected depending on whether the two voters had persuaded the remaining three of its merits (or the three non-voters had persuaded the two voters of the item's faults). Staff from RotoVision offered contextual information and translations for specific entries when required.

The simplicity of the judging method is important. This Annual does not seek to offer a scientific analysis of graphic design in Europe; the mission for the judges is simply to select what they consider to be the most imaginative, accomplished, entertaining, thought-provoking, or unusual work from the entries before them.

This task would not have been possible without the expertise and energy of the EDA team at RotoVision, and particularly Sarah Jameson and her assistant, Alex Matwijisyn. To gather and manage entries from so many countries is an enormous logistical challenge, but one that they met in every way. Their work has been vital to the success of the Annual, and the judges would particularly like to thank them for making the viewing of entries an efficient and enjoyable experience.

Following the 2-day judging session, each of the five jury members was asked to choose their own personal favourite from the thousands of pieces they had seen. Their choices and explanations can be found on the following pages, along with comments from the designers behind the selected works.

ISTVAN OROSZ, HUNGARY: "FACE OF SHAKESPEARE"
Chosen by Andrew Kner

Andrew Kner was born in Hungary, and after moving to the United States became Executive Art Director at the New York Times in the 1970s. He left to join Backer & Spielvogel as Senior Vice President and Creative Director and later joined RC Publications as Creative and Art Director of Print Magazine. A winner of over 150 awards for design and art direction, his posters are part of the permanent collections of the Museum of Modern Art, the Smithsonian and the Louvre. He served as President of the New York Art Directors Club from 1983 to 1985.

"I first became aware of Istvan Orosz's work when he won the student design competition for the cover of the November/December 1974 Print Magazine. The design was both playful and sophisticated — amazingly so for a young student.

In the decades since then I have seen his work, particularly posters, win awards in various competitions around the world. His particular combination of technical complexity and playful disregard for conventional laws of perspective and spatial relationships, combined with a great seriousness of purpose, are unmistakably all his. So when this 'portrait' of Shakespeare showed up at the judging it was familiarly his; and also fresh and unique. The use of the two theatrical musicians to create Shakespeare's face says all there is to say about Shakespeare as a creature of the theatre.

The fact that a Hungarian designer was asked to create this for the Victoria & Albert Museum in London added to my decision to choose this poster as my particular favourite in this most European of competitions."
Andrew Kner, New York, USA

"All poster designers dream of generous commissions like this one for a poster history exhibition, "The Power of the Poster", at the Victoria & Albert Museum, London.

The genre of the poster has close connections with the theatre for me (I was the resident poster designer for a Hungarian theatre for a long time). London and the theatre are also closely linked together: what could be a more obvious choice for a subject than Shakespeare ?

For me, there are several different Shakespeares. There is the Shakespeare for those who read him in the original, another for those who read him in translation, then another for those who meet him in the theatres or in the cinemas …So I decided to present the ambiguity of Shakespeare. I wanted to combine the different styles of contemporary engravings and the colourful atmosphere of the poster in our own age. I wanted to give the viewer an opportunity to choose from the meanings: if you happen to be close to the poster you can see two musicians of Shakespeare's age performing on stage, but if you look at the poster from further away the figures 'acquire' Shakespeare's own features, and the stage turns out to be the playwright's famous collar, or ruff.

Here's a short passage from Shakespeare's "Richard II", which inspired me:

"For sorrow's eye, glazed with blinding tears,
Divides one thing entire to many objects;
Like perspectives, which rightly gaz'd upon,
Show nothing but confusion, ey'd awry,
Distinguish form"

("Richard II", Act II, Scene II, lines 16-20)

The word 'perspective' had a wider meaning at that time and referred to every strange and new method for opening up spaces and to all anamorphic pictures (i.e. those that change their meaning if seen from another viewpoint or distance).

I was reminded of Marcell Duchamp's saying: 'It is the viewer who makes the art' when working on the poster."
Istvan Orosz, Budapest, Hungary

**"FACE OF SHAKESPEARE" POSTER FOR AN EXHIBITION
ENTITLED "HISTORY OF THE POSTER"
DESIGN FIRM:** Utisz, Budapest
DESIGNER/ ILLUSTRATOR: Istvan Orosz
CLIENT: Victoria and Albert Museum, London

AHLQVIST & CO. REKLAMBYRÅ, SWEDEN:
NORDSJÖ COMPANY PRESENTATION
Chosen by Carol Stevens

Carol Stevens studied at the Università degli Studi in Florence, and graduated from Smith College with a major in Art History. She joined Print Magazine in New York where she served as managing editor and writer. She has written articles for the Encyclopaedia of World Art, the French publication, Connaissance des Arts, and several editions of Print casebooks. She is a contributory editor to Print.

"The ads for Dutch Boy paints I saw as a child in American periodicals of the 1940s and 1950s always disturbed me. There was something too perfect about them. It was clear that those houses, those rooms didn't belong to ordinary people. They didn't look lived in. Thus I was delighted to find among the entries for this year's European Design Annual a brochure for the Swedish paint manufacturer, Nordsjö, that offers an honest point of view.

Entitled Where Colour is Needed, it invites the reader to use Nordsjö products, while at the same time imparting a truth about paint: it ages, it peels. What's more, tattered colours are beautiful, this brochure reminds us – with photographs of a weathered pink and green shack; decorative hinges on a window frame covered with a thick but ageing coat of white paint and tinged with rust; empty rooms – the way of life they sheltered as faded as their vanishing hand-painted ceilings; and an oil-storage tank umber with wear.

Featuring these images on consecutive spreads as if they were in an album, art director Christer Strandberg appropriates their colours to use as backgrounds for the text, which runs unobtrusively in the margins and manages to combine a thoughtful discussion of aesthetics with an overview of Nordsjö's history and of the services it offers to both private and industrial consumers."
Carol Stevens, New York, USA

"The original assignment was a fairly traditional company presentation. Together with our client, we started to elaborate some ideas that would deal with the issues in a different way. We both felt that the world had had enough of company presentations showing businessmen in suits, lab personnel in white coats and pictures from the manufacturing process.

Nordsjö is a manufacturer and distributor of paint. It's part of the world-wide Akzo Nobel industries, the world's largest producer of paint. So we started with the question: "Why does Nordsjö exist (which is also the headline on the third page)?" This led to the idea of showing only pictures of houses and interiors which are in desperate need of a new paint finish.

This is of course quite a different way of presenting a company, and we were lucky to have a client with both courage and foresight – Anders Maxe, commercial director of Nordsjö in Sweden."
Tuula Niinipuu, Ahlqvist & Co. Reklambyrå, Sweden

NORDSJÖ COMPANY PRESENTATION
FOR A PAINT MANUFACTURER
DESIGN FIRM: Ahlqvist & Co. Reklambyrå, Malmö
ART DIRECTOR: Christer Strandberg
COPY DIRECTOR: Klas Tjebbes

PHOTOGRAPHER: Gerry Johansson
CLIENT: Akzo Nobel Decorative Coatings AB

To reflect the rapid increase in Internet design across Europe, I've taken the liberty of choosing a print best of and a Web best of. Traditional graphic design media and so-called new media share much but also work in significantly different ways. Choosing two may be cheeky but I think recognising the differences involved is important at the current time.

AMDL ARCHITECTURES, ITALY: OLIVETTI BOOK
Chosen by Tim Rich

Tim Rich is a London-based contributing editor to Print magazine and a columnist for Design Week magazine, London. He provides writing, editorial and web consultancy to a range of organisations, including British Telecommunications, Bass plc and Photodisc, is the co-founder of new sports publishing brand Extraordinary World and is the editor of extraordinaryworld.com

"This brochure brings together some of the most important works created by various graphic, industrial and architectural designers for Olivetti. It was designed by a team that includes Michele de Lucchi, a co-founder of the Memphis design group. For those that don't know about them, Memphis were a colourful bunch who caused a stir by eschewing hard functionalism in favour of whimsicality and experimentation with surface materials. They were enormously influential and played a key role in establishing Olivetti as a design innovator. This brochure offers the reader little in the way of grounded learning (the text is sparse and caption-like) and yet it somehow manages to evoke a broad and profound sense of the design heritage of Olivetti, not least the beauty that lies around and within what are – ironically – highly functional business objects. From the serious symmetry of Italy's first typewriter through the ever-more self-aware dials, sprockets, wheels, knobs, levers and buttons that followed; this is a warm and personal celebration from de Lucchi and his colleagues. In today's world the most fascinating design challenges probably lie in shaping invisible creations like networks and experiences; this brochure is a timely celebration of what pioneering design used to be about."
Tim Rich, London, UK

"The history and design culture of Olivetti Spa is well known. After a long and successful history manufacturing office products and systems, the company has more recently turned its attention to telecommunications and information technology services.

This is one of the reasons why we accepted the challenge of designing a book covering 90 years of design culture; we knew that this was one of the last opportunities to produce something innovative for Olivetti, without any marketing constraints.

Our counterpart within the company was Vittorio Meloni, the director of communications, who suddenly understood our vision and encouraged it through the process.

The main issues we had to work with were: was it possible to design a very sophisticated book, reproducing the culture of Olivetti and a book designed something like an object? Was it possible to blend between the book's covers a

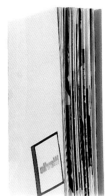

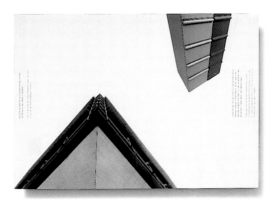

history of Olivetti's product and graphic design activities as well as its cultural initiatives and – on the other hand – the new technology of telecommunications, such as cables, call centres and 'invisible' services?

We decided that the book had to be printed in a very sophisticated black and white, to give us the opportunity of mixing pictures from different periods and photographers. In reality, the book was printed in 6 colours (two layers of black, and then grey, matt and gloss, with a special metallic green for the cover).

Furthermore, we decided with the client to mix images related to different fields of activities or to different periods, in order to echo Olivetti's 'holistic' approach to design.

The company decided to print a very limited edition of this book (less than 1,000 copies) just for distribution to managers and politicians during the Olivetti conference organised in Rome for the company's anniversary."
Mario Trimarchi, designer, AMDL Architectures, Italy

SPREADS FROM PROMOTIONAL BOOK FOR OLIVETTI SPA
DESIGN FIRM: AMDL Architectures, Milan
DESIGNERS: Michele de Lucchi, Mario Trimarchi, Katrin Schmitt-Tegge
PHOTOGRAPHER: Luca Tamburlini

ANDERS BJÖRK GMBH, GERMANY:
WEBSITE: WWW.BJOERK.DE

"I've seen so many yawn-inducing sites for designers and illustrators so I didn't expect too much when I went to look at the one for the design company Anders Björk. But this is different. The designer has really thought about the viewer and the entire experience of visiting the site, from the way the story is constructed to the dissolve on each page. Rather than simply pin his images up as if the Web were a notice board, he's really engaged with the medium. I like the images too – bizarre, dark, sort of noir-ish."
Tim Rich, London, UK

"Advertising agencies are creative, however they rarely seem to use their knowledge and potential creativity for marketing themselves. They seem to believe that the image of the advertising agency is most effective when it resembles a lawyer's office (something which in Germany is never advertised): austere ladies and gentlemen, symbols of sterile elegance, preferably dressed in black, or in black and dark grey. Thus, they do not show their customers what creativity is, but merely what 'business' is.

An idea is a real idea only when it is new or original. However originality means breaking with everything old and being able to afford losses. It means being brave. This is Anders Björk. Naturally Mr Björk is not a real person. He is an idea or, even better, he is the sum of all the ideas that are created under his name. He is an image created from kneaded rubber.

Kneaded rubber is great stuff since it can compete with the increasing demand for animation in today's World Wide Web. There are several Björk images, all about 30cm high. The image could not be made smaller since the detail can only be modelled with very little fingers or with special toolkits. The different parts of the body can be combined exactly like a child's box of bricks, so that we can have different shapes and images. The finished image can be photographed in any desired pose or it can be pasted into an old photograph. The colours come from an auto-defined colour palette which can be modified or redefined in PhotoShop.

Most companies invent a product and they build a world around it in which this product is made to shine under the most attractive light. We create a world in which it is not the product or the service that shines, but where Anders itself is the centre. His world tells stories, generates curiosity and shows that ideas are the driving force. Therefore it's the content and not the design that is decisive ... but of course exciting content without exciting design is like soup without salt."
Andreas Trumpler, Anders Björk, Germany

SELF-PROMOTIONAL WEB SITE (www.bjoerk.de)
DESIGN FIRM: Anders Björk GmbH, Lübeck
ART DIRECTOR/ DESIGNER/ ILLUSTRATOR: Andreas Trumpler

JERLOV & COMPANY, SWEDEN:
FISHERMAN'S FRIEND AD CAMPAIGN
Chosen by Dragan Sakan

Dragan Sakan is Chairman and founder of award-winning agency S Team Bates Saatchi & Saatchi in Eastern and Central Europe. He is also an ad man, business man, creative director, author, university lecturer, founder-publisher of New Moment, the magazine for Art and Advertising as well as New Ideas Campus.

"We are living in a visual time. We must now send messages by visual means and ensure that no explanations are needed. The Fisherman's Friend campaign does this brilliantly. To work, the message must be based on a truth, and this is. I almost voted for the Fender guitar ad with the key instead (also by Jerlov & Company) — I used to play the guitar and I know that what it's saying is true!"
Dragan Sakan, Ljubljana, Slovenia

"We have produced over 30 different versions of the Fisherman's Friend advert since 1996, all using the packaging as the creative basis. Now at the beginning of the year 2000, we have won more than 27 advertising prizes for the campaign: rather remarkable since the advertisements were shown almost exclusively in Sweden.

We have asked ourselves many times what it is about our Fisherman's Friend campaign that makes it so special, but there is no simple answer. One clear factor, however, is the strategy we used, which is very different from a great deal of other candy and food advertising. Our goal is to communicate the concept of 'Strength': the lozenge itself is strong, but also — more importantly — the brand has a strong sense of self-confidence in its relationship with its target group. We communicate this self-confidence by daring to forgo the obviousness found in most advertising in this category. There is no room for captions or 'payoffs' in our concept: we let these appear in the mind of the reader instead, where their impact matters most.

Our Fisherman's Friend ads have won many first prizes in reader surveys; our posters are stolen from advertising stands and they are a popular subject of debate on the Internet. Research has shown that brand loyalty has increased .... we are very proud of this campaign."
Fredrik Jerlov, Creative Director, Jerlov & Company, Sweden

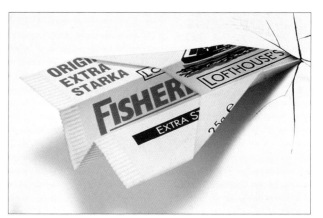

ADVERTISEMENTS FOR FISHERMAN'S FRIEND CONFECTIONERY
AGENCY: Jerlov & Company, Gothenburg
ART DIRECTOR: Madelene Wallström
PHOTOGRAPHER: Magnus Pajnert

HTB DESIGN, FRANCE: "MANIFESTO FOR THE ROAD"
Chosen by François Sargologo

François Sargologo divides his time between France and the Middle East. He is Creative Director for the consultancy Groupe Theorem in Paris and founder of the Ethno-Design programme in Lebanon, which aims to promote local knowledge of design, print and typography. He lectures at the Academy of Fine Arts and the American University in Beirut.

"I think France should seek more international visibility in terms of design. The lack of good French entries in the European Design Annual reflects this, but one French piece I particularly liked was "Manifeste pour la Route", a promotional book for a road builder. The text and the imagery creates a great rhythm throughout. But I don't feel this is about style – the designer did not consciously do it to please the audience, but did it this way simply because it was objectively the right way to do it."
François Sargologo, Paris, France

"We are two young freelance designers, and have been working together for more than 4 years, after having been together at les Arts Decos in Paris. We have worked for London-based companies like Pentagram and Vogue, and in Paris we work both for design companies and for direct clients. Our motto is "to learn and enjoy every day."

The Manifesto was a commission from EURO RSCG Omnium, the advertising agency in charge of the annual report for Colas, an asphalt manufacturer, who proposed adding a 'communicative' document to the report dedicated to the road. They contacted us to create the concept, design and spirit of it.

The raw material given to us were 15 texts written by French intellectuals, colour photographs and the client's logo.

The brief was a very free one, and we decided to create graphic 'incidents' following the words of the text, more for the reader than the viewer. We wanted to look at the road from another angle and put the design at the service of the text.

The other challenge was the lack of time: only 3 weeks from concept to printing !

Our only regret is that given more time, it would have been much better ...."
HTB Design, Paris, France

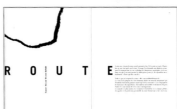

COVER AND SPREADS FROM "MANIFESTE POUR LA ROUTE", A PROMOTIONAL BOOK FOR A ROAD BUILDER
AGENCY: EURO RSCG Omnium, Paris
DESIGN FIRM: HTB Design, Paris
ART DIRECTORS: Krista Sochor, Zoé Vayssières
ILLUSTRATOR: Véronique Bour
CLIENT: Colas

AUSTRIA: COUNTRY FILE

HOTELS

MARTINSPARK HOTEL, MOZARTSTRASSE 2, DORNBIRN. T (+43) 5572 3760 A good half way stop-off between Zürich and Munich, in the centre of Dornbirn, this hotel has elegant internal spaces and is notable for its contemporary art by Flatz, Laszlo Moholy-Nagy and bed quilts designed by Maria Baumschlager-Dünser. (Virginia Pepper, Public Relations, Switzerland)

RESTAURANTS, CAFÉS & BARS

THE AMERICAN BAR, KÄRNTNERSTRASSE 10, KÄRNTNER DURCHGANG, VIENNA. Designed in 1908 by Adolf Loos, a luxurious bar with a mahogany and marble interior, best visited in the early hours of the morning when the regular clientele can be avoided.

THE PALMENHAUS, BURGGARTEN, VIENNA. T (+43) 1 533 10 33 Originally the Winter Garden of the Viennese Imperial Palace built 1901-1907, it is now a restaurant and bar serving very good food .... you can sit amongst the palms and view slides projected above the bar, or sit outside on the terrace in summer, overlooking the lush park.

WRENKH, BAUERNMARKT 10, VIENNA. T (+43) 1 533 15 26 Excellent vegetarian food (including a vegetarian schnitzel), eaten in a stylish Jasper Morrison interior. (The Lounge, Media Design Company, Vienna)

MAK-CAFÉ, STUBENRING 3-5, VIENNA. T (+43) 1 714 01 21 International and Viennese cuisine and a beautiful courtyard garden in the Museum of Applied Arts (MAK).

PLANTER'S CLUB, ZELINKAGASSE 4, VIENNA. T (+43) 1 533 33 93 One of the most extravagantly equipped bars in Vienna. Main room designed in the style of a Darjeeling hill station, with palm trees and a glass roof. (Markus Göbl, Designer, Vienna)

TRZESNIEWSKI-BUFFET, DOROTHEERGASSE 1, VIENNA. Rushing from one museum, exhibition or bookstore to another eventually builds up an appetite. T'shesh-nyéfskee (as it is pronounced) is a small buffet offering about two dozen excellent open sandwiches on rye bread. All beautifully garnished to please a designer's eye. (Ernst Roch, Designer, Montreal)

MUSEUMS, GALLERIES & LIBRARIES

SAMMLUNG ESSEL, AN DER DONAU-AU 1, KLOSTERNEUBURG. T (+43) 2243 37 050, www.sammlung-essl.at/ Recently opened, check out the website for all you need to know. The museum is founded by the president of Austria's biggest hardware store chain and focuses on contemporary art. (The Lounge, Media Design Company, Vienna)

GRAPHISCHE SAMMLUNG ALBERTINA, AUGUSTINERSTRASSE 1, VIENNA. Just behind the State Opera House lies the largest collection of graphic art in the world. The Albertina, founded by Duke Albert von Sachsen-Teschen (1738-1822) holds over 44,000 drawings and around 1.5 million prints by virtually every artist from the beginning of the 15th-century until the present. The special collections also contain miniatures, sketchbooks, architectural drawings, illustrated books, maps, plans, posters, playing cards &c., as well as original 15th-century printing blocks.

JOSEPHINUM, INSTITUTE FOR THE HISTORY OF MEDICINE, UNIVERSITY OF VIENNA, 9 WÄHRINGER STRASSE 25, VIENNA. If you have ever wondered what's hiding under your skin, pay a visit to the Josephinum's collection of anatomical wax models. Beautiful males and females lying around in a leisurely fashion, stretched out on silk pillows — exhibiting their muscles, their circulatory and nervous systems. (Ernst Roch, Designer, Montreal)

STAATSBIBLIOTHEK, JOSEFSPLATZ, VIENNA. Behind an unimposing entrance in the Hofburg complex is the world's most beautiful library. In the huge, magnificent baroque interior you can view changing exhibitions and — upon request — visit the map and globe room. Particularly stunning are the consummately skillful trompe l'oeil decorations. (Henry Steiner, Designer, Hong Kong)

The best places to see contemporary art:

KUNSTHALLE, KARLSPLATZ 4, VIENNA. T (+43) 1 521 890 and MAK (MUSEUM OF APPLIED ARTS), STUBENRING 3-5, VIENNA. T (+43) 1 711 360 (Markus Göbl, Designer, Vienna)

PLACES OF INTEREST

NASCHMARKT, 7, LINKE WIENZEILE-RECHTE WIENZEILE, VIENNA. The Jugendstil stalls, protected as historic monuments, are part of this fascinating market. Many Middle-Eastern specialities are also sold here (olives stuffed with garlic cloves, a vast array of spices, and the best baklava in Vienna). On Saturdays there is a huge flea market selling everything from limbless Barbie dolls to pricey collectables. (The Lounge, Media Design Company, Vienna)

BOOKSHOPS

LIA WOLF VERLAGSBÜRO, BÄCKERSTRASSE 2, VIENNA. T (+43) 1 512 4094 For graphic design books

Area	1,000 km2	083.9	Capital City	Vienna	Monetary Unit	Austrian schilling &
Population	1,000	8,134	Capital City Population	1,000	2,060		euro
Design Population	1,000	002.5	Languages	German	GDP per Capita (US $)	29,006
					International Dialling Code	+43

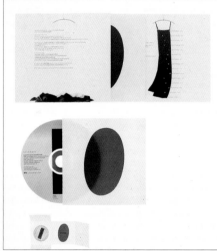

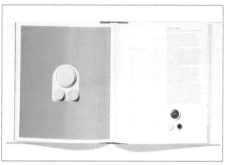

1, 2 THEATRE POSTERS FOR GRUPPE 80
DESIGN FIRM: Markus Göbl Graphic Design, Vienna
DESIGNER/ PHOTOGRAPHER/ ILLUSTRATOR: Markus Göbl

3, 4 MUSIC CD PACKAGING
(The cover consists of two images over-printed and to view the hidden image, the first layer must be scratched off)
DESIGN FIRM: Kopf & Korn, Vienna
ART DIRECTORS/ DESIGNERS: Elisabeth Kopf, Werner Korn
CLIENT: azizamusic

5 - 8 COVER AND SPREADS
FOR A BOOK ON AUSTRIAN PRODUCT CULTURE
DESIGN FIRM: A(l)lessandri, Vienna
ART DIRECTOR: Cordula Alessandri
DESIGNERS: Stefanie Ackermann, Marcus Sterz
PHOTOGRAPHER: Bernhard Angerer
CLIENT: Bibliophile Edition

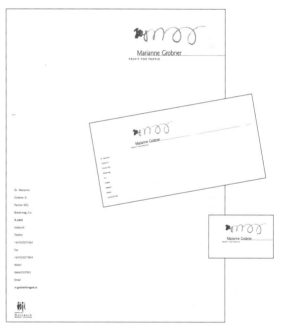

9 SELF-PROMOTIONAL COTTON FLAG POSTCARDS
STIFFENED WITH LACQUER
DESIGN FIRM: Kopf & Korn, Vienna
ART DIRECTORS/ DESIGNERS: Elisabeth Kopf, Werner Korn

10 BOOKLET OF CLUB FLYERS
DESIGN FIRM: The Lounge, Vienna
ART DIRECTOR: Tom Koch
ILLUSTRATOR: Claudine Deleau
PHOTOGRAPHER: Thomas Topf
CLIENT: B72 Club

11 - 14 DIRECT-MAIL CARDS FOR WÄLDERHAUS
DESIGN FIRM: Caldonazzi Grafik-Design, Frastanz
ART DIRECTOR/ DESIGNER: Martin Caldonazzi

15 STATIONERY FOR D+P DRÜCKEREI, A PRINTER
DESIGN FIRM: Caldonazzi Grafik-Design, Frastanz
ART DIRECTOR/ DESIGNER: Martin Caldonazzi
ILLUSTRATOR: Wilma Zündel

16 STATIONERY FOR MARIANNE GROSSNER,
A BUSINESS SERVICES CONSULTANT
DESIGN FIRM: Caldonazzi Grafik-Design, Frastanz
ART DIRECTOR/ DESIGNER/ ILLUSTRATOR: Martin Caldonazzi

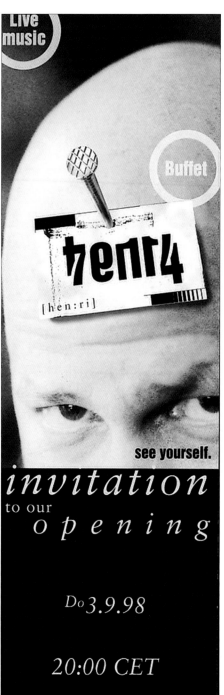

Live music

Buffet

henr4

[hen:ri]

see yourself.

invitation
to our
opening

Do 3.9.98

20:00 CET

fe & Bar "Henry" • A-4722 Peuerbach • Hauptstraße 7 • Tel: 07276 / 23 65-14

Cash or Gonzo.

henr4

[hen:ri]

see yourself.

Introducing Afustin Vasquez-Mendoza

henr4
[hen:ri]
see yourself.

the FBI's ten most wanted fugitives

One of many guys not to meet at Henry's (or anywhere else)

Unlawful Flight to Avoid Prosecution; Murder (First Degree)

Agustin Vasquez-Mendoza is being sought for his alleged participation in a drug conspiracy involving a Drug Enforcement Administration Special Agent who was killed on 6/30/94, during an undercover drug transaction in Glendale, Arizona.

Gravity control.

henr4
[hen:ri]
see yourself.

17, 18 CORPORATE IDENTITY AND STYLE GUIDE FOR ÖGB,
THE AUSTRIAN FEDERATION OF TRADE UNIONS
DESIGN FIRM: Projekt21: mediendesign GmbH, Vienna
ART DIRECTORS: Martin Berger, Alexander Gamper
DESIGNERS: Christian Modlik, Georg Metnik

19 - 23 LOGO POSTCARDS AND FLYERS FOR HENRY, A NEW PUB
DESIGN FIRM: Gerhard Schild Werbeteam, Linz
ART DIRECTOR: Selam Ebead
DESIGNER: Stefan Simader
CLIENT: Obermayr Gasthaus & Kino Gastronomie

Area | 1,000 km2	207.6	Capital City	Minsk	Monetary Unit	Belarussian rouble
Population | 1,000	10,409	Capital City Population | 1,000	1,766	GDP per Capita (US $)	994
Design Population | 1,000	000.1	Languages	Byelorussian, Russian	International Dialling Code	+375

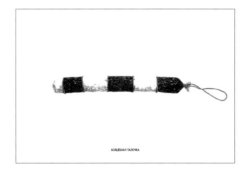

1 ADVERTISEMENT FOR "CHRONICLES" NEWSPAPER
AGENCY: Belaya Karona, Minsk
ART DIRECTOR: Oleg Usstinovitch
DESIGNER: Dmitry Galutsky
PHOTOGRAPHER: George Livshits

2 ADVERTISEMENT PROMOTING ECOLOGICAL AWARENESS
AGENCY: Belaya Karona, Minsk
ART DIRECTOR: Oleg Usstinovitch
DESIGNERS: Dmitry Galutsky, Andrew Snezko, Oleg Usstinovitch
PHOTOGRAPHER: George Livshits
CLIENT: Ministry of Housing and Communal Services

3 NATIONAL ANTI-ALCOHOLISM ADVERTISEMENT
AGENCY: Belaya Karona, Minsk
ART DIRECTOR: Oleg Usstinovitch
DESIGNER: Shamil Hayrulin
PHOTOGRAPHER: George Livshits

4 ADVERTISEMENT FOR SERGE UNDERWEAR
AGENCY: Belaya Karona, Minsk
ART DIRECTOR: Oleg Usstinovitch
DESIGNER/ PHOTOGRAPHER: Dmitry Galutsky
CLIENT: Hempic Ltd

5 ADVERTISEMENT PROTESTING AT POLICE CORRUPTION
AGENCY: Belaya Karona, Minsk
ART DIRECTOR: Oleg Usstinovitch
PHOTOGRAPHER: George Livshits

BELGIUM: COUNTRY FILE

HOTELS

AUBERGE DU MOULIN HIDEUX, NOIREFONTAINE, ARDENNES. T (+32) 61 46 70 15 The charm of an old mill nestled away in its valley. An atmosphere alive with the finer things in life; private fishing and walks in the forest. If you come to Belgium, don't miss a stop in this marvellous place lost in the Ardennes forest. (Gilles Fiszman, Designer, Brussels)

RESTAURANTS, CAFÉS & BARS

RESTAURANT CHRISTINA, NAPOLEONKAAI 45-47, ANTWERP. T (+32) 3 233 5526 Enjoy, in season (September-April) a lunch of mussels in one of the small dockside restaurants in Antwerp. The best of these in my experience is Restaurant Christina, overlooking Willem Dok, where one can savour a dish of about 50 mussels cooked in one of a dozen ways. (Herbert Spencer, Designer, London)

L'ECALLIER DU PALAIS ROYAL, 18 RUE BODENBROEK, BRUSSELS. T (+32) 2 512 87 51 A wonderful restaurant. Famous and classic. Seafood and fish. Old men in blue aprons behind the zinc bar opening fresh oysters. Necessary to make table reservations. (Ove Pihl, Art Director, Stockholm)

MUSEUMS & GALLERIES

MUSEUM PLANTIN-MORETUS, VRIJDAGMARKT 22, ANTWERP. T (+32) 3 23 30 294 Christopher Plantin (1514-1589), was printer to King Philip II of Spain. The museum's 20 rooms are hung with priceless works of art, but also include the original workshops, the type foundry and two of the world's oldest presses still in working order.

VICTOR HORTA HOUSE, AMERIKASTRAAT 23-25, SAINT GILLES, BRUSSELS. T (+32) 2 537 1692 Victor Horta (1861-1947), the famous Art Nouveau architect who designed a great number of the most beautiful buildings in Brussels, built this house for himself in 1898, when he was at the peak of his creative activity. Today a museum dedicated to his work, it is one of Europe's most complete, perfect and undamaged examples of Art Nouveau architecture. Closed Mondays. (Wim Crouwel, Designer, Amsterdam)

CENTRE BELGE DE LA BANDE DESSINÉE (BELGIAN COMIC STRIP CENTRE), RUE DES SABLES, 20, BRUSSELS. T (+32) 2 21 91 980 Housed in a splendid Art Nouveau building, this museum celebrates the comic strip and focuses especially on Hergé, Tintin's creator.

PLACES OF INTEREST

THE FALLEN ANGEL, JAN BREYDELSTRAAT 29, GHENT. T (+32) 9 23 94 15 A little shop from your dreams, stocking artists' supplies long out of stock elsewhere …you can find an unopened bottle of Renard ink, nibs in shapes we don't even remember existed, boxes of crayons from the '40s and lots of other treasures. The place is packed with old toys, fantasy postcards, bizarre prints and other rarities. It will seem even more unreal after a cherry beer in the bar next door. (Andrzej Dudzinski, Artist, New York)

Area | 1,000 km2	030.5	Capital City	Brussels	Monetary Unit	Belgian franc & euro
Population | 1,000	10,174	Capital City Population | 1,000	1,122	GDP per Capita (US $)	26,582
Design Population | 1,000	001.0	Languages	Dutch, French,German	International Dialling Code	+32

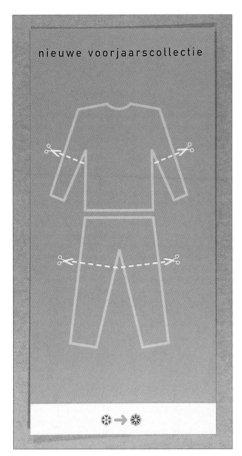

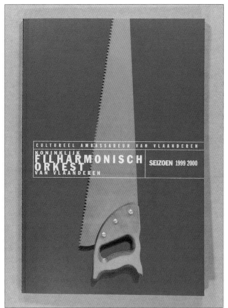

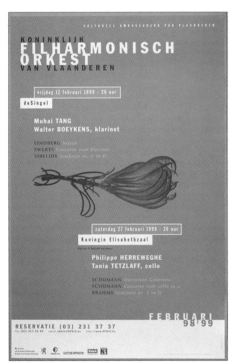

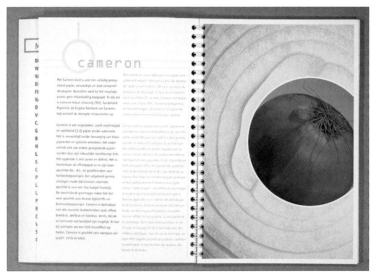

1 ADVERTISEMENT PROMOTING SPRING AND SUMMER 1999
COLLECTION FOR A CLOTHING STORE
DESIGN FIRM: Zizó!, Antwerp
DESIGNER: Marc Huyck
CLIENT: Piramide

2 POSTER FOR THE FLEMISH ROYAL PHILHARMONIC ORCHESTRA
DESIGN FIRM: Zizó!, Antwerp
ART DIRECTORS: Jan Hendrickx/ Ingrid de Decker
DESIGNERS: Ingrid de Decker, Marc Huyck

3 BOOKLET PROMOTING 1999-2000 SEASON OF
THE FLEMISH ROYAL PHILHARMONIC ORCHESTRA
DESIGN FIRM: Zizó!, Antwerp
ART DIRECTOR/ DESIGNER: Jan Hendrickx

4 SELF-PROMOTIONAL DATEBOOK
DESIGN FIRM: Zizó!, Antwerp
ART DIRECTOR/ DESIGNER: Jan Hendrickx
CLIENTS: Zizó!, Gramma/ GPG

5 SPREAD FROM A SWATCH PROMOTION FOR CAMERON PAPER
DESIGN FIRM: Zizó!, Antwerp
ART DIRECTORS/ DESIGNERS: Jan Hendrickx, Ingrid de Decker
PHOTOGRAPHER: Ingrid de Decker
CLIENTS: Gramma/ GPG

CROATIA: COUNTRY FILE

RESTAURANTS, CAFÉS & BARS

The following are all very nice cafés in Zagreb:

ART NET CLUB, PRERADOVICEVA 25, ZAGREB. Internet: www.haa.hr Open 9 am-11pm. Cyber cafe and photo and art exhibitions.

SUBLINK, TESLINA STREET, ZAGREB (another cyber café)

DOBAR ZVUK, GAJEVA STREET, ZAGREB

CAFÉ 7, MEDULICEVA STREET, ZAGREB (Nedjeljko Spoljar, Art Director, Zagreb)

MUSEUMS & GALLERIES

MUSEUM MIMARA, ROOSEVELTOV TRG. 5, ZAGREB. T (+385) 1 48 28 100 One of the finest art galleries in Europe housed in a neo-Renaissance former school building. Houses the collection of Ante Topic Mimara, who spent most of his life in Austria and donated nearly 4,000 priceless objects to his native Zagreb. Closed Mondays & Thursdays.

MUZEJ ZA UMJETNOST I OBRT (MUSEUM OF ARTS AND CRAFTS), TRG MARSALA TITA 10, ZAGREB. T (+385) 1 48 26 922 Permanent display of Arts and Crafts of Croatia. Closed Mondays.

HDLU, TRG HRVATSKIH VELIKANA B.B., ZAGREB. T (+385) 1 46 11 818 Puts on various exhibitions (even design exhibitions from time to time).

GALERIJA ULUPUH (GALLERY OF CROATIAN ASSOCIATION OF APPLIED ARTS ARTISTS), TKALCICEVA 14, ZAGREB. T (+385) 1 48 13 746 Various exhibitions of members of ULUPUH. Closed Sundays. (Nedjeljko Spoljar, Art Director, Zagreb)

ST MARK'S CHURCH, MARKOV TRG., ZAGREB. With its colourful painted-tile roof, this church houses the work of Ivan Mestrovic, Croatia's most famous modern sculptor.

PLACES OF INTEREST

MIROGOJ. 20 minute bus ride (No.106) from the cathedral. One of Europe's most beautiful cemeteries with English-style landscaping enclosed by a long 19th-century neo-Renaissance arcade. Some gorgeous mausoleums.

EUPHRAISAN BASILICA, POREC. A World Heritage Site with wonderfully preserved gold Byzantine mosaics. Entry to the church is free, and for a small fee you can visit the 4th-century mosaic floor of the adjacent Early Christian basilica.

EXHIBITIONS

ZGRAF. An international triennial exhibition of design founded in 1975. For more information: ulupuh@zg.tel.hr

BOOKSHOPS

ALGORITAM, GAJEVA 1, ZAGREB. T (+385) 1 481 8674 For graphic design books

Area	1,000 km2	088.1	Capital City	Zagreb	Monetary Unit	Croatian kuna
Population	1,000	4,700	Capital City Population	1,000	700	GDP per Capita (US $)	4,000
Design Population	1,000	000.2	Languages	Croatian	International Dialling Code	+385

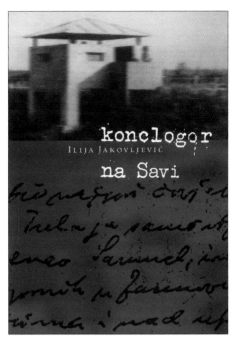

1 BOOK JACKET FOR AN AUTOBIOGRAPHY BY ILIJA JAKOVLJEVIC
DESIGN FIRM: Sensus Design Factory, Zagreb
DESIGNER/ ILLUSTRATOR: Nedjeljko Spoljar
PHOTOGRAPHER: Marko Dragicevic
CLIENT: Konzor

2 SELF-PROMOTIONAL BROCHURE FOR MENS DESIGN
DESIGN FIRM: Mens Design, Zagreb
DESIGNER: Suncana Matijasevic

3 LOGO FOR A TELEVISION/ BROADCASTING COMPANY
DESIGN FIRM: Korzinekdizajn, Zagreb
ART DIRECTOR/ DESIGNER: Marko Korzinek
CLIENT: Kanal Ri

4 SPREAD FROM "GODINE NOVE", A CULTURE MAGAZINE
DESIGN FIRM: Sensus Design Factory, Zagreb
ART DIRECTOR/ DESIGNER/ TYPOGRAPHER: Nedjeljko Spoljar
CLIENT: Konzor

5 LOGO FOR THE CROATIAN POST
DESIGN FIRM: Designsystem, Zagreb
DESIGNER: Boris Malesevic

6 IDENTITY FOR POLA HONORA, A WATER PURIFICATION SYSTEM
DESIGN FIRM: Likovni Studio D.O.O., Sveta Nedjelja
ART DIRECTOR: Tomislav Mrcic
DESIGNER: Danko Jaksic

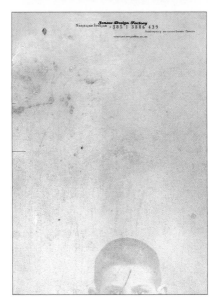

7 CALENDAR FOR THE CROATIAN BLIND UNION
DESIGN FIRM: Castelvenere Design, Zagreb
ART DIRECTOR: Tadej Bratelj
DESIGNERS: Tadej Bratelj, Sanja Rocco

8 STATIONERY FOR SENSUS DESIGN FACTORY
DESIGN FIRM: Sensus Design Factory, Zagreb
ART DIRECTOR/ DESIGNER: Nedjeljko Spoljar
PHOTOGRAPHER: Domagoj Lakos

9 COVER OF A CATALOGUE FOR ZELJKO PUSIC,
A HANDWEAVING ARTIST
ART DIRECTOR/ DESIGNER: Rajna Ljubicic, Zagreb
PHOTOGRAPHER: Robert Les
CLIENT: Galerija Klovicevi dvori

10 EXHIBITION POSTER FOR HDD CROATIAN DESIGN ASSOCIATES
DESIGN FIRM: Studio International, Zagreb
ART DIRECTOR: Boris Ljubicic
DESIGNERS/ ILLUSTRATORS: Boris Ljubicic, Igor Masniak

11 1999 CALENDAR FOR CROATIA AIRLINES
DESIGNER: Ivana Ivankovic, Zagreb
PHOTOGRAPHER: Damir Fabijanié

12 SELF-PROMOTIONAL 2001 CALENDAR
DESIGN FIRM: Studio International, Zagreb
DESIGNER/ PHOTOGRAPHER: Boris Ljubicic

DENMARK: COUNTRY FILE

HOTELS

HOTEL NYHAVN 71, NYHAVN 71, COPENHAGEN. T (+45) 33 11 8585 In a 200-year old warehouse, this quiet hotel overlooks the old ships of Nyhavn. The maritime interiors have been preserved and the tiny rooms with warm woollen bedspreads and leather armchairs make for a cosy stay.

SKOVSHOVED HOTEL, STRANDVEJEN 267, CHARLOTTENLUND, COPENHAGEN. T (+45) 39 64 0028 Originally a fishermen's pub, this small unpretentious hotel lies just off the coast in the leafy suburbs of Copenhagen near Arne Jacobsen's Klampenborg housing scheme of the early fifties. City centre fifteen minutes south, Louisiana Modern Art Museum 30 minutes north. Eat in the elegant conservatory with its sinewy steel ribs inset with frameless glass panels. (John Young, Architect, London)

THE ADMIRAL HOTEL, TOLDBODGADE 24, COPENHAGEN. T(+45) 33 74 1414 This building, dating from 1787, used to be a warehouse and is now a nautical-themed hotel. Located by the water front it has by far the best view of the port of Copenhagen. When weather allows, you can even see the west coast of Sweden.

THE RADISSON SAS ROYAL, HAMMERICHSGADE 1, COPENHAGEN. T (+45) 33 42 6000 The SAS Royal is a monument to Danish Modern Design. It was designed by the famous Danish architect Arne Jacobsen, and is located downtown just across the Tivoli Gardens. (Ulrik Westergaard, Copenhagen)

RESTAURANTS, CAFÉS & BARS

LUMSKEBUGTEN, ESPLANADEN 21, COPENHAGEN. T (+45) 33 15 6029 Wonderful restaurant near the harbour and old fortress, serving marvellous seafood.

DEN GULE COTTAGE, T (+45) 31 64 06 91 Tiny thatched cottage restaurant, a mile up the road from the Skovshoved Hotel. (John Young, Architect, London)

KROGS FISKERESTAURANT, GAMMEL STRAND 38, COPENHAGEN. T (+45) 33 15 8915 This seafood restaurant is located at Copenhagen's old fish market. They honour tradition here, and there is an atmosphere of warmth and "good old days".

ZELESTE, STORE STANDSTRÆDE 6, COPENHAGEN. T (+45) 33 16 0606 Café and restaurant in one. A popular spot in the Nyhavn area, and with good reason: fantastic dishes and excellent service. (Ulrik Westergaard, Copenhagen)

MUSEUMS & GALLERIES

CARLSBERG MUSEUM, VALBY LANGGADE 1, COPENHAGEN. TEL: (+45) 33 27 1274 A beer museum where you can see all their bottle and label designs. The Carlsberg Archives contain the entire design history of the Carlberg brand.

KUNSTINDUSTRIMUSEET, BREDGADE 67, COPENHAGEN. T (+45) 33 14 9452 The Museum of Decorative Art. Exhibitions here vary from clothes to jewellery.

LOUISIANA MUSEUM OF MODERN ART, GAMMEL STRANDVEJ 13, COPENHAGEN. T (+45) 49 19 0719 Although a train ride away north of Copenhagen, this place offers a wonderful all-round experience of nature, fine art and architecture. Their fine art exhibitions change rapidly. (Ulrik Westergaard, Copenhagen)

KOLDING Situated on the east coast of Jutland, Kolding is particularly well-placed for visiting three outstanding museums of 20th-century art: the Asger Jorn Collection at Silkeborg; the Emil Nolde Museum at Seebüll; and one of the world's most elegant museums, Nordjyllands Kunstmusem — by the Finnish architect, Alvar Aalto at Aalborg. (Herbert Spencer, Designer, London)

DANSK DESIGN CENTER, H.C. ANDERSENS BOULEVARD 27, COPENHAGEN. T (+45) 33 69 3369 The Danish Design Centre follows the movements in design very closely. They have just moved into a new building in which they house their showrooms and bookstore. They publish a wide range of design publications, all in English and all available in their bookstore.

DANSK ARKITEKTUR CENTER, GAMMEL DOK, STRANDGADE 27, COPENHAGEN. T (+45) 32 57 1930 The Danish Architectural Centre. Something of a development and discussion forum. In their bookstore you will find a large selection of books about design and architecture. (Ulrik Westergaard, Copenhagen)

THE VIKING SHIP MUSEUM, STRANDEGEN, ROSKILDE, SJÆLLAND. T (+45) 42 35 6555 In the late fifties amateur divers discovered some fragments which led to a major archaeological find. In all five Viking boats were lifted, preserved and reassembled. The museum, designed for the purpose, is exemplary. Sited right at the water's edge it displays the ships beautifully and shows how they were constructed and sailed. Terrific gift shop. (Michael Glickman, Inventor, London)

PLACES OF INTEREST

PAUSTIAN, KALKBRAENDERILØBSKAJ 2, COPENHAGEN. T (+45) 33 18 5501 Purpose-built showroom for contemporary furniture and textiles designed by Jorn Utzon in Copenhagen's Docklands. Utzon's use of simple materials and details make a perfect backdrop to view Corb, Eames, Aalto, Breuer and lesser mortals in acres of space. Part of the ground floor is given over to an excellent restaurant. (John Young, Architect, London)

See "COPENHAGEN THIS WEEK" at www.ctw.dk Information not included on this site is not worth knowing ... (Ulrik Westergaard, Copenhagen)

BOOKSHOPS

TEGNECENTER, STORE KONGENSGADE 21, COPENHAGEN. T (+45) 33 63 9033 For graphic design books and supplies.

BRANNERS BIBLIOFIL , APS BREDGATE 10, COPENHAGEN. The place for rare books in Copenhagen. (Lars Olaf Laurentii, Designer, Stockholm)

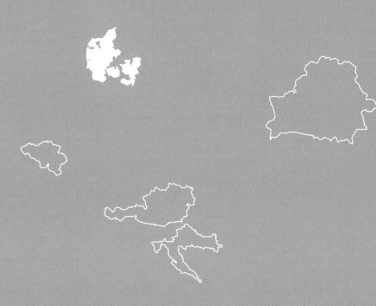
Area | 1,000 km2	043.1	Capital City	Copenhagen	Monetary Unit	Danish krone	
Population | 1,000	5,334	Capital City Population | 1,000	1,326	GDP per Capita (US $)	33,191	
Design Population | 1,000	000.6	Languages	Danish	International Dialling Code	+45	

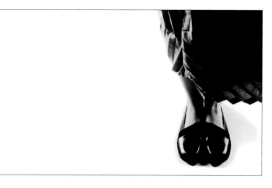
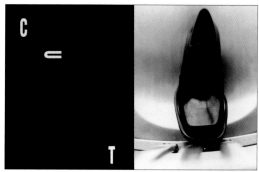

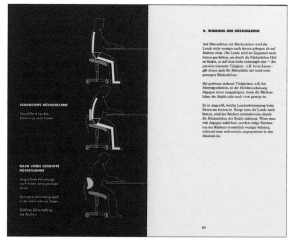

1, 2 PROMOTIONAL BROCHURES FOR A LINE OF SHOES BY ECCO
DESIGN FIRM: Black Pencil, Copenhagen
ART DIRECTOR: Anders Majgård
PHOTOGRAPHER: Morten Bjarnhof

3 LOGO FOR THE CITY OF AALBORG
DESIGN FIRM: Griffin Grafisk Design, Aalborg
ART DIRECTOR/ DESIGNER: Leo Griffin
CLIENT: Aalborg Kommune

4 LOGO CELEBRATING THE YEAR 2000
IN CHRISTIAN CHURCHES THROUGHOUT DENMARK
DESIGNER/ ILLUSTRATOR: Kim Broström, Copenhagen
CLIENT: Kirkefondet (Church Foundation)

5 1999 PROMOTIONAL CALENDAR
FOR A GRAPHIC DESIGN AND PRODUCTION COMPANY
DESIGN FIRM: Datagraf Auning AS, Auning
ART DIRECTOR: Susanne Mejlgaard
PHOTOGRAPHER: Ann Malmgren

6 PRODUCT BINDER AND BROCHURES FOR FRITZ HANSEN,
A FURNITURE COMPANY
DESIGN FIRM: Kühnel Design AS, Copenhagen
ART DIRECTOR/ DESIGNER: Jakob Kühnel
PHOTOGRAPHY: Piotr & Co

7 PUBLIC INFORMATION PAMPHLET
OFFERING GUIDELINES FOR PROPER POSTURE AT WORK
DESIGN FIRM: Kühnel Design AS, Copenhagen
ART DIRECTOR: Jakob Kühnel
DESIGNER/ ILLUSTRATOR: Mathias J Mathiesen
CLIENT: Fritz Hansen AS

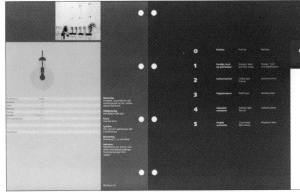

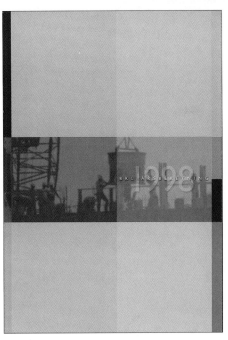

8 BROCHURE INTRODUCING THE NEW DANISH ELECTRONIC
RESEARCH LIBRARY ON THE WEB
DESIGN FIRM: Kühnel Design AS, Copenhagen
ART DIRECTOR: Jakob Kuhnel
DESIGNER: Matilda Plöjel
CLIENT: DEF

9 LOGO FOR THE SEMINARIUM FOR HÅNDVÆRK OG DESIGN
(COLLEGE OF ARTS, CRAFTS AND DESIGN)
DESIGN FIRM: Griffin Grafisk Design, Aalborg
ART DIRECTOR/ DESIGNER: Leo Griffin

10 LOGO FOR SOLSKOVGAARD, A JUVENILE CORRECTION CENTRE
DESIGN FIRM: Griffin Grafisk Design, Aalborg
ART DIRECTOR/ DESIGNER: Leo Griffin

11 COVER OF "DEBY", A HEALTH-CARE MAGAZINE FOR
YOUNG PEOPLE
DESIGN FIRM: Hovedkvarteret Aps, Copenhagen
ART DIRECTOR/ DESIGNER/ ILLUSTRATOR: Klaus Wilhardt
PHOTOGRAPHERS: Thyman, Maria Sattrup, Schiller & Co
CLIENT: Sundhedsstyrelsen

12 PRODUCT BINDER AND CATALOGUE
FOR A LIGHTING FIXTURES COMPANY
DESIGN FIRM: Kühnel Design AS, Copenhagen
ART DIRECTOR: Jakob Kühnel
DESIGNERS: Karsten Riis, Jakob Kühnel
PHOTOGRAPHER: Kai Lergaard
CLIENT: Arkilux

13 1998 ANNUAL REPORT FOR A CONSTRUCTION COMPANY
DESIGN FIRM: Profilen Aps, Aarhus
ART DIRECTOR: Jørn Rasmussen
PHOTOGRAPHER: Morten Larsen
CLIENT: BKL

1, 2 ILLUSTRATIONS FOR A SERIES OF BIBLE TEXTS
FOR A PARISH NEWSPAPER
DESIGN FIRM: Niko Taina Firma, Tammisaari
ILLUSTRATOR: Niko Taina
CLIENT: Vantaan Lauri

1 2

FINLAND: COUNTRY FILE

RESTAURANTS, CAFÉS & BARS

PAVILION RESTAURANT, MARIEHAMN, ALAND ISLANDS (halfway between Sweden and Finland). T (+358) 18 19141 Housed in a decorated timber building designed by Lars Sonck in an extraordinary Finnish-Japanese style and serving great seafood. In the summer you can eat on the balcony projecting out over the water. (Peter Lloyd Jones, Academic, Saltash)

SAVOY HOTEL, ETELÄESPLANADI 14, HELSINKI. T (+358) 9 176 571 Designed by Alvar Aalto, a delight to the eye as well as the palate and just the place for a designer to be and be seen ... (Niels Diffrient, Designer, Connecticut)

SARKANLINNA, JUHA ARKAD 12B, HELSINKI. T (+358) 9 440732 An unusual restaurant located on an island about ten minutes by boat from Helsinki. Housed in a traditional Finnish-style red and brown brick building, it is stunning on further exploration and approached through a beautiful courtyard. There are fine views of Helsinki and the surrounding islands from here. The food is good, varying from Finnish specialities to traditional European, all supported by a fine wine list. Closed during winter months from October. (Michael Peters, Designer, London)

MUSEUMS & GALLERIES

KIASMA MUSEUM OF CONTEMPORARY ART, MANNERHEIMINAUKIO 2, HELSINKI. T (+358) 9 17 336500, www.kiasma.fi This stunning museum was designed by the American architect, Steven Holl, and opened in 1998. The building itself is a work of art and houses the best in Finnish art, with exhibitions of well-known modern artists. (Michael Peters, Designer, London)

PLACES OF INTEREST

HVITTRÄSK, LUOMA, KIRKKONUMMI. T (+358) 2975 779 When in Finland it would be crazy not to go to Hvitträsk, the site of a community founded at the turn of the 20th-century by Eliel Saarinen. The studio-homes were inspired by William Morris and the concept of a brotherhood of working artists. Superlative setting by the lakeside and the grouping of buildings all with their Art Nouveau interiors recently and very well restored. There is also a good restaurant. We recommend the reindeer with cranberries. (David Mellor, Designer, Sheffield)

Area | 1,000 km2	338.0	Capital City	Helsinki	Monetary Unit	Finnish markka
Population | 1,000	5,158	Capital City Population | 1,000	516	GDP per Capita (US $)	20,000
Design Population | 1,000	000.9	Languages	Finnish, Swedish, Lapp, Russian	International Dialling Code	+358

FRANCE: COUNTRY FILE

HOTELS

GRAND HOTEL NORD PINUS, PLACE DU FORUM, ARLES. With its old-fashion decoration, this is where Picasso, Cocteau, and the famous toreros used to come. Full of charm.

Two hotels in Avignon: LA MIRANDE, 4 PLACE DE LA MIRANDE, AVIGNON. T (+33) 490 859 393 The most beautiful hotel-restaurant — so quiet and so lovely — in an old cardinal's palace located in a tranquil cobbled square at the foot of the Palais des Popes, and L'HÔTEL DU PALAIS DES PAPES, 1, RUE GERARD PHILIPE, AVIGNON. T (+33) 490 860 413 Very comfortable, pleasant and very "Côté Sud" in its decoration. (Pierre Berthier, Designer, Avignon)

HOTEL DUC DE SAINT-SIMON, 14 RUE DE SAINT-SIMON, PARIS 6E. T (+33) 1 45 48 35 66 One of the most stylish and discreet hotels in Paris (and probably anywhere in Europe), on a quiet street off the Boulevard St. Germain. Enter through wooden gates into a cobbled forecourt and find a 17th-century mansion full of antiques. Unpretentious, but quite small and often booked up. A short walk from some of the best cafés and jazz clubs in the city. (Michael Thierens, Designer, London)

LES DEUX FRÈRES, ROQUEBRUNE CAP MARTIN. T (+33) 93 289900 Hotel/restauarant above Monte Carlo Bay with a terrific view from the terrace over the bay, all overlooked by an ancient medieval castle. (Filippo Spiezia, Multimedia Designer, Italy)

RESTAURANTS, CAFÉS & BARS

Two cafés in Avignon: LE GRAND CAFÉ, 4 RUE ESCALIER STE ANNE, AVIGNON. T (+33) 4 90 86 86 77 Meet the people of Avignon here, as well as actors and celebrities during the international Festival of Theatre in July, and CHEZ FLORIANER, RUE SAINT AGRICOL, AVIGNON. Charming cooking (Provencal/Mediterranean food made with fresh ingredients) and charming terrace, in the centre of town. (Pierre Berthier, Designer, Avignon)

LA GRILLADE AU FEU DE BOIS, FLASSANS-SUR-ISSOLE, LE LUC-EN-PROVENCE. T (+33) 94 69 71 20 Lovely 18th-century farmhouse, where you can stay the night or just have an excellent provencal meal on a lovely terrace under a 200-year old mulberry tree. In Le Luc-en-Provence itself is the interesting National Stamp Museum. (Dick Bruna, Illustrator, Utrecht)

LE MARLY, COURS MARLY DU MUSÉE DU LOUVRE, PARIS. In the grand courtyard of the Louvre facing the Pyramid, a beautiful view and a peaceful restaurant.

BAR DE LA CROIX ROUGE, 2 CARREFOUR, CROIX ROUGE, PARIS. A nice typical Parisian café. (Krista Sochor & Zoé Vayssières, Designers, Paris)

BRASSERIE BOFINGER, 327 RUE DE LA BASTILLE, PARIS. T (+33) 1 42 72 87 82 The most classically beautiful of Parisian brasseries. The food is hearty rather than remarkable, but the décor is sublime. (Roger Mavity, Businessman, London)

AU GRAND INQUISITEUR, 18, RUE DU CHÂTEAU, ROQUEBRUNE VILLAGE. T (+33) 93 350537 In the centre of a little medieval village, built into a rock cave. The food is delicious and they have all kinds of French cheese. (Filippo Spiezia, Multimedia Designer, Italy)

MUSEUMS & GALLERIES

MUSÉE DE LA BANDE DESSINÉE (MUSEUM OF COMICS), ANGOULÊME. The largest library of comics in the world. Even the street signs are in 'speech balloon' format. (David Kingsley, Consultant, London)

LE MUSÉE DU JARDIN BOTANIQUE, CHERBOURG, NORMANDY. A small 18th-century house standing in a garden. This museum houses collections of butterflies, Chinese polychrome sculpture, Eskimo outfits, photographs of African queens, stuffed animals, paintings, oddities, beautiful things. (André François, Artist, Grisy les Plâtres)

LA FABULOSERIE, DICY. T (+33) 86 63 64 21 Two hours south of Paris, just off the A6, an 'Art Brut' Museum with some outstanding and scary work. The main reason for coming here is the manège de Petit Pierre, a carousel and assorted mechanised scenario of people, animals and machines which all springs to life at the pull of a lever. A wonder of the world .... (Jeff Fisher, Artist, Paris)

MUSÉE HISTORIQUE DES TISSUS, 34, RUE DE LA CHARITÉ, LYON. T (+33) 4 78 38 42 00 This historical textile museum is housed in a charming 18th-century building and features two floors of fabulous fabrics — Coptic, Egyptian, Middle Eastern, Oriental as well as Italian, Spanish and the famous Lyon silks. Closed Mondays.

PLACES OF INTEREST

L'ISLE SUR LA SORGUE, NEAR AVIGNON The island of antiques, down by the river. Millions of things and furniture to find ... (Pierre Berthier, Designer, Avignon)

LURS-EN-PROVENCE, NEAREST TOWN: FORCALQUIER. Each summer the premier graphic design association in the francophone world, the Rencontres Internationales de Lure, settle into their 'Chancellerie' in a tiny seductive village .... amongst a smell of thyme, olives, and if the wind is in the right direction, lavender. If you need a rest from design don't go near it in August or September. (Colin Banks, Graphic Designer, London)

OBERKAMPF VILLAGE, 11TH ARRONDISSEMENT, PARIS. About 10 years ago, many artists, architects, designers and photographers moved to this east side of Paris because of the cheap prices and because it was possible to find great lofts for working and living. Nowadays, it is one of the most lively and alternative places in Paris .... coffee shops, patisseries, restaurants, jazz bars, theatres, bookshops, architectural curiosities.... (Philippe Apeloig, Designer, Paris)

VILLA SAVOYE, CHEMIN DE VILLIERS, POISSY, PARIS. Villa Savoye was the last, and arguably the finest, of Le Corbusier's purist villas. Technically, a perfect expression of his architectural theory, but also an extraordinarily sensual building in the middle of an overgrown buttercup field. (Alice Rawsthorn, Journalist, Paris)

BOOKSHOPS & SHOPPING

LA HUNE, 170, BOULEVARD ST. GERMAIN, PARIS. The best design bookshop in town.

INTERART, 1 RUE DE L'EST, PARIS. T (+33) 1 43 49 36 60 For graphic design books.

COLETTE, 213, RUE SAINT HONORÉ, PARIS. T (+33) 1 55 35 33 90 An avant-garde art gallery of a shop selling edgy design items. The shop is a three-storey white-washed marvel. Street level has product design, the first floor has fashion for both sexes, and on the mezzanine at the back there is a small bookshop. All displays change weekly .... the total design shop experience. (Carl Christiansson, Architect, Paris)

CALLIGRANE, 4 & 6 RUE DU PONT LOUIS-PHILLIPPE, PARIS. T (+33) 1 48 04 31 89 Three little shops in a row selling fabulous papers, stationery and pens &c. (Boo Mitford, Designer, London)

Area | 1,000 km2	552.0	Capital City	Paris	Monetary Unit	French franc & euro
Population | 1,000	58,804	Capital City Population | 1,000	9,469	GDP per Capita (US $)	26,444
Design Population | 1,000	002.0	Languages	French	International Dialling Code	+33

MANIFESTE
pour la route

Les routes explorées
par les auteurs de ce Manifeste…

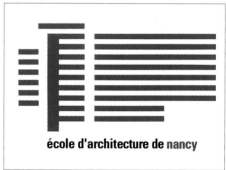

école d'architecture de nancy

1-3 COVER AND SPREADS FROM "MANIFESTE POUR LA ROUTE",
A PROMOTIONAL BOOK FOR A ROAD BUILDER
AGENCY: EURO RSCG Omnium, Paris
DESIGN FIRM: HTB Design, Paris
ART DIRECTORS: Krista Sochor, Zoé Vayssières
ILLUSTRATOR: Véronique Bour
CLIENT: Colas

4 CATALOGUE FOR AN ART EXHIBITION
DESIGN FIRM: Saluces Design & Communication, Avignon
DESIGNER: Jean-Paul Camargo
ILLUSTRATION: detail of Jean Hélion's Le Rêve et le Songe
CLIENT: RMG Palais des Papes

5 LOGO FOR ÉCOLE D'ARCHITECTURE DE NANCY
DESIGNER: Steven Vitale, Briey-en-Forêt

6 LOGO FOR LE STUDIO, A PHOTOGRAPH LIBRARY
DESIGN FIRM: Signland, Nice
DESIGNER: Yvan Balsamo

7, 8 SIGNAGE FOR HEADQUARTERS OF MECCANO,
MANUFACTURER OF BUILDING TOYS
DESIGN FIRM: Metzler & Associés, Paris
DESIGNER: Marc-Antoine Herrmann

9, 10 POSTAGE STAMPS AND SIGNAGE FOR LA POSTE
DESIGN FIRM: Dragon Rouge, Paris
DESIGNERS: Philippe de Langhé, Georges Olivereau
PHOTOGRAPHER: Nicolas Peron

11-14 POSTCARD SERIES FOR CARTES D'ART
ART DIRECTOR/ ILLUSTRATOR: Claude-Henri Saunier, Sainville

15 BOTTLE DESIGN FOR ALCOHOLIC BEVERAGE
DESIGN FIRM: Dragon Rouge, Paris
DESIGNER: Patrick Veyssière
CLIENT: United Distillers & Vintners

16 SELF-PROMOTIONAL BROCHURE
DESIGN FIRM: Metzler & Associés, Paris
ART DIRECTOR: Marc-Antoine Herrmann
DESIGNER: Anne Martirené
PHOTOGRAPHER: Didier Truffaut/ Photonica

17 AWARD CARDS FOR AN INSURANCE COMPANY
DESIGN FIRM: Printel, Paris
DESIGNER/ ILLUSTRATOR: Laurence Alessandri
CLIENT: GMF

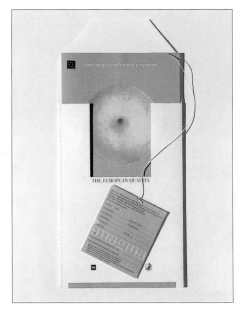

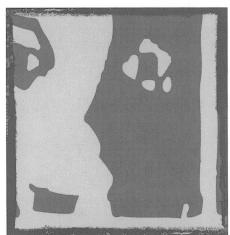

L'Arlésienne de Daudet. Devant le désaccord entre titre et distribution, les spectateurs de 1872 qui assistaient à la création de L'Arlésienne ont pu se sentir frustrés : l'héroïne attendue ne se montrait pas

...On a certes beaucoup parlé de la beauté des filles d'Arles. Cette beauté est réelle, et quelques-unes des descendantes de

---

**18 PROMOTIONAL TEABAG FOR IMAGINA,
A VIRTUAL REALITY EXHIBITION**
DESIGN FIRM: AreA Strategic Design, Paris
CREATIVE DIRECTOR: Fulvio Caldarelli
ART DIRECTOR: Niccolo Desii

19 SELF-PROMOTIONAL BOOKLET FOR A DESIGN CONSULTANCY
DESIGN FIRM: Printel, Paris
DESIGNER/ ILLUSTRATOR: Vincent Lefèvre

**20, 21 SPREAD AND COVER OF CATALOGUE
FOR THE EXHIBITION "ARLÉSIENNE: LE MYTHE?"**
DESIGN FIRM: Alyen, Marseille
DESIGNERS: Didier Mazière, Hubert Campigli
PHOTOGRAPHER: Jean-Luc Mabit
CLIENT: Museon Arlatan

GERMANY: COUNTRY FILE

HOTELS

HOTEL ROBERT MAYER, ROBERT-MAYER-STRASSE 44, FRANKFURT. T (+49) 69 970 910 A small turn-of-the-century hotel with each room decorated by a different Frankfurt artist. Furniture delights include Rietveld and Frank Lloyd Wright.

HOTEL SCHLOSS HUGENPOET, AUGUST-THYSSEN-STRASSE 51, KETTWIG, ESSEN. T (+49) 20 54 12 040 The setting of this hotel will come as something of a surprise in this area of heavy industry: a castle surrounded by a moat set in its own park, only half an hour from Essen's Poster Museum. (Thomas Manss, Designer, London)

HOTEL OPERA, HOTEL GARNI, ST ANNA-STRASSE 10, MUNICH. T (+49) 89 225 533 36 This small gem is on a quiet little street off Maximillianstrasse. The black and white facade will delight designers especially: buzz the entrance bell and the white double doors silently open to charming interiors. (Helen & Gene Federico, Designer/Illustrator, New York)

RESTAURANTS, CAFÉS & BARS

KADEWE, WITTENBERGPLATZ, TAUENTZIEN STRASSE, BERLIN.
On the sixth floor of the Kaufhaus des Westens you will find a choice of food beyond belief (pick your supper from brimming tanks of live fish). Snacks range from jacket potatoes to the 'nouvellest' cuisine. Cheeses are sold country by country. (Thomas Manss, Designer, London)

BAR AM LÜTZOWPLATZ, LÜTZOWPLATZ 7, BERLIN. T (+49) 30 262 6807 Known for its architecture and great design .... (Kyra Vögele-Müller, Art Director, Berlin)

PARIS BAR, KANTSTRASSE, BERLIN. T (+49) 30 313 8052 This restaurant gives the impression of an eternal institution of naturalness. Good wines and food, pleasant atmosphere. Famous actors, writers, and globetrotters meet here. Simple ambience. Each waiter has an individual, strong personality. (Gunter Rambow, Designer, Frankfurt)

RISTORANTE LA FATORRIA, WULSBÜTTEL. T (+49) 4746 515 Our agency's favourite restaurant is located between Bremen and Bremerhaven in a small countryside village called Wulsbüttel. On the outside it looks like a normal sort of pub, but inside you find the finest Italian restaurant in the northern hemisphere. Home-grown products (e.g. mushrooms) are used in the most delicious food we have ever tasted. We can highly recommend their ever-delicious six course meal. They also feature probably the world's largest pepper mill which has to be carried to your table by at least two waiters. And best of all: reasonable prices. (Jens Pfennig, Braue Design, Bremerhaven)

MUSEUMS & GALLERIES

MUSEUM FÜR MODERNE KUNST, DOMSTRASSE 40, FRANKFURT. T (+49) 69 2123 0447 Housed in a distinctive triangular building by Hans Hollein.

NEUE SAMMLUNG, PRINZREGENTENSTRASSE 3, MUNICH. T (+49) 89 22 78 44 An honest way of exhibiting design and design history. The Neue Sammlung has the world's biggest collection of design objects and holds two to three exhibitions a year. Information is on promotional posters designed by Mendell & Oberer. (Justus Oehler, Designer, London)

STADTISCHE GALERIE IM LENBACHHAUS, LUISENSTRASSE 33, MUNICH. T (+49) 89 23 33 2000 Formerly the residence of Franz von Lenbach, its reputation is based on the collection of works by the Blaue Reiter (Blue Rider) group. Apart from Marc, Macke and Kandinsky there are wonderful works by Jawlensky and Klee. Good small cafeteria. (Virginia Pepper, Public Relations, Switzerland)

HAUS DER WIRTSCHAFT, DESIGN CENTRE, WILLI-BLEICHER-STRASSE 19, STUTTGART. T (+49) 711 123 2500 A 19th-century building, recently re-furbished and now the showpiece of Baden-Württemberg design promotion. There are always exhibitions in its 3,000 square metres of exhibition space. Have a coffee in its cafeteria called 'Logo'. (Klaus Lehmann, Professor of Product Design, Stuttgart)

VITRA DESIGN MUSEUM, CHARLES EAMES STRASSE 1, WEIL AM RHEIN. T (+49) 7621 702 351 Designed by Frank Gehry to house the Vitra Design Foundation's collection of 1,200 furnishings from 1850 to the present. The museum has special exhibitions covering key pieces from the history of industrial furniture design. The exhibition programme also includes architecture, photography, video and graphic arts. Comprehensive library and archive of early and rare design books and sales catalogues. (Verner Panton†, Designer, Basel)

PLACES OF INTEREST

BAUHAUS DESSAU, GROPIUSALLEE 38, DESSAU. T (+49) 19 52 22 Albers, Herbert Bayer, Kandinsky and Paul Klee taught here. Lisitzky and Piet Zwart visited and lectured briefly. If you are travelling between Berlin and Leipzig, reserve a day to visit this historic UNESCO World Heritage site. (Walter Allner, Designer, New York)

BOOKSHOPS & SHOPPING

POSTER GALERIE HAMBURG, GROSSE BLEICHEN 31, HAMBURG. T (+49) 40 34 68 50 One of the largest poster shops in West Germany.

STILWERK, GROSS ELBSTRASSE 68, HAMBURG. T (+49) 40 306 210 Six indoor gallery floors with a concentration of leading international retailers, manufacturers and brands, you find nearly all kinds of design products: furniture, lighting, fabrics, giftware. (Bruno K. Wiese, Designer, Hamburg)

KOPP FACHBUCH, MAINTAL. T (+49) 6181 450 74 For graphic design books and magazines.

MAGAZIN, LAUTENSCHLAGERSTRASSE 16, STUTTGART. T (+49) 711 29 32 06 The most likely place to meet architects and designers who buy their furniture, door handles, lighting fittings or books here. An interesting store founded by designers, commercially successful and still expanding. Next door to the airport terminal. (Klaus Lehmann, Professor of Product Design, Stuttgart)

Area | 1,000 km2	357.0		Capital City	Berlin		Monetary Unit	Deutsch mark & euro
Population | 1,000	82,079		Capital City Population | 1,000	3,471		GDP per Capita (US $)	29,632
Design Population | 1,000	15.0		Languages	German		International Dialling Code	+49

Januar *January*
1 2 3 4 5 6 7 8 9 10 11 12 13 14 15 16 17 18 19 20 21 22 23 24 25 26 27 28 29 30 31

Mai *May*
2 3 4 5 6 7 8 9 10 11 12 13 14 15 16 17 18 19 20 21 22 23 24 25 26 27 28 29 30 31

September *September*
1 2 3 4 5 6 7 8 9 10 11 12 13 14 15 16 17 18 19 20 21 22 23 24 25 26 27 28 29 30

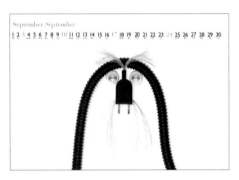

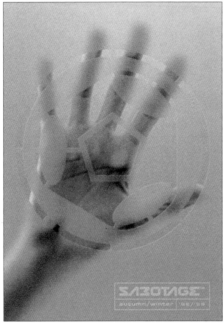

A Alligator
They have a long head and a tail and a thick, tough skin. Alligators are reptiles and live in rivers and swamps in the United States and in China.

G Giraffe
It is an large African animal with a very long neck, long thin legs and a coat with brown patches.

November *November*
1 2 3 4 5 6 7 8 9 10 11 12 13 14 15 16 17 18 19 20 21 22 23 24 25 26 27 28 29 30

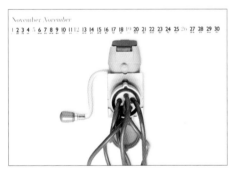

I Insect
Any of a large group of small animals without a backbone. Insects have a body divided into three parts. Flies, beetles, ants and grasshoppers are insects.

Q Quack
"Quack" is the infant word for a duck. It is a water bird that has a broad, flat bill and webbed feet that help it to swim. There are both wild and tame ducks.

1-4 CALENDAR FOR AN ELECTRICITY COMPANY
DESIGN FIRM: AReA Strategic Design, Frankfurt
CREATIVE DIRECTOR: Antonio Romano
ART DIRECTOR: Stefano Aureli
CONCEPT: Silvio Pasquarelli
DESIGNER: Mario Catizone
CLIENT: Verlags-und Wirtschaftsgesellschaft der Elektrizitätswerke

5 LOGO FOR A NUDIST CLUB
DESIGNER/ ILLUSTRATOR: Frederic Herring, Karlsruhe
CLIENT: LBK

6,7 CATALOGUE FOR SABOTAGE, A FASHION COLLECTION
DESIGN FIRM: Metzger & Schmidt
(Designbüro MESCH), Manheim
ART DIRECTOR: Gianni Macario
DESIGNERS: Manuela Schmidt, Martina Metzger
PHOTOGRAPHER: Matt Wilson
CLIENT: Profashion GmbH

8-11 ANIMAL ALPHABET FLASH CARDS
ART DIRECTOR/ ILLUSTRATOR: Nina David, Düsseldorf

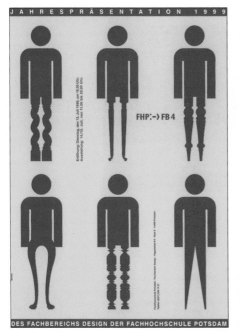

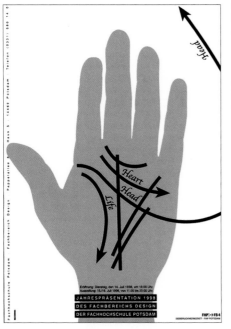

12, 13 POSTERS FOR STUDENT DESIGN COMPETITIONS
DESIGNER/ ILLUSTRATOR: Prof Lex Drewinski, Berlin
CLIENT: Fachhochschule Potsdam

14 INSIDE COVER FROM A PROMOTIONAL CD FOR THE NEW MERCEDES 'S' CLASS
DESIGN FIRM: Scholz & Volkmer, Wiesbaden
ART DIRECTOR: Anette Scholz
DESIGNERS: Katja Rickert, Susanne Schwalm
CLIENT: Daimler Chrysler AG

15-17 SLEEVE ART FOR RELEASES ON THE PLASTIC CITY LABEL
DESIGN FIRM: U C Graphic, Neckargemünd
ART DIRECTORS: Ulrich Ambach, Evelyn Gögele

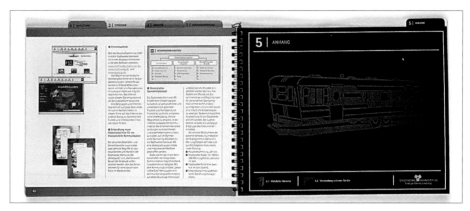

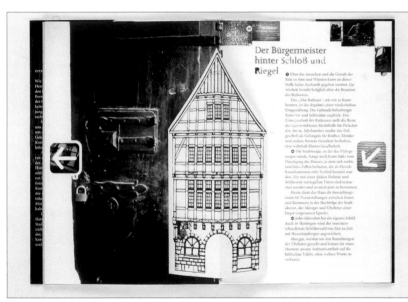

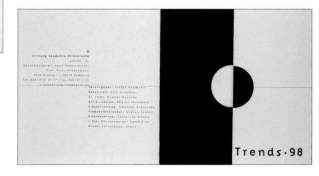

*Never run
an advertisement
you would not
want your own
family to see.*

David Ogilvy

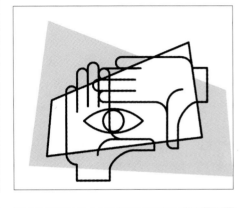

26 SELF-PROMOTIONAL BOOK FOR AD AGENCY
AGENCY: Ogilvy & Mather, Frankfurt
ART DIRECTOR: Lutz Augustin

27 LOGO FOR BURKHARD HENRICHS PHOTOGRAPHY STUDIO
DESIGN FIRM: Voss Design, Essen
ART DIRECTOR/ DESIGNER: Axel Voss

28 SELF-PROMOTIONAL BROCHURE
FOR ILLUSTRATOR SABINE KUSSMAUL
DESIGN FIRM: Volker Müller Grafik Design, Königsbach-Stein
ART DIRETOR/ DESIGNER: Volker Müller

29 BROCHURE FOR PRESENTATION TO THE CLIENTS OF K5,
A MANAGEMENT SERVICE COMPANY
DESIGN FIRM: Kyra Design, Berlin
DESIGNER: Kyra Vögele-Müller
ILLUSTRATOR: Christian C Haider
PHOTOGRAPHER: Rhomberg & Kaufmann

30 LOGO FOR WALKING CULTURE GALLERY
DESIGN FIRM: Voss Design, Essen
ART DIRECTOR/ DESIGNER: Axel Voss

31 STATIONERY BOX, USED IN PLACE OF A CATALOGUE
FOR THE MUSEUM DER DINGE (MUSEUM OF OBJECTS)
DESIGN FIRM: Im Stall GmbH, Berlin
DESIGNER: Claudius Lazzeroni

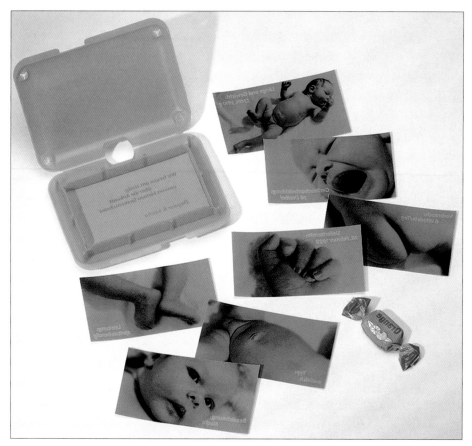

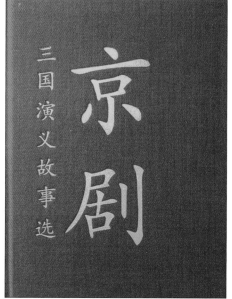

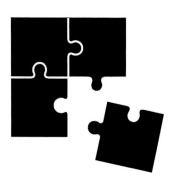

32 BIRTH-ANNOUNCEMENT PACKAGE
DESIGN FIRM: Artwork Station Graphikbüro, Biberach
DESIGNER/ PHOTOGRAPHER: Sascha Weihs

33 LOGO FOR CHRIST'S SAKE, A ROCK BAND
DESIGN FIRM: Braue Design, Bremerhaven
ART DIRECTOR/ DESIGNER/ ILLUSTRATOR: Marçel Robbers

34 LOGO FOR PORTOFINO, A RESTAURANT
DESIGN FIRM: Braue Design, Bremerhaven
ART DIRECTOR/ DESIGNER/ ILLUSTRATOR: Marçel Robbers

35 LOGO FOR URBAN GÖRGE, AN INVESTMENT COMPANY
DESIGN FIRM: Braue Design, Bremerhaven
ART DIRECTOR/ DESIGNER: Kai Braue
ILLUSTRATOR: Raimund Fohs

36 DESIGNS FOR A SET OF COFFEE CANS
DESIGN FIRM: Heinemann Nagel Blöck, Hamburg
DESIGNERS/ ILLUSTRATORS: Sönke Wildt, Alex Specht

37 BOOK ON THE PEKING OPERA FOR A GALLERY
DESIGN FIRM: Art Direction + Design, Stuttgart
ART DIRECTOR: Michael Kimmerle
CLIENT: Institut für Auslandsbeziehungen

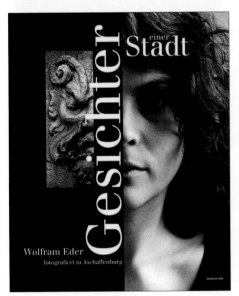

38, 39 COVER AND SPREAD FROM "MACHTSPIELE",
A BOOK DOCUMENTING A TYPE/ DESIGN CONFERENCE
DESIGNER: Marion Wagner, Berlin
CLIENT: Fachhochschule Potsdam

40 BOOK OF PHOTOGRAPHIC PORTRAITS
ART DIRECTOR: Herbert Wurm, Aschaffenburg
DESIGNER: Axel Bär
PHOTOGRAPHER: Wolfram Eder

41 DESIGN ANNUAL BOOK
DESIGN FIRM: Büro für Gestaltung, Offenbach
ART DIRECTORS/ DESIGNERS: Christoph Burkardt, Albrecht Hotz
CLIENT: Verlag form

42 LOGO FOR A MOTORCYCLE ACCESSORY LABEL
DESIGN FIRM: Sandra Müller Grafik Design, Stuttgart
DESIGNER: Sandra Müller

43 "VANISHED" POSTER FOR A FISHING MATERIALS COMPANY
DESIGN FIRM: Springer & Jacoby Werbung GmbH, Hamburg
ART DIRECTOR: Torsten Rieken
PHOTOGRAPHER: Gerd George
CLIENT: Deutsche Angelgeräte Manufaktur GmbH

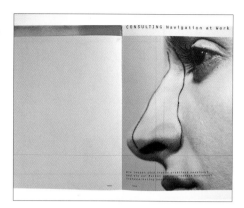

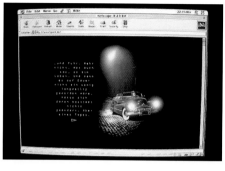

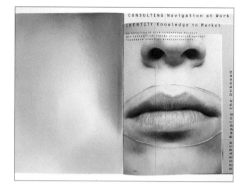

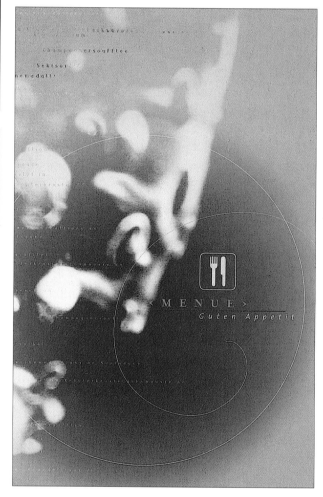

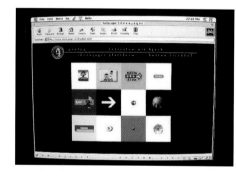

44, 45 BROCHURE FOR A RESEARCH CONSULTANCY
DESIGN FIRM: Büro Hamburg, Hamburg
ART DIRECTOR/ DESIGNER: Régine Thienhaus
ILLUSTRATOR: Birgit Eggers
PHOTOGRAPHERS: Nathaniel Goldberg, Claudia Kemp
CLIENT: Trendbüro

46-49 SELF-PROMOTIONAL WEB SITE (www.bjoerk.de)
DESIGN FIRM: Anders Björk GmbH, Lübeck
ART DIRECTOR/ DESIGNER/ ILLUSTRATOR: Andreas Trumpler

50, 51 MENU AND BOOKLET FOR A MILLENNIUM EVENT
DESIGN FIRM: Alles wird gut, Munich
DESIGNER: Katja Deml
CLIENT: Sport A

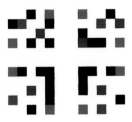

VOGELSANG
KONZEPTAGENTUR

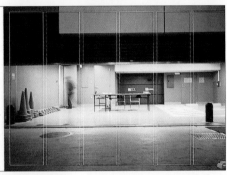

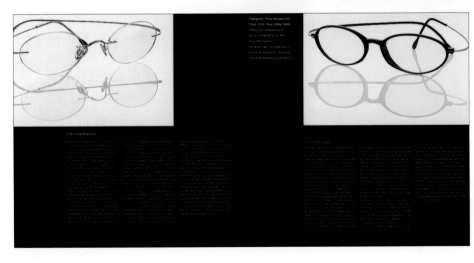

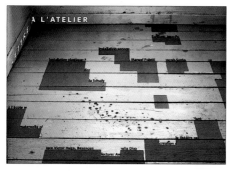

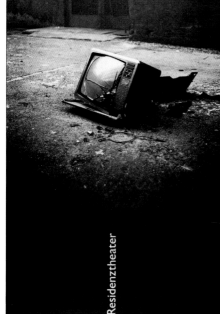

60-63 ILLUSTRATIONS FROM THE 1997 ANNUAL REPORT FOR AN INSURANCE COMPANY
DESIGN FIRM: Bernhard Kunkler, Freiburg
ART DIRECTOR: Karin Warzecha
ILLUSTRATOR/ PHOTOGRAPHER: Bernhard Kunkler
CLIENT: Marquard & Bahls AG

64 EXHIBITION POSTER FOR THREE ARTISTS
DESIGNER: Fons M Hickmann, Düsseldorf
PHOTOGRAPHER: Nicola Schudy
CLIENTS: Manuel Poletti, Nicola Schudy, Jean Françoise Santoro

65 PROMOTIONAL POSTER FOR A THEATRE
AGENCY: Jung von Matt an der Isar, Munich
ART DIRECTORS: Tobias Eichinger
DESIGNER: Oliver Voss
PHOTOGRAPHER: Peter Weber
CLIENT: Bayerisches Staatsschauspielhaus

66, 67 POSTERS FOR MORE THAN FOOD RESTAURANT
AGENCY: Jung von Matt an der Isar, Munich
ART DIRECTORS: Mathias Lamken, Oliver Voss, Claudia Schnaars
CLIENT: Hörzu

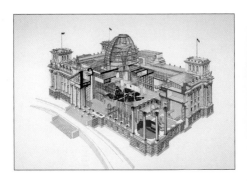

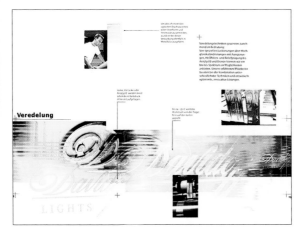

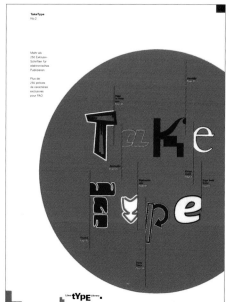

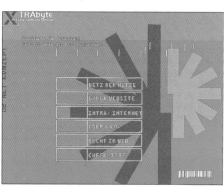

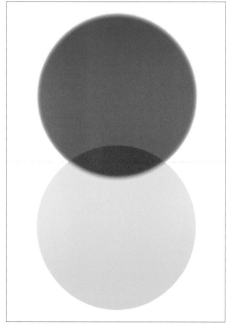

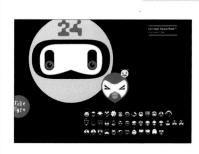

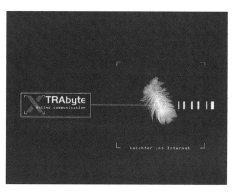

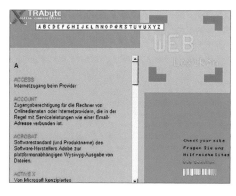

75 LOGO FOR THE AGRICULTURAL UNION
DESIGN FIRM: Stankowski & Duschek, Stuttgart
ART DIRECTOR: Karl Duschek
DESIGNER: Udo Schliemann

76 POSTER FOR AN EXHIBITION
BY THE CHINESE POSTER DESIGN ASSOCIATION
ART DIRECTOR/ DESIGNER: Fons M Hickmann, Düsseldorf

77, 78 TAKE TYPE CATALOGUE AND CD
DESIGN FIRM: Büro für Gestaltung, Offenbach
ART DIRECTORS/ DESIGNERS: Christoph Burkhardt,
Albrecht Hotz

79-81 POSTCARDS FEATURING FONTS
FROM THE TAKE TYPE CATALOGUE
DESIGN FIRM: Büro für Gestaltung, Offenbach
ART DIRECTORS/ DESIGNERS: Christoph Burkhardt,
Albrecht Hotz

82-85 SELF-PROMOTIONAL WEB SITE (www.xbyte.de)
DESIGN FIRM: XTRAbyte Online Communication, Düsseldorf
ART DIRECTOR: Pit Mayen

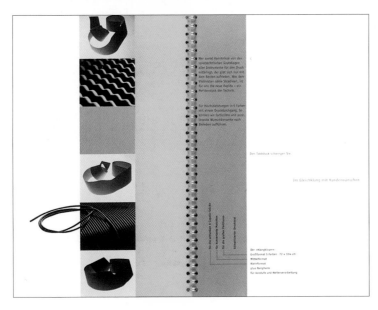

86 SPREAD FROM A PROMOTIONAL BOOK FOR A PRINTING COMPANY
DESIGN FIRM: Zink & Kraemer, Trier
ART DIRECTOR: Stephan Kraemer
DESIGNER: Matthias Schmitz
PHOTOGRAPHER: Hans-Georg Merkel
CLIENT: Bastian

87 "EMOTIONAL", A SELF-PROMOTIONAL BOOK FOR A PAPER COMPANY
DESIGN FIRM: Maassen & Francke Agentur für Kommunikationsdesign, Wuppertal
CLIENT: Deutsche Papier Vertriebs

88 BROCHURE FOR A PRINTING COMPANY
DESIGN FIRM: Grundies Design, Freiburg
ART DIRECTOR/ DESIGNER: Claudia Grundies
PHOTOGRAPHER: Hanspeter Trefzer
COPYWRITER: Gerhard Reiter
CLIENT: Furtwängler

89 ADVERTISEMENT FOR A STOCK PHOTOGRAPHY SERVICE
AGENCY: Heye + Partner, Unterhaching
CREATIVE DIRECTORS: Ralph Taubenberger, Peter Hirrlinger
ART DIRECTOR: Oliver Oelkers
DESIGNER: Jessika Menke
COPYWRITER: Doris Haider
CLIENT: Tony Stone

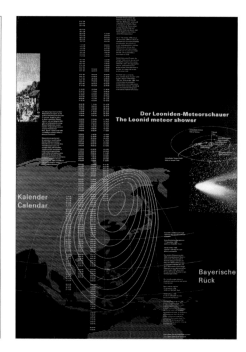

90 SELF-PROMOTIONAL MAILING
DESIGN FIRM: Braue Design, Bremerhaven
ART DIRECTORS: Kai Braue, Marçel Robbers
DESIGNERS/ ILLUSTRATORS: Marçel Robbers, Kai Braue,
Raimund Fohs

91 POSTER ANNOUNCING A LIGHT SHOW IN SAARBRÜCKEN
DESIGN FIRM: Maksimovic & Partners, Saarbrücken
ART DIRECTORS: Ivica Maksimovic, Patrick Bittner
DESIGNERS: Patrick Bittner, Isabel Bach
PHOTOGRAPHERS: Natascha Maksimovic
CLIENT: Versorgungs-und Verkehrgesellschaft Saarbt

92 POSTER FOR A DESIGN SYMPOSIUM
DESIGN FIRM: Baumann & Baumann, Schwäbisch Gmünd
DESIGNERS: Gerd Baumann, Barbara Baumann
CLIENT: Design Zentrum, Munich

93-95 POSTERS/ CALENDARS DEPICTING THE BEST TIME AND
PLACE TO SEE METEOR SHOWERS
DESIGN FIRM: Baumann & Baumann, Schwäbisch Gmünd
DESIGNERS: Gerd Baumann, Barbara Baumann
CLIENT: Bay. Rück Versicherungs AG

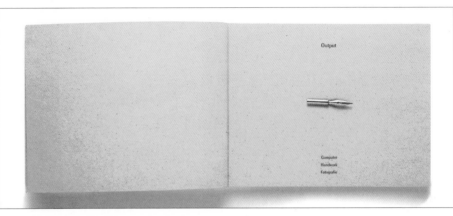

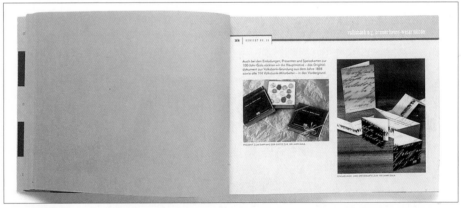

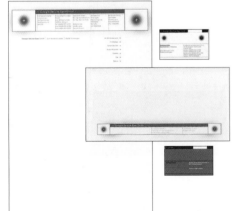

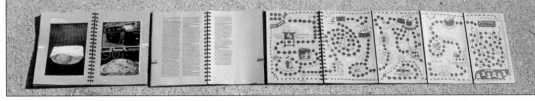

96 SPREAD FROM "APOGEO", A BOOK OF POEMS BY THE NICARAGUAN AUTHOR GIOCONDA BELLI
DESIGNER/ PHOTOGRAPHER: Feh A Reichl, Darmstadt

97 BROCHURE FOR A CLEANING COMPANY
DESIGN FIRM: Imago 87 Design, Freising
ART DIRECTOR: Maite Herzog
DESIGNER: Peter Krüll
CLIENT: Max Schmidt

98, 99 SELF-PROMOTIONAL BROCHURE
DESIGN FIRM: Artwork Station Graphikbüro, Biberach
DESIGNERS: Sascha Weihs, Dagmar Weihs

100, 101 SELF-PROMOTIONAL BROCHURE
DESIGN FIRM: Braue Design, Bremerhaven
ART DIRECTORS: Kai Braue, Marçel Robbers
DESIGNERS/ ILLUSTRATORS: Kai Braue, Marçel Robbers, Raimund Fohs

102 STATIONERY FOR ENERGIE SERVICE SAAR
DESIGN FIRM: Maksimovic & Partners, Saarbrücken
ART DIRECTORS: Ivica Maksimovic, Patrick Bittner
DESIGNER: Patrick Bittner

103 AN INTERACTIVE BOOK DIVIDED INTO THREE PARTS: PHOTOS, TEXT, AND ILLUSTRATION
DESIGN FIRM: Eigenhufe, Berlin
DESIGNER/ ILLUSTRATOR/ PHOTOGRAPHER: Thomas Richter Eigenhufe
CLIENT: Edition Hammeraue

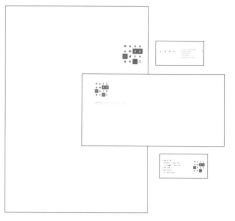

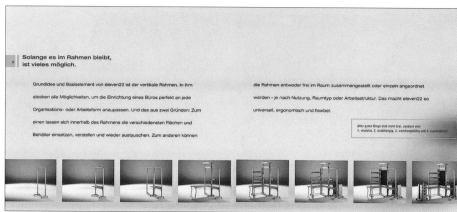

Solange es im Rahmen bleibt,
ist vieles möglich.

Grundidee und Basiselement von eleven22 ist der vertikale Rahmen. In ihm
stecken alle Möglichkeiten, um die Einrichtung eines Büros perfekt an jede
Organisations- oder Arbeitsform anzupassen. Und das aus zwei Gründen: Zum
einen lassen sich innerhalb des Rahmens die verschiedensten Flächen und
Behälter einsetzen, verstellen und wieder austauschen. Zum anderen können

die Rahmen entweder frei im Raum zusammengestellt oder einzeln angeordnet
werden – je nach Nutzung, Raumtyp oder Arbeitsstruktur. Das macht eleven22 so
universell, ergonomisch und flexibel.

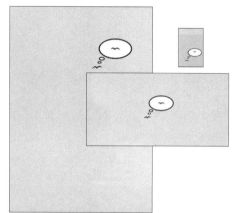

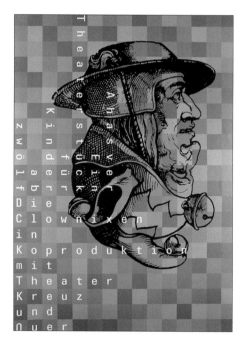

104 STATIONERY FOR THE MUSEUM DER DINGE
(MUSEUM OF OBJECTS)
DESIGN FIRM: Im Stall, Berlin
DESIGNER: Prof Claudius Lazzeroni

105 STATIONERY FOR R LAUGALLIES, A FLYING SCHOOL
DESIGN FIRM: Heye + Partner, Unterhaching
DESIGNERS: Detlev Schmidt, Frank Widmann

106 POSTER FOR CLOWNIXEN, A CHILDREN'S THEATRE GROUP
DESIGN FIRM: Hickmann & Grotrian, Düsseldorf
ART DIRECTORS: Fons M Hickmann, Gesine Grotrian

107 BROCHURE FOR A NEW LINE OF OFFICE FURNITURE
DESIGN FIRM: Scholz & Volkmer, Wiesbaden
ART DIRECTOR: Michael Volkmer
DESIGNERS: Heike Brockmann, Susanne Schwalm
CLIENT: U S M

108 SPREAD FROM "MÄUSETRÄUME", A CHILDREN'S BOOK
DESIGN FIRM: VE&K Werbeagentur, Essen
ART DIRECTOR/ DESIGNER/ ILLUSTRATOR: Gaby van Emmerich
CLIENT: Arena/ Edition Bücherbär

109 POSTER FOR CLOWNIXEN, A CHILDREN'S THEATRE GROUP
DESIGN FIRM: Hickmann & Grotrian, Düsseldorf
ART DIRECTORS/ DESIGNERS: Fons M Hickmann, Gesine Grotrian
ILLUSTRATOR: Gesine Grotrian-Steinweg

110 POSTER FOR A PRODUCTION OF "HAMLET" BY THEATERHAUS
ART DIRECTOR/ DESIGNER: Fons M Hickmann, Düsseldorf

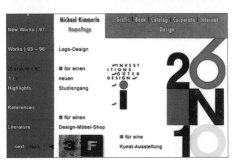

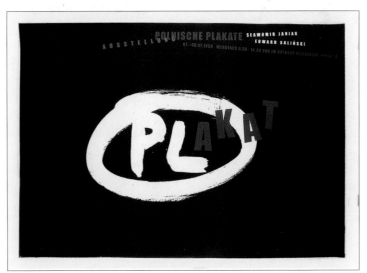

111–113 SELF-PROMOTIONAL WEB SITE (www.kimmerle.de)
DESIGN FIRM: Art Direction + Design, Stuttgart
DESIGNER/ ILLUSTRATOR/ PHOTOGRAPHER: Michael Kimmerle

114 SELF-PROMOTIONAL CALENDAR
DESIGN FIRM: VE&K Werbeagentur, Essen
ART DIRECTOR: Tilo Kare
ILLUSTRATOR: Gaby van Emmerich

115 SPREAD FROM 1998 ANNUAL REPORT
DESIGN FIRM: Vorwerk & Co, Wuppertal
ART DIRECTORS/ DESIGNERS/ ILLUSTRATORS: Herrmann Michels,
Regina Göllner

116 SELF-PROMOTIONAL CALENDAR
DESIGN FIRM: Falkenthal-Fotografie, Bielefeld
ART DIRECTOR/ PHOTOGRAPHER: Achim Falkenthal
DESIGNER: Diana Holtmann
COPYWRITER: Hartwig Frankenberg

**117 LETTERHEAD, BUSINESS CARD, AND BROCHURE
FOR A DERMATOLOGIST**
DESIGN FIRM: Bettina Huchtemann Art Direction & Design,
Hamburg
DESIGNER/ ILLUSTRATOR: Bettina Huchtemann
CLIENT: Dr Med Krausse

118 POSTER FOR AN EXHIBITION OF POLISH POSTER ART
DESIGNER: Prof Gerd Finkel, Kreiensen
CLIENTS: Slawomir Janiak, Edward Salinski

119 POSTER FOR AN OPERA PRODUCTION
DESIGNER: Jürgen Haufe(†), Dresden
CLIENT: Staatsoperette, Dresden

120 POSTER FOR AN EXHIBITION OF WORK
BY RUSSIAN EMIGRÉ ARTISTS
DESIGN FIRM: Büro für Gestaltung, Offenbach
ART DIRECTORS/ DESIGNERS: Christoph Burkardt, Albrecht Hotz
CLIENT: Stadt Frankfurt am Main

121 POSTER FOR AN EXHIBITION OF BRITISH DESIGN
DESIGN FIRM: Büro für Gestaltung, Offenbach
ART DIRECTORS/ DESIGNERS: Christoph Burkardt, Albrecht Hotz
PHOTOGRAPHER: Norbert Miguletz
CLIENT: Museum für Kunsthandwerk

122 POSTER FOR CLOWNIXEN, A CHILDREN'S THEATRE GROUP
DESIGN FIRM: Hickmann & Grotrian, Düsseldorf
ART DIRECTORS: Fons M Hickmann, Gesine Grotrian
DESIGNER: Fons M Hickmann

123, 124 POSTERS FOR THE INTERNATIONAL SOCIETY
FOR HUMAN RIGHTS
DESIGNER: Friedhelm Plassmeier, Brakel

125 POSTER FOR AN EXHIBITION OF PRIZE-WINNING
PHOTOGRAPHS IN THE EUROPEAN ARCHITECTURAL
PHOTOGRAPHY COMPETITION
DESIGN FIRM: Typoware, Stuttgart
ART DIRECTOR/ DESIGNER: Christine Rampl
PHOTOGRAPHERS: David Hiepler, Fritz Brunier
CLIENT: Deutsche Bauzeitung Architektur Schwarz-weiss

HUNGARY: COUNTRY FILE

RESTAURANTS, CAFÉS & BARS

CLUB VERNE RESTAURANT, VACI UTCA 60, BUDAPEST. T (+36) 1 318 9952 A club-restaurant with outstanding interior design and exquisite cuisine.

HADES 'JAZZTAURANT', VOROSMARTY UTCA 31, BUDAPEST (virtually next door to the Academy of Fine Arts). T (+36) 1 352 1503 A pub cellar with live music and very popular among artists, art teachers and art students alike. (Laszlo Lelkes, Designer, Budapest)

GUNDEL, BUDAPEST. Fabulous restaurant run by the well-known and charming owner of the Café des Artistes in New York. Extensive menu features Hungarian specialities and showcases the country's food products and wines, including its famous foie gras. (Paul Prejza & Deborah Sussman, Designers, Los Angeles)

NEW YORK CAFÉ, VII, ERZSÉBET KÖRÚT 9-11, BUDAPEST. A Budapest institution since 1895 with its fin-de-siècle décor. Open from noon until midnight.

COQUAN'S KAVÉ, V, NÁDOR UTCA 5 & IX RÁDAY UTCA 15, BUDAPEST. Come here for the best coffee in town.

FÉSZEK, VII, KERTÉSZ UTCA 36 (corner of Dob utca), BUDAPEST. T (+36) 1 322 6043 Hidden inside the 100-year old Fészek Artists' Club in downtown Pest is this large neo-classical dining room. An extensive menu offers Hungarian classics (the venison stew with tarragon is outstanding). In summer dine outdoors in the Venetian-style courtyard.

MUSEUMS, GALLERIES & LIBRARIES

KERESKEDELMI ES VENDEGLATOIPARI MUZEUM, 1 FORTUNA UTCA 4 (on Castle Hill) BUDAPEST. T (+36) 1 175 6249 A delightful museum with 19th-century pastry moulds, ancient culinary gadgets of all descriptions, old coffee-makers, packs and posters. If you enjoy café/Konditorei culture, you will have a lot of fun looking around here. (Pat Schleger, Designer, London)

MÜCSARNOK (PALACE OF EXHIBITIONS), XIV, DÓZSA GYÖRGY ÚT 37, BUDAPEST. Striking structure, built in 1895 holding exhibitions of contemporary Hungarian and international art and a rich series of films, plays and concerts.

NÉPRAJZI MÚZEUM (MUSEUM OF ETHNOGRAPHY), V, KOSSUTH LAJOS TÉR 12, BUDAPEST. T (+36) 1 332 6340 An elegant, impressive museum with exhaustive exhibits of folk costumes and traditions — those authentic pieces you cannot find in the tourist shops.

THE LIBRARY OF THE HUNGARIAN ACADEMY OF FINE ARTS, ADRASSY UTCA 69-71, BUDAPEST. T (+36) 1 342-1738, www.arts7.hu This is really worth a mention, for it has a huge and recently-discovered collection of photographs from around the turn of the 19th/20th century (still being catalogued). (Laszlo Lelkes, Designer, Budapest)

KOVÁCS MARGIT MÚZEUM, VASTAG GYÖRGY UTCA 1, SZENTENDRE. Lively artists' colony first settled in the 14th century. The narrow cobbled streets are lined with painted houses, many now art galleries.

PLACES OF INTEREST

THERMAL BATHS IN BUDAPEST. This is a major spa town with numerous thermal baths to choose from. THE GELLÉRT BATHS (off XI, Kelehegyi út) maintain a constant temperature of 40°C; the RUDAS BATHS (I, Döbrentei tér 9), built by the Turks in 1566 still retain a strong Turkish ambience.

JÁNOSHEGY (JÁNOS HILL), BUDAPEST Take the chairlift to the summit and the highest point in Budapest. Climb the lookout tower for the best view of the city.

Area	1,000 km2	093.0	Capital City	Budapest	Monetary Unit	forint
Population	1,000	10,208	Capital City Population	1,000	2,017	GDP per Capita (US $)	4,325
Design Population	1,000	000.7	Languages	Hungarian	International Dialling Code	+36

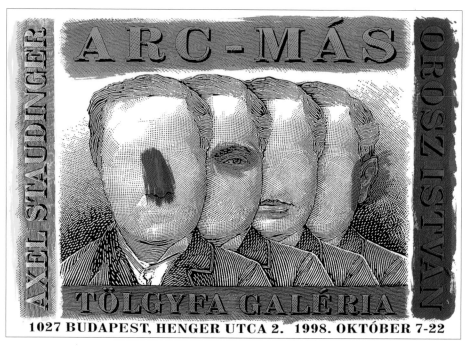

1 POSTER FOR AN EXHIBITION AT MORAVIAN COLLEGE'S
GALLERY OF ART IN BETHLEHEM, PA
DESIGN FIRM: Utisz, Budapest
DESIGNER/ ILLUSTRATOR: Istvan Orosz

2 POSTER FOR AN EXHIBITION AT TOLGYFA GALLERY,
A UNIVERSITY GALLERY IN BUDAPEST
DESIGN FIRM: Utisz, Budapest
DESIGNER/ ILLUSTRATOR: Istvan Orosz

3 POSTER FOR AN ANIMATED FILM CALLED "MIND THE STEPS!"
DESIGN FIRM: Utisz, Budapest
DESIGNER/ ILLUSTRATOR: Istvan Orosz
CLIENT: Pannonia Flims

4 "FACE OF SHAKESPEARE" POSTER FOR AN EXHIBITION
ENTITLED "HISTORY OF THE POSTER"
DESIGN FIRM: Utisz, Budapest
DESIGNER/ ILLUSTRATOR: Istvan Orosz
CLIENT: Victoria and Albert Museum, London

5 PAINTED WALL ADVERTISEMENT FOR MATÁV,
A TELECOMMUNICATIONS COMPANY
AGENCY: Lowe/ GGK Budapest
ART DIRECTOR/ DESIGNER: Balázs Vargha
ILLUSTRATOR: Tonio

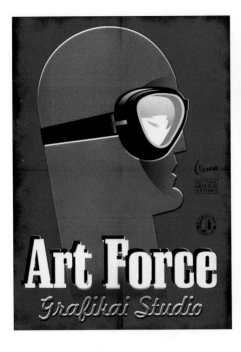

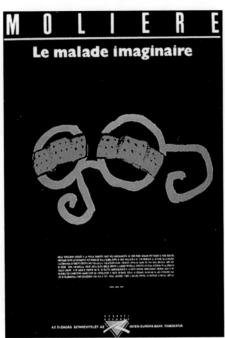

6 SELF-PROMOTIONAL POSTER
DESIGN FIRM: Art Force Studio, Budapest
ART DIRECTOR/ DESIGNER/ ILLUSTRATOR: Veress Tama's

7, 8 THEATRE POSTERS FOR THE HUNGARIAN GRAPHIC
DESIGN BIENNIAL
DESIGNER: Laszlo Lelkes, Budapest

9 LOGO FOR THE HUNGARIAN ACADEMY OF DRAMA AND FILM
DESIGNER: Laszlo Lelkes, Budapest

10 POSTER TO MARK THE HAND-OVER OF HONG KONG TO CHINA
DESIGNER: Laszlo Lelkes, Budapest
CLIENT: Political Poster Triennial in Mons (Belgium)

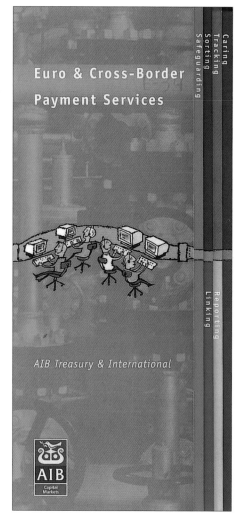

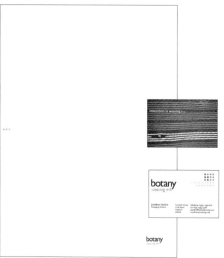

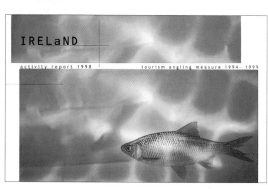

1 INFORMATIONAL BROCHURE FOR AIB,
A FINANCIAL SERVICES ORGANIZATION
DESIGN FIRM: Corporate Graphics, Dublin
DESIGNER: Larry Byrne
ILLUSTRATOR: Brian Fitzgerald

2 STATIONERY FOR BOTANY WEAVING MILL
DESIGN FIRM: Rain design partners, Dublin
ART DIRECTOR: Cliona Geary
DESIGNERS: Cliona Geary, Garrett Reil

3 SELF-PROMOTIONAL BROCHURE
DESIGN FIRM: BFK Design Ltd, Dublin
ART DIRECTOR: Paul Hogan
DESIGNER: Neil O'Keeffe
PHOTOGRAPHERS: Tony Higgins, Eoghan Kavanagh

4 BROCHURE FOR BARRE FITZPATRICK, IMAGINEER
DESIGN FIRM: The Identity Business, Dublin
ART DIRECTOR: Garrett Reil
DESIGNER: Marie Vahey

5 1998 ACTIVITY REPORT FOR THE CENTRAL FISHERIES BOARD
DESIGN FIRM: Averill Brophy Associates, Dublin
ART DIRECTOR/ DESIGNER: Siobhan O'Carroll

IRELAND: COUNTRY FILE

HOTELS

SCHOOLHOUSE HOTEL, 2-8 NORTHUMBERLAND ROAD, BALLSBRIDGE, DUBLIN 2. T (+353) 1 667 5013 Situated close to Dublin's city centre, this hotel offers superb 4-star standard accommodation, good food and a lively traditional pub for the discerning visitor. (Larry Byrne, Art Director, Dublin)

RESTAURANTS, CAFÉS & BARS

NUDE, 21 SUFFOLK STREET, DUBLIN 2. Nude is Dublin's first healthy fast-food restaurant. Organic produce is used wherever possible: wraps, soups, smoothers, juices, snacks and daily specials are all wrapped up in award-winning packaging. Open 7 days.

FRONT LOUNGE, PARLIAMENT STREET, DUBLIN 2 Spacious, comfortable and very popular. Large sofas and armchairs create a very relaxing atmosphere. Interiors often display local artists' work. Great cappuccinos

GURU, CAPE STREET, DUBLIN 1. One of Dublin's newest bars set in a new area of the city. The interiors have been designed by Peter O'Kennedy and are reminiscent of New York in style. (Maria Vahey, Designer, Dublin)

HOGAN'S PUB, 35 GREAT GEORGE'S STREET SOUTH, DUBLIN 2. Trendy pub full of designer-type people. Great atmosphere on a Friday night after work.

JOHNNIE FOX'S PUB, GLENCULLEN, CO. DUBLIN. T (+353) 1 295 5647 Traditional style pub. Good atmosphere, great seafood, great Irish music and dance, great pint of Guinness. Its location in the Dublin mountains is an added bonus. (Larry Byrne, Art Director, Dublin)

MUSEUMS & GALLERIES

THE IRISH MUSEUM OF MODERN ART, ROYAL HOSPITAL KILMAINHAM, DUBLIN. T (+353) 1 612 9900 Located in a restored 17th-century building, this museum presents international and Irish art of the 20th-century through its permanent collections and temporary exhibitions. Associated educational and community programmes, performances, theatre and music. (Larry Byrne, Art Director, Dublin)

NATURAL HISTORY MUSEUM, MERRION SQUARE WEST, DUBLIN 2. T (+353) 1 677 7444 A 19th-century museum that is truly a monument to taxidermy. The typography on the signs and labels is stunning and best of all are the hand-blown glass anemone and jellyfish, reminiscent of Louise Bourgeois sculptures. (Carin Goldberg, Designer, London)

PLACES OF INTEREST

ARTHOUSE, CURVED STREET, TEMPLE BAR, DUBLIN 2. T (+353) 1 605 6800, www.arthouse.ie Multimedia Centre for the Arts situated in the heart of the Temple Bar area of Dublin. An innovative centre for the Arts for creative people who wish to work with multimedia and information technology. (Larry Byrne, Art Director, Dublin)

GLEBE HOUSE, CHURCH HILL, NEAR LETTERKENNY, CO. DONEGAL. Derek Hill's own home, given to the Irish nation and an example of an artist's eye gorged on pattern. Gallery and tearoom. (Nancy Gorman, Painter, Chicago)

Try the following websites for more information on places of interest in Ireland: www.temple-bar.ie & www.modernart.ie

Area	1,000 km2	070.3	Capital City	Dublin	Monetary Unit	Irish pound & euro
Population	1,000	3,619	Capital City Population	1,000	911	GDP per Capita (US $)	17,500
Design Population	1,000	000.5	Languages	English, Irish (Gaelic)	International Dialling Code	+353

ITALY: COUNTRY FILE

HOTELS

HOTEL PAGGERIA MEDICEA, ARTIMINO (PRATO). T (+39) 055 8792030 A very ancient and special 'hotel-agriturismo' in the green hills of Tuscany. Nearby try the Restaurant Biagio Pignatta, T (+39) 055 8718086. (Filippo Spiezia, Multimedia Designer, Pescara)

VILLA SAN MICHELE, FIESOLE, FLORENCE. Although not the cheapest, certainly the most laid-back luxury hotel and restaurant there ever was. Set on a hillside within a former monastery attributed to Michelangelo, the surroundings are exquisite. The loggia, where summer meals are served, must be one of the most romantic places in Europe — over 100 feet long, an arched colonnade lit by candles overlooking the roofscape of Florence. (Michael Manser, Architect, London)

HOTEL SPADARI AL DUOMO, VIA SPADARI, MILAN. T (+39) 02 722 2371 Small, clean, quiet, friendly hotel with well-designed contemporary rooms, furniture and art. Only about two blocks from the Galleria, La Scala, the Duomo, and many terrific restaurants. (James Stockton, Designer, San Francisco)

RESTAURANTS, CAFÉS & BARS

OSTERIA CON CUCINA LUCHIN, VIA BIGHETTI 51, CHIAVARI, LUGURIA. T (+39) 0185 301 063 This trattoria has existed since 1907, and the food is still cooked as it was 93 years ago: on charcoal. The best dish is 'Farinata' — an indescribable delicacy. Long bare tables, people of all kinds from local plumbers to big publishers from Milan. Shut during October. (Giannetto Coppola, Illustrator, Chiavari)

BRANCALEONE, TERRANOVA, FRAZ. DI ROCCAMONTEPIANO, CHIETI. T (+39) 0871 77571 Delicious, traditional Abruzzo regional cuisine, and each guest has a different style of plate design!

ANZICHÉ, PIAZZA DEL CARMINE 29, FLORENCE. T (+39) 055 212 532 Technically a private club, but easy to 'crash' since you become a member by walking through the door. Upstairs is a small bar and art gallery. Downstairs a combination of kitchen and dining room that feeds an imaginative assortment of Neapolitan food from 20.30 to 04.00. Inexpensive and informal and with a clientele so eclectic you think you are eating your way through a Fellini film. (Ralph Caplan, Writer, New York)

I MALAVOGLIA, VIA LECCO 4, MILAN. T (+39) 02 29 53 13 87 An exceptional fish restaurant. The wife is the wonderful cook and the husband and daughter serve. Medium priced despite the quality. Closed Mondays. (Bruno & Jacqueline Danese, Design Gallery, Milan)

RISTORANTE RIGOLO, VIA SOLFERINO, 11, MILAN. T (+39) 02 805 9678 Very undesignerly, patronised less by the Milan smart set than the solid citizenry. Excellent unflamboyant food and soothingly professional service. (David Mellor, Designer, Derbyshire)

OSTERIA DEL GESSO, VIA FERDINANDO MAESTRI, 11, PARMA. T (+39) 0521 230505 All the traditional flavours of Parmesan Cuisine. Visit after a trip to the cinema or theatre. (Filippo Spiezia, Multimedia Designer, Pescara)

PASTICCERIA M. ZANON, TOLETTA 1169/A, VENICE. T (+39) 041 22 619 Their ricotta cheesecake surpasses anything you have eaten. (Carl Christiansson, Designer, Paris)

MUSEUMS & GALLERIES

MAURIZIO CORRAINI, VIA MADONNA DELLA VITTORIA 5, MANTOVA. T (+39) 0376 322753 This gallery and art publisher has dedicated itself in recent years to publishing the written, designed and illustrated output of Bruno Monari and to bringing his children's books back into print. The gallery also shows the work of contemporary Italian artists and designers, and sells a selection of design objects from around the world. (Steven Guarnaccia, Illustrator, New York)

FONDAZIONE PRADA, 10 CORSO COMO, MILAN. T (+39) 02 654 831, www.fondazioneprada.org Photographers' gallery and café. (Valeria Brancaforte, Illustrator, Milan)

BIBLIOTECA-PINACOTECA AMBROSIANA, PIAZZA SAN SEPOLCRO, MILAN. Excellentlly renovated by Carlo Cigolotti, the newly restored Ambrosiana Library is five minutes from the Duomo. You can gaze at Cardinal Frederico Borromeo's extraordinary collection of 16th-century drawings and paintings, including superb Leonardos. A real visual treat. (Fiona MacCarthy, Writer, Derbyshire)

GALLERIA NAZIONALE DI PARMA, PALAZZO DELLA PILOTTA, PARMA. The huge, old Palace of La Pilotta, in the former barracks and granary of the Farnese family is now the seat of the National Gallery of Parma. The entrance through the 17th-century wooden theatre is breathtaking. There are beautiful works by Leonardo, Parmigiano, Holbein, Correggio and many others. The visit is a must. (Italo Lupi, Designer/Editor, Milan)

PLACES OF INTEREST

FRANCO CASONI-INTAGLIATORE, PIAZZA SAN GIOVANNI 73, CHIAVARI, LIGURIA. You can find Franco Casoni in his workshop at the heart of the historical town centre of Chiavari (32 km from Genoa). He is one of the last carvers of figureheads and his work is seen in great halls and gracing the bows of many fine ships. (Gianetto Coppola, Illustrator, Chiavari)

IL BISONTE PRINT WORKSHOP, VIA SAN NICOLO 24, FLORENCE. T (+39) 055 234 425 85 The leading Fine Arts print workshop and school in Italy since the 1950s. Picasso, Calder, Tamayo, Severini created and printed their works on the Bisonte Presses. Dedicated to the maintenance of traditional technical skills, as well as modern techniques in print techniques, Il Bisonte attracts major present-day artists to its workshops, and offers short courses. Located in the elegantly-restored stables of the Palazzo Demidoff, just across the river from the Uffizi. (Germano Facetti, Designer, Sarzana)

GRAZIE DI CURTATONE The small town of Grazie is host to a yearly (mid-August) festival of art of the most ephemeral sort: chalk drawing on pavement. Chalkers participate from all over the world, and the entire town square is plotted out in masking taped blocks. Much of the imagery is based on classical painting. Makes painting a true spectator sport. (Steven Guarnaccia, Illustrator, New York)

IL CARTABOLO, CORSO GARIBALDI, 89, MILAN. T (+39) 02 659 2949 In her workshop, Clare Rota produces beautiful and unusual custom-made paper, putting her expertise at the disposal of designers or simply aficionados, creating books and notebooks with refined handicraft and care. (Giuseppe Basile, Designer, Milan)

FONDERIA MARIANI, VIA TRE LUCI 51, PIETRASANTA (LUCCA). T (+39) 0584 71 095 A bronze foundry specialising in artists' work. Mr Mariani will discuss the alloy and surface finishes with great knowledge. He can cast (or enlarge) your sculpture to any size from six inches to thirty feet. For those who like a working holiday, studios and materials are available close by. Pleasant open-air wine drinking evenings with a cosmopolitan crowd of artists and local craftsmen. (Germano Facetti, Designer, Sarzana)

BOOKSHOPS & SHOPPING

GIANNINO STOPPANI, VIA RIZZOLI 1F, PIAZZO RE ENZO, BOLOGNA. T (+39) 051 227 337 Well-stocked children's bookstore that also mounts exhibitions of international children's book illustrators. The catalogue that they publish for the exhibitions is lavishly produced. (Steven Guarnaccia, Illustrator, New York)

L'ARCHIVOLTO, VIA MARSALA 2, MILAN. T (+39) 02 659 2734 The best bookstore in town for architecture, design and graphics, they also sell old (antique) editions of rare books. They have interesting shows of architectural drawings in the vaulted basement. Good coffee shops in the vicinity, and an excellent restaurant — La Briciola — just across the street. (Emanuela Frattini Magnusson, Architect, New York)

DRIADE SRL, VIA MANZONI, 30, MILAN. F (+39) 02 720 02434 Well-known designers' furniture shop. (Valeria Brancaforte, Illustrator, Milan)

CORSO COMO 10, 10, VIA CORSO COMO, MILAN. T (+39) 02 29 00 26 74 We would suggest only one place: it is a fashion shop, bookshop, restaurant and bar and you can also find CDs, art, graphics, fashion and photography books and magazines, stylish objects for the house and very interesting exhibitions. It's very, very, very expensive and the owner is a well-known guru in the milanese fashion milieu. (David Mack & Paolo Prossen, Executive Director/Designer, Milan)

CESARE CRESPI, 28A VIA BRERA, MILAN. T (+39) 02 86 28 93 Old-fashioned (since 1840), old-mannered art materials store with the largest range of rare, hand-made, western and oriental papers and cards. 150 years behind La Scala, worth a visit to collect samples. (Germano Facetti, Designer, Sarzana)

LEGATORIA PIAZZASI (PAPER SHOP), SAN MARCO 2511, SAN MARIO DEL GIGLIO, VENICE. They sell Carta Varese, the way paper was made using 15th-century techniques. The patterns are printed by hand, using woodcut of the same age. The ink is specially made from natural dyes (wild grass &c). Also beautiful handmade marble paper. (Yusaku Kamekura, Designer, Tokyo)

Area	1,000 km2	301.0	Capital City	Rome	Monetary Unit	Italian lira & euro
Population	1,000	56,782	Capital City Population	1,000	2,700	GDP per Capita (US $)	19,121
Design Population	1,000	005.0	Languages	Italian	International Dialling Code	+39

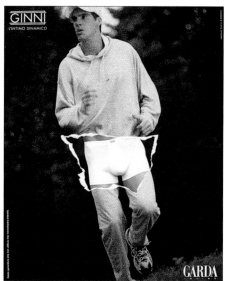

1 POSTER FOR "ITINERARIA", PROMOTING MUSEI IN TAVOLA,
AN EVENT THAT CONNECTS RESTAURANTS AND MUSEUMS
DESIGN FIRM: BCPT Associati, Perugia
ART DIRECTOR: Marco Tortoioli Ricci
ILLUSTRATOR: Andrea Medri

2, 3 ADS FOR AN ATHLETIC UNDERWEAR MANUFACTURER
AGENCY: Lorenzo Marini & Associati, Milan
ART DIRECTOR: Francesco Degano
COPYWRITER: Pino Pilla
PHOTOGRAPHER: Carlo Miari Fulcis
CLIENT: Confezioni Garda

4 PROMOTIONAL BOOKLET FOR ENTERTAINER
DARIO MANFREDINI
DESIGN FIRM: Studio Grafico Fausta Orecchio, Rome
DESIGNER: Fausta Orecchio
ILLUSTRATOR: Dario Manfredini
CLIENT: Cadmo

5 ADVERTISEMENT FOR VOLKSWAGEN BEETLE
AGENCY: Lorenzo Marini & Associati, Milan
ART DIRECTOR: Arianna Conti
PHOTOGRAPHER: Ambrogio Gualdoni
CLIENT: Bburago

6, 7 COVERS OF "NESSUNO TOCCHI CAINO" ("HANDS OFF CAIN"),
A BI-MONTHLY MAGAZINE ON LITERATURE, POLITICS, AND ART
DESIGN FIRM: Studio Grafico Fausta Orecchio, Rome
ART DIRECTOR: Fausta Orecchio
DESIGNERS: Fausta Orecchio, Sara Verdone, Silvana Amato (6),
Simone Tonucci (6)
ILLUSTRATORS: Jordan Isip (6), Fabian Negrin (7)

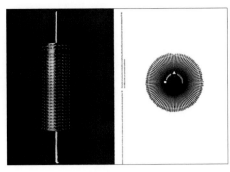

End of the Millennium

DECEMBER

8, 9 SPREADS FROM PROMOTIONAL BOOK FOR OLIVETTI SPA
DESIGN FIRM: AMDL Architectures, Milan
DESIGNERS: Michele de Lucchi, Mario Trimarchi,
Katrin Schmitt-Tegge
PHOTOGRAPHER: Luca Tamburlini

10 LOGO AND IDENTITY FOR RESTAURANT MILCH
DESIGN FIRM: Studio FM, Milan
ART DIRECTORS/ DESIGNERS: Barbara Forni, Sergio Menichelli

11, 12 SELF-PROMOTIONAL CALENDAR USING FLORA AND FAUNA
TO INDICATE THE NEED FOR NATURE IN THE NEW MILLENNIUM
DESIGN FIRM: AReA Strategic Design, Rome
ART DIRECTOR: Stefano Aureli
ILLUSTRATOR: Francesca Montosi
PHOTOGRAPHERS: Marco Tempera, Giuseppe Fadda
CREATIVE DIRECTOR: Antonio Romano

13 LOGO AND IDENTITY FOR +A
(POSITIVE ARCHITECTURE STUDIO)
DESIGN FIRM: Studio FM, Milan
ART DIRECTORS/ DESIGNERS: Barbara Forni, Sergio Menichelli

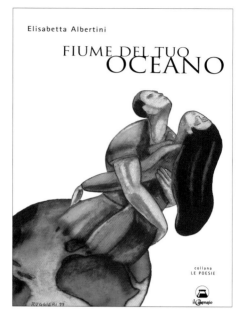

14 BOOK COVER FOR IL CALAMAIO PUBLISHING
DESIGN FIRM: Vertigo Design, Rome
ILLUSTRATOR: Alberto Ruggieri
ART DIRECTORS: Alberto Ruggieri, Mario Rucco

15, 16 ORDINARY PEOPLE FASHION COLLECTION
DESIGN FIRM: Studio Falavigna, Milan
ART DIRECTOR: Ciro Falavigna
ILLUSTRATOR: Sandro Fabbri
COPYWRITER: Michela Gattermayer

17 BROCHURE FOR NATIONAL CONFERENCE ON ENERGY AND ENVIRONMENT
DESIGN FIRM: AReA Strategic Design, Rome
ART DIRECTOR: Niccolo Desii
CREATIVE DIRECTOR: Fulvio Caldarelli

18 POSTER FOR ITALIAN STATE THEATRE CORP
DESIGN FIRM: Studio Grafico Fausta Orecchio, Rome
ART DIRECTOR: Fausta Orecchio
DESIGNERS: Fausta Orecchio, Lorenzo Mattotti

19-21 SELF-PROMOTIONAL WEB SITE PORTFOLIO
(www.ideagrafica.it)
DESIGN FIRM: Ideagrafica, Pescara
DESIGNER/ ILLUSTRATOR: Filippo Spieza

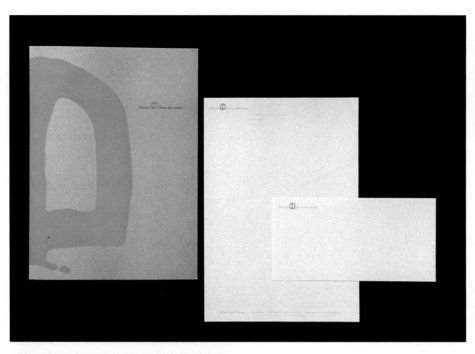

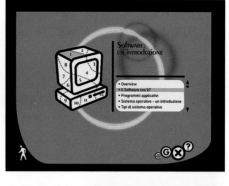

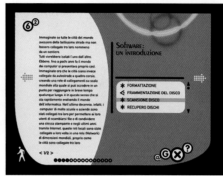

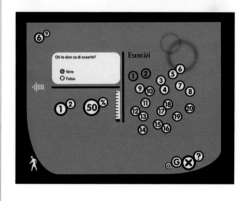

22-24 LOGO AND IDENTITY
FOR BRUNO MONDADORI PUBLISHING
DESIGN FIRM: Studio FM, Milan
ART DIRECTORS/ DESIGNERS: Barbara Forni, Sergio Menichelli

25, 26 STATIONERY (23) AND LOGO (24)
FOR L'ANCORA PUBLISHING
DESIGN FIRM: Studio Grafico Fausta Orecchio, Rome
DESIGNER: Fausta Orecchio

27-29 CD-ROM THAT TEACHES BASIC COMPUTER SKILLS
DESIGN FIRM: Jekyll & Hyde, Milan
DESIGNERS: Marco Molteni, Margherita Monguzzi
CLIENT: McGraw-Hill

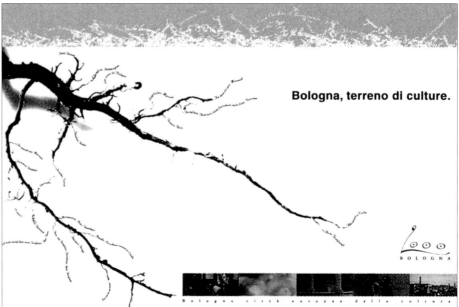

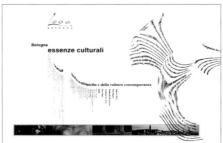

30 POSTER FOR EMILIA ROMANA THEATRE AND COMMUNAL
THEATRE OF FERRARA
DESIGN FIRM: Studio Magni, Ferrara
ART DIRECTOR: Laura Magni
PHOTOGRAPHER: Tilde de Tullio

31, 32 ADVERTISEMENTS FOR "BOLOGNA 2000",
A MILLENNIUM CELEBRATION
DESIGN FIRM: Kuni, Bologna
ART DIRECTOR: Barbara Cuniberti
DESIGNERS: Elena Corradini, Martina Zucchini
PHOTOGRAPHERS: Piero Casadei, Luciano Leonotti

33, 34 SIGNAGE FOR A MOTORCYCLE MANUFACTURER
DESIGN FIRM: Giacometti Associati, Treviso
ART DIRECTOR: Franco Giacometti
DESIGNERS: Stefano Martignago, Stefano Russo,
Massimo Cerruti
PHOTOGRAPHER: Marco Zanta
CLIENT: Aprilia SPA

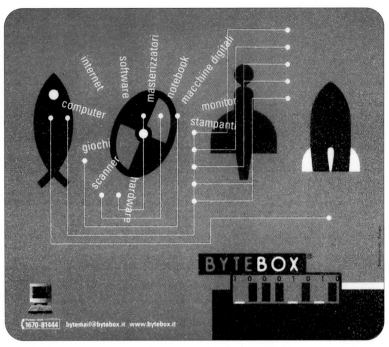

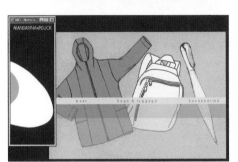

35 THEATRE POSTER FOR ITALIAN THEATRE CORP
DESIGN FIRM: Studio Grafico Fausta Orecchio, Rome
ART DIRECTOR: Fausta Orecchio
DESIGNER: Silvana Amato
ILLUSTRATOR: Fabian Negrin

36, 37 WEB SITE FOR MANDARINA DUCK (www.mandarina.com),
A CLOTHING AND ACCESSORIES MANUFACTURER
DESIGN FIRM: Orchestra Srl, Milan
ART DIRECTOR: Renata Prevost
DESIGNER: Roberta Maculan

38 PROMOTIONAL MOUSE PAD FOR A COMPUTER
HARDWARE MANUFACTURER
DESIGN FIRM: BCPT Associati, Perugia
ART DIRECTOR: Marco Tortoioli Ricci
DESIGNER/ ILLUSTRATOR: Lucia Noscini
CLIENT: Ecobyte

39, 40 BOOK JACKETS FOR CHILDREN'S EXERCISE BOOKS
DESIGNER: Valeria Brancaforte, Milan
ART DIRECTOR: Robert Clemente
CLIENT: GUT

41 PACKAGING FOR A CHOCOLATE MANUFACTURER
DESIGN FIRM: Designroom, Milan
DESIGNER: Paolo Prossen
CLIENT: Lindt & Sprungli

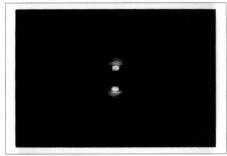

50 TITLE SEQUENCES FOR A CULTURAL TV PROGRAMME
DESIGN FIRM: Elica, Milan
ART DIRECTORS: Carmen Lo Maglio, Gianluigi Toccafondo
ILLUSTRATOR: Gianluigi Toccafondo
TYPOGRAPHY: Carmen Lo Maglio
CLIENT: RAI

51, 52 BROCHURE FOR PERCEPTION, AN INTERNATIONAL BRAND-
ING AND COMMUNICATIONS COMPANY
DESIGN FIRM: Studio Falavigna, Milan
ART DIRECTOR: Ciro Falavigna
DESIGNER: Leone Di Sebastiano

53 ADVERTISEMENT FOR FISCHER BEER
DESIGN FIRM: Simbol, Milan
ART DIRECTOR: Marco Castori
CLIENT: Heineken Italia

54 SELF-PROMOTIONAL DIRECTORY
DESIGN FIRM: Studiotto, Rome
ART DIRECTOR: Claudia Ravello de Santi
DESIGNER: Chiara Mammì
ILLUSTRATOR: Paola Chartroux
PHOTOGRAPHER: Lorenzo Sechi

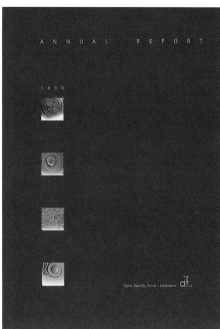

1 CALENDAR FOR VILNIUS UNIVERSITY
DESIGN FIRM: RIC Ltd, Vilnius
ART DIRECTOR: Giedrius Laurusas
DESIGNER: Vilmas Narecionis

2 COVER OF 1998 ANNUAL REPORT
FOR THE OPEN SOCIETY FUND OF LITHUANIA
DESIGN FIRM: RIC Ltd, Vilnius
ART DIRECTOR/ DESIGNER: Vilmas Narecionis

3 LOGO FOR LINE, AN INTERNATIONAL TEXTILE EXHIBITION
DESIGN FIRM: jsc "LIEPA", Kaunas
DESIGNER: Ausra Lisauskiene
CLIENT: Lithuania Artists' Association

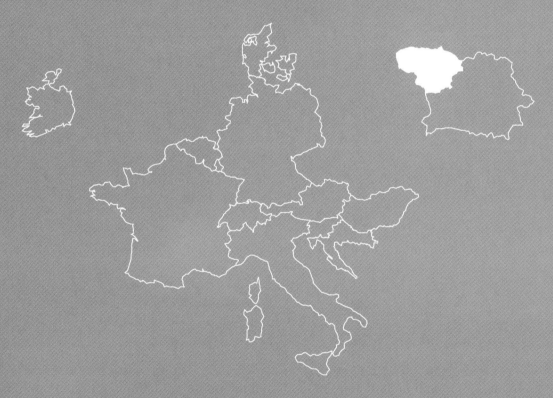

LITHUANIA: COUNTRY FILE

RESTAURANTS, CAFÉS & BARS
RESTAURANT "ZEMAICIU UZEIGA", VOKIECIU ST. 24, VILNIUS. Famous for its Lithuanian cuisine and located in the old part of city. (Eugenijus Tinfavicius, Design Company Managing Director, Vilnius)

MUSEUMS & GALLERIES
MUSEUM OF EUROPE CENTRE, RAJ. JONEIKISKIU K., VILNIUS. T +370 2 652 368 This museum of modern sculpture is located near the capital, Vilnius, and surrounded by a nice grove. It's in the geographic centre of Europe. (Eugenijus Tinfavicius, Design Company Managing Director, Vilnius)

BOOKSHOPS
HUMANITAS, DONELAICIO 52, KAUNAS. T (+370) 7 229 555 For graphic design books.

Area | 1,000 km2	065.2	Capital City	Vilnius	Monetary Unit	Lithuanian lita
Population | 1,000	3,600	Capital City Population | 1,000	598	GDP per Capita (US $)	1,595
Design Population | 1,000	000.2	Languages	Lithuanian, Russian, Polish	International Dialling Code	+370

NETHERLANDS: COUNTRY FILE

HOTELS

HOTEL "NEW YORK", KONINGINNEHOOFD 3072, ROTTERDAM, T (+31) 10 439 0500 A new Rotterdam hotel and restaurant housed in an historic Art Nouveau building, the former head office of the 'Holland-Amerika Line' shipping company. Each room is different and all retain the flavour of the old office rooms with super beds and splendid views over the old harbour sites. The restaurant is excellent and the 'hit' of Rotterdam. (Wim Crouwel, Designer, Amsterdam)

RESTAURANTS, CAFÉS & BARS

JEAN JEAN, AMSTERDAM. Nice — and quite big — restaurant in 'the Jordaan', the most cosy, artistic and friendly part of downtown Amsterdam. They have the best 'salade gourmande', a perfect menu (f.43,50 with three dishes) and a constantly changing décor. (François Gervais, Illustrator, Amsterdam)

SEAFOOD RESTAURANT LUCIUS, SPUISTRAAT 247, AMSTERDAM. T (+31) 20 624 1831 A small and popular restaurant, serving delicious seafood. (Ruedi Rüegg, Designer, Zürich)

PANCAKE BAKERY, PRINSENGRACHT 191, AMSTERDAM. T (+31) 20 625 1333 Pancakes laden with sweet and savoury fillings. Not far from the Anne Frankhuis.

L'ORAGE, OUDE DELFT 111B, DELFT. T (+31) 15 212 3629 A fresh and classically-designed restaurant serves delicious fish dishes on the canal side by award-winning chef.

MUSEUMS & GALLERIES

NEW METROPOLIS (SCIENCE & TECHNOLOGY MUSEUM), OOSTERDOK 2, PRINS HENDRIKKADE, AMSTERDAM. T (+31) 20 531 3233 A stunning and very modern science and technology centre, designed by Renzo Plano, architect of the Pompidou Centre in Paris. Get a fantastic view of the city from the rooftop terrace.

KRÖLLER-MÜLLER MUSEUM, NATIONAL PARK DE HOGE VELUWE, APELDOORN. T (+31) 318 591 241 In the middle of the woods of the Hoge Veluwe Park is one of the world's best collections of modern art, housing nearly 300 works by Vincent Van Gogh, as well as paintings, drawings and sculpture from masters like Seurat, Redon, Braque, Picasso and Mondriaan.

NATIONALMUSEUM VAN SPEELKLOK TOT PIEREMENT (NATIONAL MUSEUM OF MECHANICAL MUSICAL INSTRUMENTS), BUURKERKHOF 10, UTRECHT. T (+31) 30 231 2789 Devoted solely to music machines — from music boxes to street organs and musical chairs to a self-playing Steinway grand piano — this museum is located in a medieval church house in the centre of town.

BOOKSHOPS & SHOPPING

BRUIL & VAN DE STAAIJ, ZUIDELINDE 64, MEPPEL. T (+31) 522 261 303 For graphic design books.

HET ARSENAL Formerly an arsenal, now an interior decorating showroom by Jan Des Bouvrie. Everything for the house from top to bottom. Plus coffee corner and top restaurant. 20 minutes from Amsterdam by car, this little 18th-century stronghold town has many antique shops.

Area | 1,000 km2	040.8	Capital City	Amsterdam	Monetary Unit	Netherlands guilder, gulden, florin & euro	
Population | 1,000	15,731	Capital City Population | 1,000	1,109			
Design Population | 1,000	003.0	Languages	Dutch	GDP per Capita (US $)	25,635	
				International Dialling Code	+31	

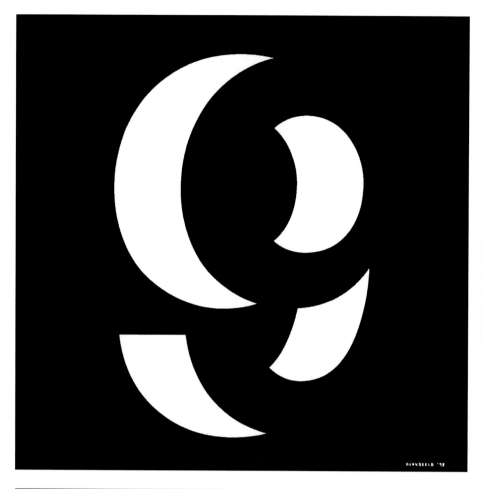

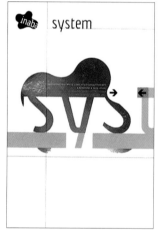

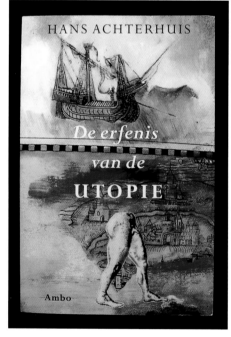

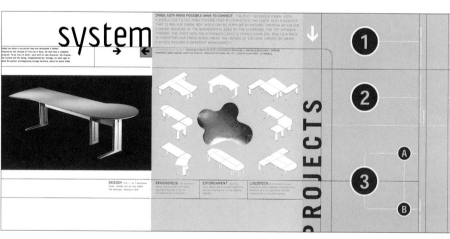

1 SELF-PROMOTIONAL NEW YEAR'S POSTER
DESIGN FIRM: Denkbeeld, Utrecht
DESIGNER: Carlo Knoef

2 STATIONERY FOR A PRODUCT AND PACKAGING DESIGN FIRM
DESIGN FIRM: Shape bv, Amsterdam
ART DIRECTOR/ DESIGNER: Hans Versteeg
PHOTOGRAPHER: Maxim Meekes
CLIENT: Going Dutch

3 COVER FOR "DE ERFENIS VAN DE UTOPIE" BY HANS ACHTERHUIS
DESIGN FIRM: IRISK, Rotterdam
ILLUSTRATOR: Iris Kiewiet
CLIENT: Ambo/ Anthos

4,5 BROCHURE FOR INABA SYSTEM DESKS
DESIGN FIRM: Limage Dangereuse, Rotterdam
CLIENT: Safimex

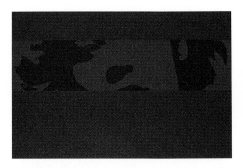

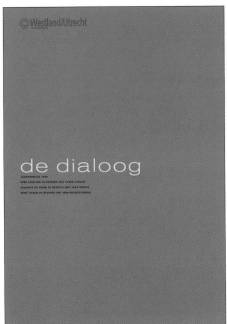

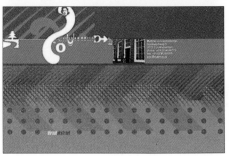

6-9 FRAMES FROM A SELF-PROMOTIONAL WEB SITE
(www.mattmo.nl)
DESIGN FIRM: Mattmo, Amsterdam
ART DIRECTOR: Paul van Ravestein; interaction
DESIGNER: Loes Kalb
CREATIVE DIRECTOR: Monique Mulder

10 COVER OF 1998 ANNUAL REPORT
DESIGN FIRM: Total Design bv, Amsterdam
DESIGNER: Bas Masbeck
PHOTOGRAPHER: Dirk W de Jong
CLIENT: Westland/ Utrecht Hypotheekbank

11 COVER OF 1999 GRADUATION CATALOGUE
DESIGN FIRM: Limage Dangereuse, Rotterdam
CLIENT: VOF Autonoom

12 SELF-PROMOTIONAL CALENDAR
DESIGN FIRM: Limage Dangereuse, Rotterdam

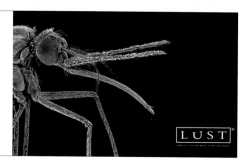

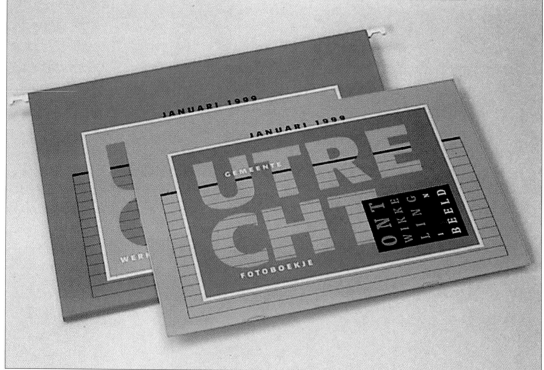

13, 14 CATALOGUE FOR LUST, A SHOE MANUFACTURER
DESIGN FIRM: Uittenhout Design Studio, Wijk en Aalburg
ART DIRECTOR: Eric Eykhout
DESIGNERS: Jessica Zeelenberg, Eric Eykhout
COPYWRITER: Kees Uittenhout

16 TANGO, A POSTER FOR VERKERKE GALLERY
ILLUSTRATOR: François Gervais, Amsterdam

16 IDENTITY PROGRAMME FOR THE CITY OF UTRECHT
DESIGN FIRM: Anker X Strybos, Utrecht
DESIGNER: Menno Anker

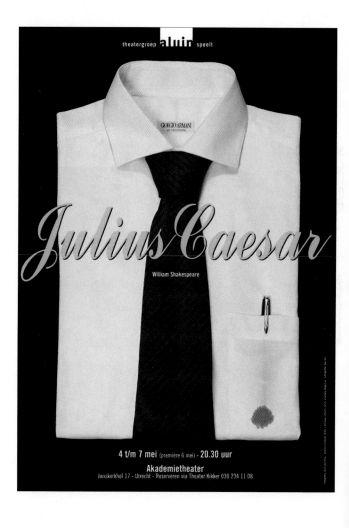

17-19 FRAMES FROM www.lowlands.nl WEBSITE
DESIGN FIRM: Fabrique, Delft
ART DIRECTOR: Marc Fabels
DESIGNERS: Marc Fabels, Djie Han Thung, Peter te Bos
PROGRAMMER: Maarten van Hoogdalem

20 1998 ANNUAL REPORT
FOR A TRADE FAIR AND CONFERENCE COMPANY
DESIGN FIRM: Shape bv, Amsterdam
ART DIRECTOR/ DESIGNER: Hans Vertsteeg
PHOTOGRAPHER: Taco Anema
CLIENT: RAI

21, 22 SOFTWARE AND MAILER FOR A COURIER SERVICE
DESIGN FIRM: KSDP Design, Amsterdam
ART DIRECTOR: Michael King
DESIGNERS: John Comitis (21), Michael King (20),
Adrian van Wyck
PHOTOGRAPHER: Henk Wildschut
CLIENT: TNT

23 POSTER FOR ALUIN THEATRE GROUP
DESIGN FIRM: Anker X Strybos, Utrecht
ART DIRECTOR/ DESIGNER: Hans Strybos
PHOTOGRAPHER: Door van Herp

NORWAY: COUNTRY FILE

HOTELS

FJAERLAND FJORDSTUE HOTEL, FJAERLAND. T (+47) 57 69 32 00 Perched along the edge of the Sognefjord, at the base of the glacier. The veranda overlooking the water offers breath-taking views of the valley and the towering mountains (be sure to ask for a room on the water). Nearby is the Glacier Museum (Norsk Bremuseum) by the Norwegian architect, Sverre Fehn, recipient of the Pritzker Prize. (Andrea Simitch/Val Warke, Architects, New York)

WALAKER HOTEL & GALLERI, SOLVORN, SOGNEFJORD. T (+47) 5 68 42 07 If sheer natural beauty and a small, quaint water-side hotel with home-cooking in the heart of the country will do, this is the place. Located on the very edge of the fjord this old frame building sits in a garden filled with fruit trees. The ferry crosses the fjord in just 20 minutes to one of Norway's best stave churches, Urnes. (Niels Diffrient, Designer, Connecticut)

RESTAURANTS, CAFÉS & BARS

FINNEGAARDS STUENE, ROSENKRANTZGATAN 6, BERGEN. T (+47) 555 50320 A classic Norwegian restaurant in a medieval merchant's house, with four snug rooms and an emphasis on seafood. The venison and reindeer are outstanding and the traditional Norwegian desserts like cloudberries and cream are wonderful.

THEATERCAFEEN, STORTINGSGATAN 24-26, OSLO. T (+47) 22 824 050 A great fun large café with music rather like something you might have found in Paris in the '30s. Very simple, noisy and packed. (Edward Booth-Clibborn, Publisher, London)

LITTLE SAIGON CAFÉ, BERNT ADELS GATE, OSLO A café with an 'intense' yet laid-back atmosphere. Low priced but delicious food!

MOTHER INDIA, BISLETT, OSLO Oslo's best tandoori kitchen (according to some)! (Bryce Bennett, Art Director, Sofiemyr)

MUSEUMS & GALLERIES

EDVARD MUNCHS EKELY, TØYENGATA 53, OSLO. T (+47) 22 552 163 Munch lived and worked for 28 years at Ekely until his death at the age of 80 in 1944. Only his 'winteratelier' remains, and this will be the site of the 'Edward Munch at Ekely' commemorative exhibition in the summer of year 2000.

KON-TIKI MUSÉET, BYGDØYNESVN. 36, OSLO. T (+47) 22 438 050 Take the ferry from Rådhusbryggen (City Hill Wharf) to this museum where Thor Heyerdahl's Kon-Tiki raft and his reed boat RAII are now on view. He crossed the Pacific on the raft and the Atlantic on the boat.

NORSK FOLKEMUSEUM (NORWEGIAN FOLK MUSEUM), MUSEUMSVN. 10, OSLO. T (+47) 22 123700 Again, the ferry will take you over to this park where historic farmhouses have been collected and re-assembled from all over the country.

PLACES OF INTEREST

HÅ GAMLE PRESTEGARD, VARHAUG. T (+47) 51 43 30 61 An exposed settlement which consists of a lighthouse with rooms that you can book, an art gallery (permanent and changing exhibitions) converted from a beautiful group of stone buildings, a stunning painted wooden house that combines an historical centre and café (no staff – help yourself and leave some money). Also, don't miss the Viking graves. (Brian Webb, Designer, London)

BOOKSHOPS & SHOPPING

LUTH, OSTRE AKER VEI 213, OSLO. T (+47) 22 25 48 20 For graphic design books.

Area	1,000 km2	324.0	Capital City	Oslo	Monetary Unit	Norwegian krone
Population	1,000	4,420	Capital City Population	1,000	681	GDP per Capita (US $)	33,734
Design Population	1,000	000.6	Languages	Norwegian	International Dialling Code	+47

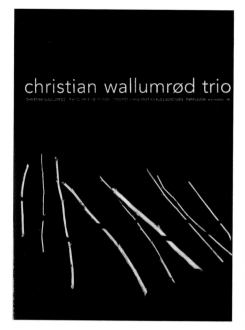

1, 2 POSTERS FOR A JAZZ TRIO
DESIGN FIRM: Aina Griffin, Oslo
ART DIRECTOR/ DESIGNER: Aina Griffin
PHOTOGRAPHER: Petter Martinsen
CLIENT: Rikskonsertene

3, 4 FLYER AND POSTER FOR A MODERN DANCE PERFORMANCE
DESIGN FIRMS: Aina Griffin/ Observatoriet, Oslo
ART DIRECTOR/ DESIGNER: Aina Griffin
ILLUSTRATOR: Observatoriet
CLIENT: Demodans/ Eva Cecilie Richardsen

Introduction

Agresso

Agresso Group ASA is a manufacturer and supplier of international administrative software. The AGRESSO product consists of a number of closely-integrated program modules which together provide a complete system for accounting, financial control, project management, logistics and payroll and personnel administration. The company's product range includes software, services and support. Sales and distribution take place both through partners/distributors and directly to the customer.

Goal Agresso Group ASA's goal is to be a leading international supplier of standard administrative software for medium-sized and large organisations.

Strategy Agresso's products are to be continuously developed, so that the product is among the best as regards both technology and functionality. Product developments that lead to a reduction in the cost of installing, implementing and operating AGRESSO will be given priority. AGRESSO's quality function must be strengthened. Strong growth, a prerequisite for success as an independent company, is to be achieved through a combination of organic growth and acquisitions.

Competitive advantages Agresso supplies products that provide the customer with better and more flexible solutions at lower acquisition and operating costs. Furthermore, Agresso has a cost-effective distribution network, made possible by the fact that all the program modules are standardised with a common program code irrespective of market, language or technical platform.

Organisation The Agresso Group consists of the parent company, Agresso Group ASA, and wholly-owned subsidiaries in UK, Sweden, USA, France and Norway. As at 1 March 1998, there were 249 employees in the Group, of whom 116 work outside Norway.

Important events in 1997
➤ A rise in turnover of 110 per cent
➤ 67 per cent of the turnover takes place outside Norway
➤ The UK is the largest individual market, with 38 per cent of the turnover
➤ A share issue of approximately NOK 60 million in August
➤ Merger with Ampersand Systems Ltd in the UK
➤ The launch of a new main version: AGRESSO 5
➤ Letters of intent regarding mergers with
   Engsoft AS in Norway
   Visionary Solutions Corp in Canada
   BG Partner in France

In order to act upon the trends affecting their organisations, business managers must have up-to-date information instantly available and at all times. AGRESSO delivers strong complex reporting potential - at any time.

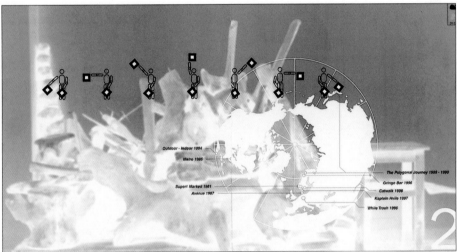

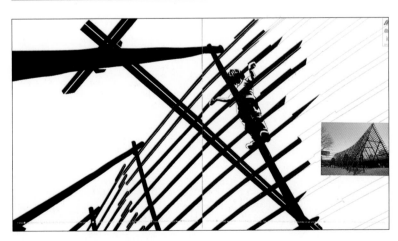

5 1997 ANNUAL REPORT
FOR A BUSINESS AND FINANCIAL SOFTWARE COMPANY
DESIGN FIRM: Bryce Bennett Communications, Sofiemyr
ART DIRECTOR: Bryce Bennett
ILLUSTRATOR: Rolf Jansson
CLIENT: Agresso Group

6, 7 SPREADS FROM AN EXHIBITION CATALOGUE ABOUT THE
WORK OF ARTIST INGHILD KARLSEN
DESIGN FIRMS: Aina Griffin, Oslo/ ORG Studio, Oslo
ART DIRECTORS: Aina Griffin, Stein Sørlie
ILLUSTRATOR: Stein Sørlie

POLAND: COUNTRY FILE

HOTELS

HOTEL ELEKTOR, UL. SZPITALNA 28, KRAKÓW. T (+48) 12 423 2317 This small hotel is just outside the old town's walls, within walking distance of all the main sites in Kraków. Intimate atmosphere and friendly service. An ideal location for exploring the medieval capital of Poland, Kazimierz (a Jewish district), churches and the Wieliczka Salt Mine (which is a must). (Tomasz Lachowski, Designer, Warsaw)

RESTAURANTS, CAFÉS & BARS

KUCHNIA ARTYSTYCZNA, CENTRUM SZTUKI WSPOLCZESNEJ, ALEJE UJAZDOWSKIE 6, WARSAW. T (+48) 22 628 12 78 Café with a remarkable interior and very pleasant atmosphere — not really a tourist hot spot either. (Mark Rozycki, Designer, Warsaw)

LOLEK, ROKITNICKA 20 (POLE MOKOTOWSKIE), WARSAW. T (+48) 22 825 62 02 Inside, this pub resembles a prehistoric cave with fireplace. Offers a choice of beers, grilled meats and delicious salads. A great place to spend some spare time, meet friends and listen to live music. Especially worth visiting in summer when you can eat outdoors.

MODULAR CAFÉ BAR, PL. TRZECH KRZYZY 8, WARSAW. T (+48) 22 627 26 03 One of the most interesting pubs in Warsaw in terms of interiors: French in style, one might say. Ideal for Saturday breakfast, casual lunches and nice evenings. Many foreign visitors. Warning: metal furniture is dominant. Everything is simple and very modern.

PIWNICA PRZY HOZEJ, HOZA 50, WARSAW. T (+48) 22 622 13 30 A calm, enclosed place to eat. Inside is wood, wood, stones and more wood. Delicious salads.

LOKOMOTYWA (LOCOMOTIVE), KRUCZA 17, WARSAW. T (+48) 22 621 78 74 Café-pub much visited by young people. Offers Polish cuisine in surroundings resembling a train's interior. Very cosy atmosphere. (Agnieszka Galas, Copywriter, Warsaw)

QCHNIA ARTYSTYCZNA, ZAMEK UJAZDOWSKI, WARSAW. T (+48) 22 625 7627 If you like to see artists, designers or architects, come here. There is usually a group of eccentrics wanting to mix with a fancy crowd. Good food (even better named). After lunch, we recommend visiting the Centre of Modern Art (see below). Book first.

POD BARYLKA, UL. GARBARSKA 7, WARSAW. T (+48) 22 826 6239 A lovely, cosy pub in the square famous for its festivals in the '50s. Close to the Old Town, but off the beaten track. Variety of Polish beers served in warm summer evenings by the fountain. (Tomasz Lachowski, Designer, Warsaw)

MUSEUMS & GALLERIES

MUZEUM PLAKATU (POSTER MUSEUM), UL. ST. KOSTKI POTOCKIEGO 10/16, WARSAW. T (+48) 22 842 2606 Constant exhibition of posters from the '20s and '30s, including masterpieces by Tadeusz Gronowski, as well as interesting temporary shows. Before or after the museum, do visit the Wilanów Royal Castle and Gardens.

CENTRUM SZTUKI WSPÓLCZESNEJ (CENTRE OF MODERN ART), ZAMEK UJAZDOWSKI, WARSAW. T (+48) 22 628 1271 Located in Ujazdowski Castle — one of the worst buildings in Warsaw — but the unfinished structure, unpainted walls and ceilings create an unusual environment for contemporary art exhibitions. Films, 'happenings', posters, glass — you can find almost everything here. Lovely surroundings, including Lazienki Royal Park, help you contemplate the impressions of your visit.

MUZEUM KARYKATURY (CARTOON MUSEUM), UL. KOZIA 11, WARSAW. T (+48) 22 827 8895 Located on narrow Goat Street where you feel like you're in medieval Warsaw. Dozens of cartoons on show. (Tomasz Lachowski, Designer, Warsaw)

BOOKSHOPS

ARTES, UL. MAZOWIECKA 11A, WARSAW. T (+48) 22 282 64758 ext. 112 For graphic design books.

Area | 1,000 km2	323.0	Capital City	Warsaw	Monetary Unit	Polish zloty
Population | 1,000	38,607	Capital City Population | 1,000	1,642	GDP per Capita (US $)	3,058
Design Population | 1,000	000.8	Languages	Polish	International Dialling Code	+48

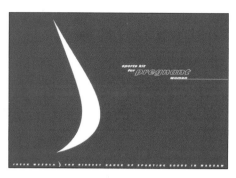

1 POSTER FOR THE ACADEMY OF FINE ARTS IN POZNAN
DESIGNER: Miroslaw Adamczyk, Poznan

2 EXHIBITION POSTER FOR GALERIA U JEZUITÓW
DESIGNER: Miroslaw Adamczyk, Poznan

3-5 ADVERTISEMENTS FOR JACEK WSZOLA SPORTSWEAR
DESIGN FIRM: Ammirati Puris Lintas Warsaw
ART DIRECTOR: Chris Matyszczyk
DESIGNERS: Karolina Czarnota, Magdalena Berent,
Artur Dynowski

6-8 ADVERTISEMENTS FOR SONY POLAND
AGENCY: Leo Burnett, Warsaw
CREATIVE DIRECTORS: Kerry Keenan, Darek Zatorski
ART DIRECTOR: KC Arriwong
COPYWRITERS: Kerry Keenan, Lechoslaw Kwiatkowski
PHOTOGRAPHER: Jonathan Root

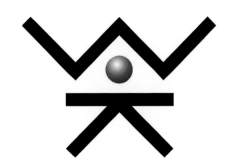

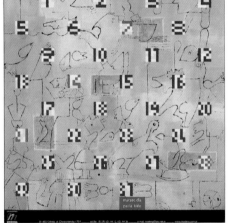

9 ILLUSTRATION FOR "MAX" MAGAZINE
ART DIRECTOR: Tomek Drzewinski, Warsaw
ILLUSTRATOR: Piotr Lesniak
CLIENT: WPTS Sp.zo.o.

10 SELF-PROMOTIONAL CALENDAR FOR DRUKARNIA MODENA, GDYNIA, A PRINTING HOUSE
DESIGNER: Bartek Ignaciuk

11 LOGO FOR DESIGNER WALDEMAR KWIATKOWSKI
DESIGN FIRM: Korek Studio, Warsaw
DESIGNER/ ILLUSTRATOR: Wojciech Korkuc

12,13 KETCHUP AND MUSTARD PACKAGING
DESIGN FIRM: Atelier Tadeusz Piechura, Lodz
DESIGNER: Tadeusz Piechura
PHOTOGRAPHER: Piotr Tomczyk
CLIENT: SUWARY S.A.

14 POSTER FOR "CAMERIMAGE '98", A FILM FESTIVAL
DESIGN FIRM: Studio Pro, Torun
ART DIRECTOR: Edward Malinowski
DESIGNER: Krysztof Bialowicz
CLIENT: Fundacja Tumult

15 ADVERTISEMENT FOR NEWSPAPER "GAZETA POMORSHA"
DESIGN FIRM: Studio Pro, Torun
ART DIRECTOR: Edward Malinowski
DESIGNER: Krysztof Bialowicz

foood   drink

toilets   stairs

exit

NA MINUSIE

Media Polska

MEDIALNE
ŁUPY

16-20 SELF-PROMOTIONAL SIGNAGE
AGENCY: Corporate Profiles DDB, Warsaw
ART DIRECTORS/ DESIGNERS: Jacek Dyga, Filip Gebski

21 KIOSK FOR KREATURA '98,
A NATIONAL ADVERTISING COMPETITION
DESIGN FIRM: Korek Studio, Warsaw
DESIGNER/ ILLUSTRATOR: Wojciech Korkuc
PHOTOGRAPHER: Wlodek Krzeminski
CLIENT: VFP Communications

22 12-YEAR REPORT FOR A FURNITURE MANUFACTURER
DESIGN FIRM: Zdanowicz & Pawrowski, Poznan
DESIGNER: Piotr Zdanowicz
PHOTOGRAPHER: Andrzej Grabowski
CLIENT: Adriana

23, 27 SPREADS FROM "MEDIA POLSKA" MAGAZINE
ART DIRECTOR: Mark Rozycki/ VFP Communications, Warsaw
ILLUSTRATOR: Andrzej Saganowski

24-26 COVERS FROM "MEDIA POLSKA" MAGAZINE
ART DIRECTOR: Mark Rozycki/ VFP Communications, Warsaw
ILLUSTRATORs: Andrzej Saganowski (24, 25), Piotr Lesniak (26)

MATKI, ŻONY, KOCHANKI

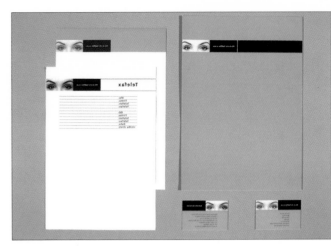

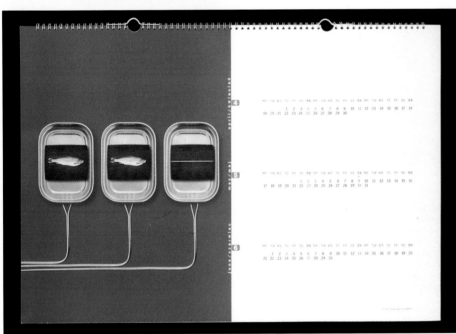

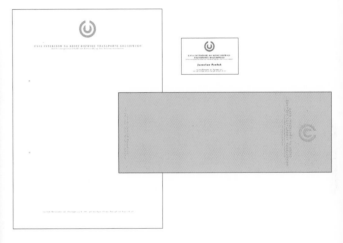

ANATOMIA SUKCESU

PORTUGAL: COUNTRY FILE

HOTELS

RESIDENCIA YORK HOUSE, RUA DAS JANELAS VERDES, 32, LISBON. T (+351) 21 60 66 36 Small hotel west of the city centre located in a 16th-century convent on rising ground above the River Tagus. Clean, simple rooms, no luxuries, but sublime peace. Get on one of Lisbon's wonderful trams at the next corner and eat in the city centre, 5 minutes' ride away. (John Young, Architect, London)

ESTALAGEM SANTA CATARINA, RUA SANTA CATARINA 1347, OPORTO. Wonderful, hidden, unknown hotel, typically forties and seldom mentioned in tourist guides. Set around a beautiful inner garden with tropical plants and fountains, the three-block building is covered with blue azulejos. Bedrooms are sumptuous and full of antique furniture. Not expensive and very comfortable. (Christina Lucchini, Fashion Editor, Milan)

HOTEL PALÁCIO DE SETEAIS, 8 AV. BARBOSA BOCAGE, SINTRA. T (+351) 21 92 33 200 Formerly a palace completed in 1878. Today the rooms are furnished with fine furniture some with original painted wallpapers. The restaurant is very attractive; the food could be better, but one stays here because it is really quite an amazing place and only half an hour from Lisbon. (Edward Booth-Clibborn, Publisher, London)

RESTAURANTS, CAFÉS & BARS

OS TIBETANOS, RUA DO SALITRE, 117, LISBON. T (351) 21 3142030 / 3151524 Great vegetarian food and a great place to rest from the your client's deadlines.

PATO BATON, TV. FIÉIS DE DEUS, 28, LISBON (BAIRRO ALTO). T (351) 21 3426372 Excellent food, excellent wines and excellent service in a Lisbon 'hot spot'.

W.I.P. - WORK IN PROGRESS: CLOTHES, HAIR, BAR, RUA DA BICA DUARTE BELO, 47/49, LISBON (BAIRRO ALTO). T (351) 21 3461486 Open till 4am, where designers and architects meet and there's live music — and no tourists! (Nuno Alves, Art Director/Designer, Lisbon)
The old part of Lisbon has lots of small great bars. Go to the Bairro Alto part of the city to find them — FRÁGIL is one. (Lizá Defossez Ramalho, Art Director/Designer, Matosinhos)

SOLMAR RESTAURANT, RUA DAS PORTAS DE SANTO ANTÃO NOS 106A-108, LISBON. T (+351) 1 342 3371 Wonderful 1950s interior — lots of curves and magnificent murals — in the heart of Lisbon. The food is good: all fish, fresh from the Atlantic, washed down with a bottle or two of Vinho Verde. (Brian Boylan, Designer, London)

RESTAURANTE LEÃO DE OURO, RUA 1º DE DEZEMBRO, LISBON. High-ceilinged, old-fashioned restaurant with traditional food — and excellent fish. Not expensive. (George Hardie, Illustrator, London)

CAFÉ NICOLA, ROSSIO SQUARE, LISBON. The old and very original coffee house at the lower end of Rossio Square is very popular thanks to the good coffee (own blend) and pastries. The perfect place to sit and watch…. (Justus Oehler, Designer, London)

ANIKI-BÓBÓ, RUA FONTE TAURINA 36/38, OPORTO. T (+351) 22 332 4619 This bar is in the old part of the city, and has interesting décor, great music and the clients are people connected with arts.

GUERNICA, RUA MIGUEL BOMBARDA, OPORTO. A small, but great restaurant serving Angolan food on Fridays and an Arabic menu on Saturdays. Lunch only served during the week. Near to several art galleries, including Artes em Partes. (Lizá Defossez Ramalho, Art Director/Designer, Matosinhos)

MUSEUMS & GALLERIES

DESIGN MUSEUM, BELÉM CULTURAL CENTER, PRAÇA DO IMPÉRIO, EDIFÍCIO CENTRO CULTURAL DE BELÉM, LISBON. T (351) 21 3612400 Industrial Design Collection and the focus for the best cultural events in Lisbon. (Nuno Alves, Art Director/Designer, Lisbon)
If you go to the DESIGN MUSEUM, visit the great tea house that serves the typical cakes of the region — Pateis de Belém. (Lizá Defossez Ramalho, Art Director/Designer, Matosinhos)

MUSEU NACIONAL DO AZULEJO, RUA MADRE DE DEUS 4, LISBON. T (+351) 21 814 7747 Housed in a former monastery founded in 1509 is a collection of tiles from the 15th-century to the present. The tiles are mainly from Portugal, but there are additional examples from Antwerp, the Netherlands and Spain.

MUSEU NACIONAL DE ARTE ANTIGA, LISBON Grim exterior, good sombre contemporary architecture within. Particularly recommended is the Hieronymous Bosch "Temptations of St. Anthony". (Helen & Gene Federico, Illustrator/Designer, New York)

CAM (CENTRO D'ARTE MODERNA), FUNDAÇAO GULBENKIAN, AV. DE BERNA, 45 LISBON. T (351) 21 798 6961 A modern museum of modern art with perhaps the best café of its kind in Lisbon run by the renowned restaurant 'Tavares'. (Justus Oehler, Designer, London)

GALERIA PEDRO OLIVEIRA, CALÇADA DE MONCHIQUE, 3, OPORTO. T (+351) 22 2007 131 In a lovely part of the city, this gallery holds exhibitions of contemporary art, and nearby (almost across the street) there is another interesting exhibition space in an old building called Alfandega.

FUNDAÇÃO DE SERRALVES, RUA D. JOÃO CASTRO, OPORTO. T (+351) 22 615 6500 The Modern Museum opened just a few months ago. It was designed by the well-known Portuguese architect, Siza Vieira. It has a beautiful garden.
(Lizá Defossez Ramalho, Art Director/Designer, Matosinhos)

PLACES OF INTEREST

COSTA NOVA, NEAR AVEIRO. A small seaside village sandwiched between a lagoon and the Atlantic on the route from Lisbon to Oporto. All the houses are immaculately painted in alternating stripes of white and a primary colour. The total effect of red/white, blue/white, yellow/white, green/white under a clear blue sky and in strong sunlight is stunning. Nothing else to do there. (John Young, Architect, London)

SINTRA Visit the all-day Sunday market with different stalls of local produce and crafts set in the middle of the beautiful old town on a hill. Try the oven-baked bread and buy some of the local sheep cheese. (Edward Booth-Clibborn, Publisher, London)

PORT WINE CELLARS

A.A. CÁLEM & FILHO, SA, AV. DIOGO LEITE, 26, APARTADO 140, VILA NOVA DE GAIA. T (+351) 22 3794041

A.A. FERREIRA, SA, RUA DA CARVALHOSA, 19 - 103, VILA NOVA DE GAIA. T (+351) 22 3700010 (José M. Da Silva, Art Director/Designer, Oporto)

Area	1,000 km2	091.9	Capital City	Lisbon	Monetary Unit	Portuguese escudos & euro
Population	1,000	9,928	Capital City Population	1,000	1,863		
Design Population	1,000	002.0	Languages	Portuguese	GDP per Capita (US $)	10,428
					International Dialling Code	+ 351

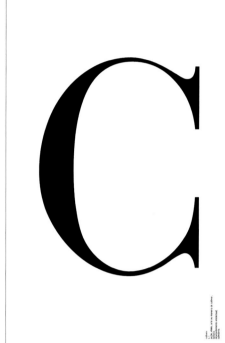

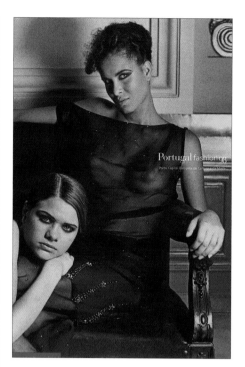

Culture, the beliefs, behaviour, language, and entire way of life of a particular group of people at a particular time. Culture includes customs ceremonies, works of art, inventions, technology, and traditions. The term also may have a more specific aesthetic interpretation.

Portugal fashion 98

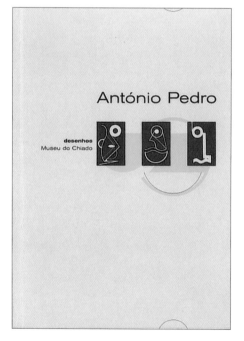

António Pedro

desenhos
Museu do Chiado

FÁBRICA
DO INGLÊS
SILVES

1, 2 SPREAD (1) AND COVER (2)
FROM "PORTUGAL FASHION 98" BOOK
DESIGN FIRM: Setezeroum Design, Oporto
DESIGNER: José Manuel Da Silva
PHOTOGRAPHER: Cassiano Ferraz
CLIENT: Associação Nacional de Jovens Empresários

3 EXHIBITION CATALOGUE FOR MUSEU DO CHIADO
DESIGN FIRM: Ricardo Mealha Atelier, Lisbon
ART DIRECTOR: Ricardo Mealha
DESIGNER: Isabel Castro

4 LOGO FOR FÁBRICA DO INGLÊS
DESIGN FIRM: HPP Comunicaçáo, Lisbon
DESIGNER: Cristováo Bartiosa
CREATIVE DIRECTOR: Pedro Oliveira

5, 6 ADVERTISING CAMPAIGN FEATURING CELEBRITIES AND HISTORICAL FIGURES FOR SOCIETY OF COLLECTIVE TRANSPORT (STCP), OPORTO
DESIGN FIRM: Novodesign, Lisbon
ART DIRECTOR: Paulo Rocha

7, 8 SIGNAGE FOR LOJA DO CIDADÃO, MUNICIPAL BUILDINGS IN LISBON AND OPORTO
DESIGN FIRM: A&L Criatividade é Comunicação, Caseris
ART DIRECTOR: Paulo Alfonso
DESIGNER: Pedro Jorge
CLIENT: Instituto para Gestão das Lojas do Cidadão

9 WEDDING INVITATION FOR KATHY XIOMANA SANTOS
DESIGN FIRM: Setezeroum Design, Oporto
DESIGNER: José Manuel Da Silva

10, 11 PROMOTIONAL BROCHURES FOR THE PLAY, "AIR"
DESIGN FIRM: R2 Design, Matosinhos
ART DIRECTORS/ DESIGNERS: Lizá Ramalho, Artur Rebelo
CLIENT: Teatro Bruto

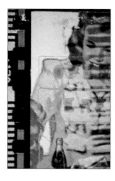

12-16 SELF-PROMOTIONAL POSTCARDS
DESIGN FIRM: Pink Design, Vila Nova de Gaia
ART DIRECTOR/ DESIGNER/ ILLUSTRATOR:
Sandra Mónia Couto Coelho

17 COVER OF "DESENHOS DOS SURREALISTAS EM PORTUGAL",
A CATALOGUE FOR A SURREALIST EXHIBITION
DESIGN FIRM: Ricardo Mealha Atelier, Lisbon
ART DIRECTOR: Ricardo Mealha
DESIGNER: Pedro Santos
CLIENT: The Institute of Contemporary Art

18 LOGO FOR MINISTERIO DA SEGURANCIA SOCIAL
(SOCIAL SECURITY)
DESIGNER: Nuno Alves, Lisbon

19 SILK SCARF PACKAGING
DESIGN FIRM: Artlandia Design, Lisbon
DESIGNER: Beatriz Horta Correia
CLIENT: Portuguese Institute of Architecture

Discoteca
DUNAS

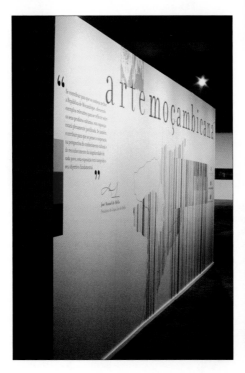

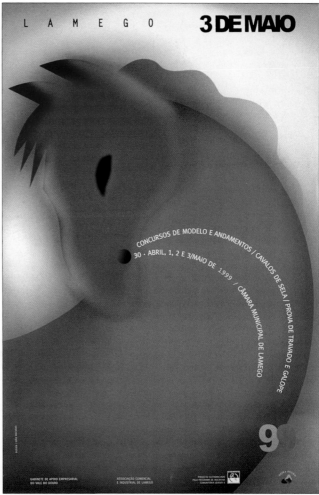

egg design office

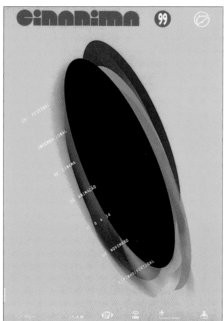

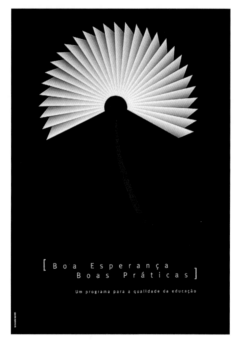

24 POSTER PROMOTING PORTUGAL'S NATIONAL WATER DAY, 1999
DESIGN FIRM: João Machado Design, Oporto
ART DIRECTOR/ DESIGNER/ ILLUSTRATOR: João Machado
CLIENT: Serviços Municipalizados de Águas e Saneamento

25 POSTER FOR "EXPODOURO '99", AN EXHIBITION FOR
BUSINESSES LOCATED IN THE DOURO REGION
DESIGN FIRM: João Machado Design, Oporto
ART DIRECTOR/ DESIGNER/ ILLUSTRATOR: João Machado
CLIENT: Associação Comercial e Industrial de Lamego

26 POSTER FOR CINANIMA 99, AN ANIMATED FILM FESTIVAL
DESIGN FIRM: João Machado Design, Oporto
ART DIRECTOR/ DESIGNER/ ILLUSTRATOR: João Machado

27 "BOA ESPERANÇA, BOAS PRÁCTICAS 98" POSTER
DESIGN FIRM: João Machado Design, Oporto
ART DIRECTOR/ DESIGNER/ ILLUSTRATOR: João Machado
CLIENT: Instituto de Inovação Educacional

28 POSTER FOR AN EXHIBITION OF THE WORK OF JOÃO MACHADO
IN MACAU
DESIGN FIRM: João Machado Design, Oporto
ART DIRETOR/ DESIGNER/ ILLUSTRATOR: João Machado
CLIENT: Fundação Oriente

29 ONE OF A SERIES OF POSTERS FOR A PAPER MANUFACTURER
DESIGN FIRM: João Machado Design, Oporto
ART DIRECTOR/ DESIGNER/ ILLUSTRATOR: João Machado
CLIENT: Sociedade de Distribuição de Papel

| 24 | 26 | 28 |
| 25 | 27 | 29 |

RUSSIA: COUNTRY FILE

HOTELS

HOTEL METROPOL, 1 PROSPEKT MARXA, MOSCOW. T (+7) 95 927 6100 This hotel by the oldest part of the Kremlin wall was Stalin's first Moscow headquarters before he moved into the Kremlin. It has large, comfortable well-decorated rooms, but the most impressive spaces are the dining rooms, such as the Europeysky, which are in the classic Empire style, and the Breakfast Room with its fountain in gold. (Edward Booth-Clibborn, Publisher, London)

MUSEUMS & GALLERIES

INTERNATIONAL ACADEMY OF ADVERTISING AND DESIGN, GENERALA BERSARINA STREET, MOSCOW. T (+7) 95 9468921 The Academy prepares the future specialists in design (graphic design, textiles, interiors) as well as in marketing and in advertising management. There is a permanent exhibition of student work here.

TSENTRAL'NY DOM KHUDOZHNIKA (THE CENTRAL HOUSE OF THE ARTIST), KRYMSKY VAL 10, MOSCOW. T (+7) 95 2389634 An exhibition centre with permanently changing shows of work from Russian and foreign painters and designers (from "classics" to modern).

SOVINCENTER, KRASNOPRESNENSKAYA NABEREZHNAYA 12, MOSCOW. T (+7) 95 2532760, 2566303 A centre of international trade and science offering a complex of shops, hotels and restaurants. There are regular press-conferences and exhibitions here dedicated to modern art and graphic design.

EXPOCENTRE ON KRASNAYA PRESNYA, KRASNOPRESNENSKAYA NABEREZHNAYA 14, MOSCOW. T (+7) 95 2553799, 2052800 Regular international exhibitions and fairs dedicated to different kinds of art and technology.

MANEZH EXHIBITION CENTRE, MANEZHNAYA SQUARE 1, MOSCOW. T (+7) 95 2028252 Holds international and local exhibitions of painting and graphic design.

PHOTOCENTRE, GOGOLEVSKY BULVAR 8, MOSCOW. T (+7) 95 2904188 For Russian and international exhibitions of photographic art.

MARAT GELMAN'S GALLERY, MALAYA POLYANKA STREET 7/7, MOSCOW. T (+7) 95 2386654 Regular exhibitions of modern design, painting and photographs. (Denis Kusnetzov, Art Director/Designer, Moscow)

TOLSTOY HOUSE MUSEUM, 21 LEV TOLSTOY STREET, MOSCOW. Take a taxi to the writer's house, a beautiful wooden building in a run-down part of Moscow. It still looks very much as it must have done in Tolstoy's lifetime. Well worth the trouble of getting there. (David Gentleman, Artist, London)

THE TILE MUSEUM AT THE NOVO-DEVICHI CONVENT, MOSCOW Down a little path in the convent grounds, this little museum displays in chronological order a fascinating collection of tiles, dating from the 16th to the 19th-centuries. Wonderful, wonderful tiles. (Marianne Ford, Set Designer, London)

Area | 1,000 km2	17,075.0	Capital City	Moscow	Monetary Unit	rouble
Population | 1,000	146,861	Capital City Population | 1,000	9,233	GDP per Capita (US $)	2,451
Design Population | 1,000	000.5	Languages	Russian	International Dialling Code	+95

1 WEB SITE FOR NOVOYE TRIO (NEW TRIO)
(www.novoye-trio.msk.ru)
ART DIRECTORS/ DESIGNERS: Gelena Melnikova,
Denis Kusnetzov, Moscow

2 LOGO FOR ARABESQUE FURNITURE COMPANY
ART DIRECTORS/ DESIGNERS: Gelena Melnikova,
Denis Kusnetzov, Moscow

3 LOGO FOR SIBIRTAYZHMASH (SIBERIAN MACHINE WORKS)
ART DIRECTORS/ DESIGNERS: Gelena Melnikova,
Denis Kusnetzov, Moscow

4 LOGO FOR THE CENTRE OF DIGITAL TELEVISION TECHNOLOGIES
ART DIRECTORS/ DESIGNERS: Gelena Melnikova,
Denis Kusnetzov, Moscow

5 LOGO FOR MAX LEVEL, AN AD AGENCY
ART DIRECTORS/ DESIGNERS: Gelena Melnikova,
Denis Kusnetzov, Moscow

SLOVENIA:COUNTRY FILE

RESTAURANTS, CAFÉS & BARS
OD ZMAUCA SOSED PA UD BRATA PRIJATU, RIMSKA 21, LJUBLJANA. T (+386) 61 210 324 The name of this café is not translatable, but it is a place where the best sandwiches in the town are served and is always full of young artistic people.
SPAJZA, GORNJI TRG 28, LJUBLJANA. T (+386) 61 125 30 94 A cool place where you can eat Mediterranean food and drink good Slovenian wines.
NOSTALGIJA, STARI TRG 9, LJUBLJANA. T (+386) 61 222 682 A pleasant, retro-designed place, for all nostalgic people from former Yugoslavia.
VINOTEKA MOVIA, MESTNI TRG 2, LJUBLJANA. T (+386) 61 125 54 48 A real wine shop, where you can taste and buy excellent Slovenian wines. (Eduard Cehovin, Art director, Ljubljana)

MUSEUMS & GALLERIES
INTERNATIONAL CENTRE OF GRAPHIC ARTS, POD TURNOM 3, GRAD TIVOLI, LJUBLJANA. T (+386) 61 126 52 40 The International Biennial Exhibitions of Graphic Arts are held here. Among past winners are Joan Miro (1965), Joe Tison (1985) and David Hockney (1995).
GOSPODARSKA ZBORNOCA SLOVENIJE (IDCO GALLERY), DIMICEVA 13, LJUBLJANA. T (+386) 61 189 80 00 The only gallery in Ljubljana exhibiting works from the field of design.
ARCHITEKTURNI MUZEJ (PLE(NIK COLLECTION), KORUNOVA 4, LJUBLJANA. T (+386) 61 335 066 Joze Plecnik was a Slovene, and the most well-known Central European architect from the beginning of the last century. He worked in Vienna and Prague, but in Ljubljana there are still many of his buildings which catch the eye. (Eduard Cehovin, Art director, Ljubljana)

PLACES OF INTEREST
CENTROMERKUR, TRUBALJEVA 1, LJUBLJANA. T (+386) 61 126 3170 One of the most glorious of all the Vienna Secessionist-style buildings. Inside this department store you'll find an extraordinary curved wrought-iron staircase leading to the upper floors. Built 1903.
PIRAN A medieval walled city perched on a dagger-shaped peninsula jutting out into the Adriatic Sea. The charming harbour is enclosed by gracious, pastel-coloured houses and the warren of steep, narrow walkways leading down to the grand marble square is overlooked by a Romanesque church. (Sarah Jameson, European Design Annual, Hove)

BOOKSHOPS
MLADINSKA KNIGA, SLOVENSKA 29, LJUBLJANA. T (+386) 61 159 7527 For graphic design books.

Area	1,000 km2	020.3	Capital City	Ljubljana	Monetary Unit	tolar
Population	1,000	1,972	Capital City Population	1,000	260	GDP per Capita (US $)	9,652
Design Population	1,000	000.1	Languages	Slovenian	International Dialling Code	+386

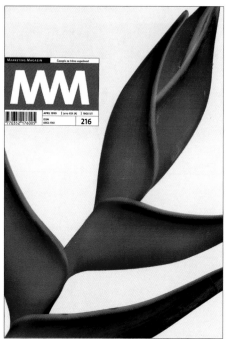

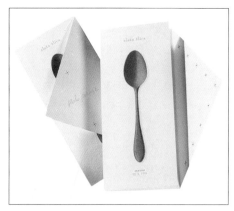

1, 2 COVERS OF JULY/ AUGUST (1) AND APRIL 1999 (2) ISSUES OF "MM" (MARKETING MAGAZINE), LJUBLJANA
ART DIRECTOR: Mateve Medja
PHOTOGRAPHER: Dragan Arrigler

3 1998 ANNUAL REPORT FOR "DELO", A NEWSPAPER PUBLISHER
ART DIRECTOR/ DESIGNER: Dusan Brajic/ Delo, Ljubljana

4 MENU DESIGN FOR MAXIM, A RESTAURANT
DESIGN FIRM: Kompas Design, Ljubljana
ART DIRECTOR/ DESIGNER: Zare Kerin
PHOTOGRAPHER: Janez Puksic

5-9 "TRICKSY TRIXIE", A HOLIDAY-GREETING FLIP BOOK FOR A FILM AND VIDEO PRODUCTION COMPANY
DESIGN FIRM: A±B (In Exile), Ljubljana
ART DIRECTOR/ DESIGNER: Eduard Cehovin
CLIENT: A Atalanta

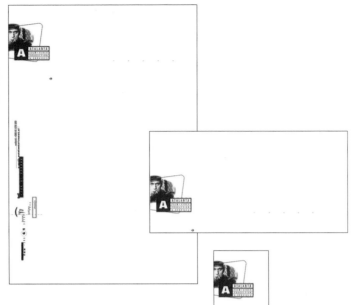

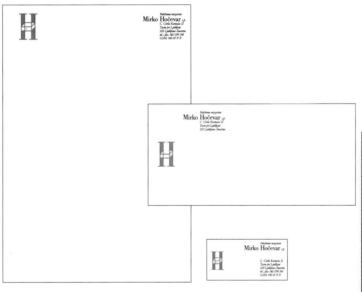

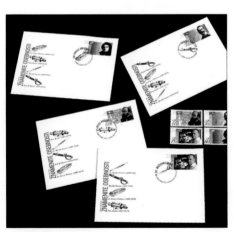

**10 1999 CALENDAR FEATURING EXAMPLES OF
SLOVENIAN CULTURE**
DESIGN FIRM: KROG, Ljubljana
ART DIRECTOR/ DESIGNER: Edi Berk
PHOTOGRAPHER: Janez Puksic
CLIENT: Kmecki glas

**11 1997 ANNUAL REPORT FOR ENVIRONMENTAL DEVELOPMENT
FUND OF THE REPUBLIC OF SLOVENIA**
DESIGN FIRM: Kraft & Werk, Maribor
ART DIRECTOR/ DESIGNER: Damijan Vesligaj

**12 POSTAGE STAMPS AND ENVELOPES
SHOWING FAMOUS SLOVENIAN MEN IN HISTORY**
DESIGN FIRM: KROG, Ljubljana
ART DIRECTOR/ DESIGNER: Edi Berk
CLIENT: Posta Slovenije

13 STATIONERY FOR A FILM AND VIDEO PRODUCTION COMPANY
DESIGN FIRM: A±B (In Exile), Ljubljana
ART DIRECTOR/ DESIGNER: Eduard Cehovin
CLIENT: A Atalanta

14 STATIONERY FOR A JOINER
DESIGN FIRM: KROG, Ljubljana
ART DIRECTOR/ DESIGNER: Edi Berk
CLIENT: Mirko Hocevar

15, 16 DESIGN FOR WINE LABELS
DESIGN FIRM: KROG, Ljubljana
ART DIRECTOR/ DESIGNER: Edi Berk
CLIENT: KG Rakican

SPAIN: COUNTRY FILE

HOTELS

HOTEL SUECIA, MARQUÉS DE CASA RIERA, 4, MADRID. T (+34) 91 231 6900 Wonderfully crisp, bright, clean, well-run hotel with a great location half-way between the Prado and the Plaza Mayor. (Jim Stockton, Deisgner, San Francisco)

HOTEL EL PORTO, PORTO KALEA 1, MUNDAKA. Forget staying in Bilbao while visiting the museum. 35 minutes north on the coast is the beautiful, secluded little fishing village of Mundaka with this fabulous little hotel. Modest and perfectly sited above the harbour with unbeatable views across the geraniums to the red, blue and green boats below. (Chris & Esther Pullman, Designers, Boston)

HOTEL SIMÓN, GARCÍA DE VINUESA 19, SEVILLE. T (+34) 95 422 6660 An 18th-century mansion a few minutes' walk away from Seville Cathedral. Prices are very reasonable and the rooms functional rather than glamorous, but the pleasures of the fountain and the staircase more than compensate. The bakery a few doors down sells ambrosial cakes, biscuits, chocolates and coffee. (Juliet Barclay, Writer, London)

RESTAURANTS, CAFÉS & BARS

SEMPRONIANA, ROSELLN, 148, BARCELONA. T (+34) 93 453 18 20 A very special and original restaurant situated in an area of Barcelona where people eat late. An important centre at night ! (Eva Arno, Index Book, Barcelona)

RESTAURANTE "SI, SENYOR", 199 MALLORCA STREET, BARCELONA. T (+34) 93 253 2149 A functional restaurant in the centre of the city, near Gaudi's buildings. The owner is an office furniture designer who enjoys art. On the walls you can see Tapies lithographies, Man Ray and Catala-Roca photographs &c. They try to serve plain dishes that preserve in their cooking the original natural tastes. After your meal you can walk along Mallorca Street, straight to Paseo de Gracia and enjoy looking at some of the modernist houses along the road. (Josep Pla Narbona, Designer, Barcelona)

BARRI DE LA RIBERA, BARCELONA. Close to the Barri Gothic and the harbour this is one of the less well-known places in Barcelona. It's a historical area now full of great restaurants, bars and antiques. Get yourself lost there, and discover what it has to offer ....

LLÀNTIA, C/ BROSOLÍ 5, BARRI DE LA RIBERA, BARCELONA. T (+34) 93 319 7510 A quiet restaurant, which will please your palate and your pocket. (Lamosca, Design and Multimedia Studio, Manso, Barcelona)

TRAINERA, CALLE LAGASCA, MADRID. T (+34) 91 275 4717 A noisy, amazing, local and bustling fish restaurant. A shot of Madrid essence, and superb raunchy food. If you're in Madrid, go! (Michael Wolff, Designer, London)

EL ESPEJO - RESTAURANTE, PASEO DE RECOLOETOS 31, MADRID. T (+34) 91 308 23 47 One part of the restaurant is a bar-room with little tables for drinks and Spanish snacks, full of people waiting for the sunrise. In the other part you can take an excellent dinner or lunch in an exclusive atmosphere. The interiors are pure Art Nouveau. Some years ago it was restored by an expert of the "Facultad de Bellas Artes" of the University of Madrid. (Professor Uwe Loesch, Designer, Düsseldorf)

BERMELL, C/ SANTO TOMÁS, 18, VALENCIA. T (+34) 96 391 02 88 Good Valencian products in one of the most atmospheric areas of the city. Local, small but very traditional.

LA ROSA, PASEO NEPTUNO, 70, VALENCIA. T (+34) 96 371 20 76 Eat paella on the shores of the Mediterranean sea. Specialities include seafood, rice dishes, shell fish &c. (Pepe Gimeno, Designer, Godella, Valencia)

MUSEUMS & GALLERIES

THE FUNDACIÓ MIRO (MIRO'S FOUNDATION), BARCELONA. On the Montjuïc Mountain in Barcelona is this luminous building designed by the architect Josep Lluis Sert, containing a large collection of Miro's paintings. There is also a very nice restaurant with a sophisticated menu. On sunny days, the tables invade the inner square of this modern, white and Mediterranean building. (Josep Pla Narbona, Designer, Barcelona)

GUGGENHEIM MUSEUM, BILBAO. Everybody should go to Bilbao and see the incredible museum Frank Gehry built. Take an hour first to walk around the outside (across the bridge and along the river too). Then spend the rest of your visit inside (at least 2 hours). It's truly a marvel. Skip lunch at the crowded, smoky café inside and go one block up the street opposite the entrance to Restaurant Zuretzat (Iparraguirre 7) for spinach crepes and local daily specials. (Chris & Esther Pullman, Designers, Boston)

IVAM (INSTITUTO VALENCIANO DE ARTE MODERNO/THE INSTITUTE OF MODERN ART OF VALENCIA), AVDA. GUILLEM DE CASTRO, 118, VALENCIA. T (+34) 96 386 30 00 As well as art exhibitions the Institute often has exhibitions with a graphic theme.

MUSEO FALLERO, PLAZA MONTEOLIVETE, 4, VALENCIA. T (+34) 96 352 54 78 Every year, during the festivals of Las Fallas, they build monuments made of cardboard and wood in the streets and burn them on 19 March. The public vote for one model to save from the fire, and this is then integrated into the museum's collection. (Pepe Gimeno, Designer, Godella, Valencia)

PLACES OF INTEREST

ALTEA, PROVINCE OF ALICANTE. A coastal town with the old quarters situated on a hill. Very picturesque. (Pepe Gimeno, Designer, Godella, Valencia)

SEMON SA, GANDUXER 31, BARCELONA. T (+34) 93 201 8366 A wonderful deli with a fantastic selection of local produce together with hams (Iberico-Serrano Halongs) and cheeses. It has a small coffee bar where you can sample the goods. A great place to spend half an hour and spend a fortune ! (Robin Partington, Architect, London)

MERCAT DE LA BOQUERIA, BARCELONA Historic market next to La Ramblas, where food is something else. Take your camera, and prepare to be amazed ! (Lamosca, Design and Multimedia Studio, Manso, Barcelona)

BOOKSHOPS & SHOPPING

INDEX BOOK, CONSEJO DE CIENTO 160, BARCELONA. T (+34) 93 454 5547 For graphic design books.

LA SALA VINÇON, PASSEIG DE GRÀCIA, 96, BARCELONA. A design department store in an extraordinary 'modernista' townhouse, this is a treasure-trove of visual surprise and delights, from its witty window displays to its exceptional collection of contemporary Spanish furniture. If you visit the second-floor tiled terrace, you can sneak a peek at the rear side of Gaudi's famed La Pedrera apartment house. (Marisa Bartolucci, Editor, New York)

ART POPULAR, 2 BIS (BARRIO GÓTICO), BARCELONA. T (+34) 93 315 0954 A beautiful shop full of designer's stuff from all over but with an amazingly diverse and unique collection of papier maché. Particularly exciting are the masks reproducing Picasso heads including minotaurs and horses. (Eddie Pond, Designer, London)

Area	1,000 km2	505.9	Capital City	Madrid	Monetary Unit	peseta
Population	1,000	39,134	Capital City Population	1,000	4,072	GDP per Capita (US $)	14,111
Design Population	1,000	000.3	Languages	Spanish, Catalan	International Dialling Code	+34

C

l'espai Travessera de Gràcia, 63
08021 Barcelona. Tel. 93 414 31 33

TEMPORADA 98-99

GENER
1999

JOAN ISAAC

MARGARET JOVA,
ELISA MORRIS,
TERESA NIETO I
DENISE PERDIKIDIS

VÍCTOR VALLS

Generalitat de Catalunya
Departament de Cultura

1-3 BROCHURE FOR L'ESPAI, A DANCE THEATRE
DESIGN FIRM: Lamosca, Barcelona

1 2 3

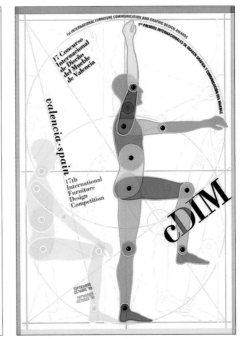

■ 1.1 La Feria Internacional del Mueble convoca el XVII Concurso de Diseño, de ámbito internacional. ■ 1.2 Este Concurso está dirigido a profesionales y a estudiantes de diseño. **2 OBJETIVOS** ■ 2.1 El propósito es destacar aquellas piezas en las que se valorarán los siguientes aspectos: Innovación formal. Innovación funcional y de uso. Posibilidades de realización técnica y aplicación a la producción. Elección de materiales que respeten el medio ambiente **3 PARTICIPANTES** ■ 3.1 Podrán participar en el apartado de estudiantes, todos aquellos que estén cursando estudios relacionados con el diseño, haciendo mención expresa, en la exposición y difusión de los trabajos seleccionados del centro de estudios correspondiente. ■ 3.2 En el apartado de profesionales la participación está abierta a todos los diseñadores **4 TEMA** ■ 4.1 El tema para profesionales es de libre elección, dentro del mobiliario para el hábitat, en todas sus variantes de uso, quedando los materiales o sistemas a emplear a libertad de los concursantes. ■ 4.2 Quedan excluidas lámparas y textiles. ■ 4.3 Es requisito imprescindible que el producto no se haya comercializado o publicado con fecha anterior al 15 de julio de 1.999. ■ 4.4 En el apartado de estudiantes, dentro del mobiliario para el hábitat, los estudiantes deberán desarrollar su trabajo dentro del siguiente tema: "MUEBLES NOMADAS, TRANSPORTABLES O MOVIBLES"; para una forma de vida abierta, cambiante y global que te permita viajar junto con tus cosas, transportar con facilidad aquello que estimas y transformar fácilmente el espacio que habitas.

1.1 The International Furniture Fair announces the 17th International Design Competition.

1.2 This competition is open to students and professionals involved in the field of design.

2 AIM

2.1 The aim is to highlight projects on the basis of the following aspects: formal innovation; functional innovation; technical and productive feasibility; use of environmentally-friendly materials.

3 PARTICIPANTS

3.1 The students category is open to students in fields related to design, provided express mention of the corresponding educational institute is made in the exhibition

and in any public presentation of projects being admitted.

3.2 The professionals section is open to all designers.

4 THEME

4.1 The theme for professionals can be freely chosen within the limits of furniture for the home, with the choice of materials and systems to be used being left to the discretion of participants.

4.2 Lamps and textiles are excluded.

4.3 Products published or commercialized before 15 July 1999 shall not be admitted.

4.4 The theme for students is "NOMADIC, PORTABLE OR

MOVABLE FURNITURE" for a constantly changing and global lifestyle - articles allowing us to travel with our personal belongings, to take our favourite possessions wherever we like and to easily transform our surroundings in the habitat.

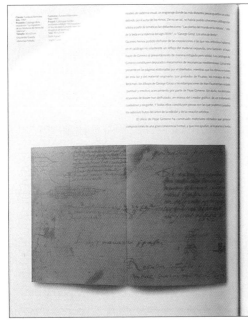

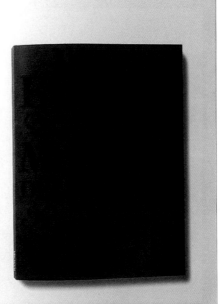

4, 5 BOOKLET (2) AND POSTER (3) FOR THE 17TH INTERNATIONAL FURNITURE DESIGN COMPETITION
DESIGN FIRM: Pepe Gimeno-Proyecto Grafico, Godella (Valencia)
DESIGNER: Pepe Gimeno
CLIENT: Feria de Valencia

6 SPREAD FROM SELF-PROMOTIONAL BOOK
DESIGN FIRM: Pepe Gimeno-Proyecto Grafico, Godella (Valencia)
DESIGNER: Pepe Gimeno
CLIENT: Experimenta

7 PACKAGING FOR FONT PICANT MINERAL WATER
DESIGN FIRM: Morera Shining SL, Barcelona
DESIGNER: Josep M Morera Gusi

SWEDEN: COUNTRY FILE

HOTELS

ESPLANADE HOTEL, STRANDVAGEN 7A, STOCKHOLM. T (+46) 8 663 0740 Authentic Art Nouveau facing Nybroviken (Harbour) across which you can see the Vasa Museum, the new Museum of Modern Art by Raphael Moneo and other sights. Modestly priced, simple breakfast included. Ask for front corner rooms. Not a fancy place, but comfortable and hospitable. (Niels Diffrient, Designer, Connecticut)

RESTAURANTS, CAFÉS & BARS

BISTRO RUBY, ÖSTERLÅNGGATAN 14, GAMLA STAN (OLD TOWN), STOCKHOLM. T (+46) 8 205 776 Small, charming, wood-panelled old bistro in the heart of the old town. Very good food without being ostentatious. Ask for Lojrom (bleak roe), great with Schnapps. (Niels Diffrient, Designer, Connecticut)

ERIK'S, ÖSTERLÅNGGATAN 17, STOCKHOLM. T (+46) 8 23 85 00 Considered by many to be one of the most outstanding kitchens in town. Intimate and classy atmosphere located in the Old Town. Created and owned by Erik Lallerstedt. Wide variety of excellent seafood dishes. (Jan Stael von Holstein, Design Management, London)

BERNS, BERZELII PARK, STOCKHOLM. T (+46) 8 566 322 22, www.berns.se Bar, restaurant, coffee shop and hotel, this is an international meeting place with a rich heritage and old, beautiful decorations. The place has recently undergone a facelift by Terence Conran. Don't miss the fantastic cocktail bar!

STUREHOF, STUREPLAN 2, STOCKHOLM. T (+46) 8 440 5730 This bar-restaurant is the hub of Stockholm's nightlife with interiors by Tomas Sandell and Swedish cooking at its best. Lots of media and design people, as well as suits. Good for lunch as well as dinner — or just a drink.

FOLKHEMMET, RENSTIERNAS GATA 30, STOCKHOLM. T (+46) 8 640 55 95 Very Swedish bar on the south side. Locals ('söderbröder'), pop stars, actors, media people in two crowded bars. Atmosphere: simple, free and easy. (Nina Fylkegård & Oki Billengren, Designers, Stockholm)

CAFÉ OPERA, OPERA HOUSE, KUNDSTRADGARDEN, STOCKHOLM. T (+46) 8 676 58 07 Housed in the old Opera House Grill with mirrored walls and old stucco ceilings, this is one of Europe's largest and most beautiful watering holes. Neighbouring the Opera House Bar, a genuine Art Nouveau shelter for the arts and letters people.

WEDHOLM FISK (WEDHOLM'S FISH RESTAURANT), NYBROKAJEN 17, STOCKHOLM. T (+46) 8 611 7874 Probably the best fish restaurant in Scandinavia. Bengt Wedholm, owner-chef, has a penchant for quality that also includes the interior. It's expensive, so better mortgage your house before going there …. (Carl Christiansson, Architect, Stockholm)

GULDAPAN (THE GOLDEN MONKEY), ÅSÖGATAN 140, STOCKHOLM. T (+46) 8 640 97 71 A really good place for a drink or a beer in a nice atmosphere. I recommend a visit in the week (less crowded than weekends). The guests are mostly local. There is a restaurant in a side room (Curtis Mayfield over the speakers!). You probably have to book in advance to get a table. (Pija Sundin, Satama Interactive, Stockholm)

MUSEUMS & GALLERIES

TÄNDSTICKSMUSEET (THE MATCH MUSEUM), TÄNDSTICKSGR. 7, JÖNKÖPING. T (+46) 36 105 543 Jönköping was the birthplace of the match, and this museum, built on the site of the first factory, contains exhibits on the history and manufacture of matches.

MODERNA MUSEÉT (MUSEUM OF MODERN ART), SKEPPSHOLMEN, STOCKHOLM. T (+46) 8 519 55 200, www.modernamuseet.se Opened in 1998 in a new building by the awarded Spanish architect Rafael Moneo, this museum has unique collections of international and Scandinavian 20th-century art, photographs, films and video. Simply the best place to go if you're interested in art. (Henrik Löwemark, Assistant Art Director, Stockholm)

CARL LARSSON GÅRDEN, CARL LARSSONSV. 12, SUNDBORN. T (+46) 23 60053 In a lovely lakeside setting, the former home of the celebrated Swedish artist where you can see a selection of his paintings.

PLACES OF INTEREST

GRYTHYTTAN For visitors to Sweden who want to see our forests and rivers, I would recommend an exclusive and beautiful country inn, Grythyttan, for weekends. About 3 hours by car from Stockholm. (Astrid Sampe, Designer, Stockholm)

BOOKSHOPS & SHOPPING

ORDNING & REDA, KRISTINELUNDSGATAN 5, GOTHENBURG. T (+46) 31 202003 An essential stop for paper freaks. Designer folders, portfolios, notebooks, stationery, files and papers. Several branches in Stockholm and one in London in New Row, Covent Garden. (Alan Fletcher, Designer, London)

MORRIS ANTIKVARIAT, JARNGATAN 3, BOX 313, SODERTALJE. T (+46) 8 550 304 10 A goldmine for designers ! Rare books in the town of Sodertalje, 30 miles south of Stockholm. Books on typography, calligraphy and graphic design a speciality. (Lars Olaf Laurentii, Stockholm)

KONSTIG BOOKSTORE, IN KONSERHUSET ON SERGELSTORG, STOCKHOLM. T (+46) 8 508 315 18 Books about everything to do with art and design. Helpful staff and good prices. A must if you know how to read … (Henrik Löwemark, Assistant Art Director, Stockholm)

DESIGNTORGET, SERGELSTORG AND GÖTGATSBACKEN, STOCKHOLM. www.designtorget.se DesignTorget (opened 1993) presents what's latest, best and most fun in art and design in their two Stockholm shops. Every week there are new designers selected by jury who rent a spot there (DesignTorget takes care of the sales). You'll always find something here for your home or your office — and it's great for gifts, too.

BO, STOCKHOLM. T (+46) 8 643 69 14 Scandinavian and international furniture from the 20th-century. Some made by the best people in 20th-century design. If you don't want to buy anything, you should visit it just for inspiration. (Henrik Löwemark, Assistant Art Director, Stockholm)

Area | 1,000 km2	450.0	Capital City	Stockholm	Monetary Unit	Swedish krona
Population | 1,000	8,887	Capital City Population | 1,000	1,545	GDP per Capita (US $)	26,253
Design Population | 1,000	001.5	Languages	Swedish	International Dialling Code	+46

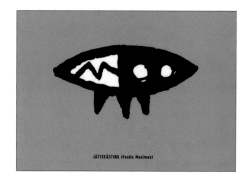

Det finns saker du aldrig glömmer.
De flesta lärde du dig som ung.

Viktor Jansson, född 1985

år 2057

Mats Theselius' guide to

1-6 PROMOTIONAL POSTCARDS FOR VOSS, A DESIGN FIRM
DESIGNER/ ILLUSTRATOR: Lars Rehnberg, Stockholm

7 PROMOTIONAL BROCHURE FOR ARENA 99, A SPORTS, MUSIC,
AND LIFESTYLE CONFERENCE CENTRE FOR TEENAGERS
AGENCY: Fenix Reklambyrå, Gothenburg
ART DIRECTOR/ DESIGNER: Joakim Ahnfelt
PHOTOGRAPHERS: Magnus Pajnert, Marléne Hamström
CLIENT: Svenska Mässen

8, 9 SELF-PROMOTIONAL BOOKLET
FOR FURNITURE DESIGNER MATS THESELIUS
DESIGN FIRM: Forsman & Bodenfors Design, Gothenburg
DESIGNER: Anders Kornestedt
PHOTOGRAPHER: Mats Theselius
CLIENT: Röhsska Museet

10 EDITORIAL ILLUSTRATION FOR AN ARTICLE ABOUT SMALL
COMPANIES MAKING THEIR OWN WAY
ILLUSTRATOR: Lars Rehnberg, Stockholm
CLIENT: Tidningen Företagaren

11 INVITATION TO THE EXHIBITION "HERRINGS AND JAZZ" AT
INREDNINGS STALLET, AN INTERIOR DESIGN SHOWROOM
DESIGN FIRM: Studio Bubblan, Borås
ART DIRECTOR/ DESIGNER/ PHOTOGRAPHER: Kari Palmqvist

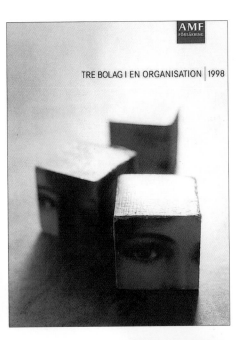

TRE BOLAG I EN ORGANISATION | 1998

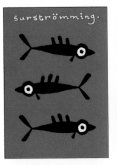

surströmming.

jul.

kräftor.

mid-sommar.

Glimtar ur historien

GLOBAL

mårten gås.

påsk.

GLOBAL

GLOBAL

---

12 EDITORIAL ILLUSTRATION FOR AN ARTICLE ABOUT DEPRESSED CHILDREN AND THEIR FAMILIES
ILLUSTRATOR: Annika Sköld Lindau, Stockholm
ART DIRECTOR: Lena Lien
CLIENT: Frimospedagogen

13-18 PROMOTIONAL POSTCARDS FOR VOSS, A DESIGN FIRM
DESIGNER/ ILLUSTRATOR: Lars Rehnberg, Stockholm

19, 20 CORPORATE INFORMATION BROCHURE
DESIGN FIRM: LOG Kommunikation, Stockholm
ART DIRECTOR: Anna Marhevärn
PHOTOGRAPHER: Daniel Lagerlöf
CLIENT: AMF Försäkring

21 T-SHIRT FOR STOCKHOLM INFORMATION SERVICE WITH ILLUSTRATIONS OF FAMOUS VIEWS OF THE CITY
ILLUSTRATOR: Annika Sköld Lindau, Stockholm
DESIGN FIRM: Idé Art
ART DIRECTOR: Annika Hansson

22 PROPOSED ILLUSTRATION OF A REINDEER FOR A GREETING CARD
ILLUSTRATOR/ DESIGNER: Annika Sköld Lindau, Stockholm
DESIGN FIRM: Elisabet Levén Förlag

23-25 ADVERTISEMENTS FOR A SET OF KITCHEN KNIVES
DESIGN FIRM: Tennis, Anyone?, Gothenburg
ART DIRECTOR: Fredrik Ganslandt
PHOTOGRAPHY: Branko
CLIENT: J A Sundqvist AB

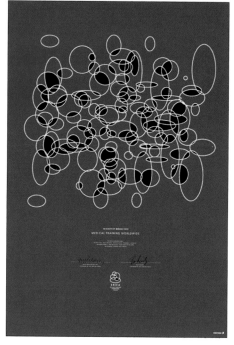

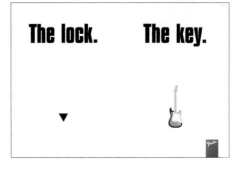

33 ILLUSTRATION FOR AN ARTICLE ABOUT SIGN LANGUAGE IN
"SAMHALL IN FOCUS" MAGAZINE
ILLUSTRATOR: Annika Sköld Lindau, Stockholm
ART DIRECTOR/ DESIGNER: Bo Holmström

34 STATIONERY FOR INTERACTIVE MEDIA COMPANY
DESIGN FIRM: Wognum Art, Stockholm

35 POSTER FOR AN EXHIBITION OF THE WORK OF GLASS AND
LIGHTING DESIGNER BRITA FLANDER AT THE RÖHSSKA MUSEET
DESIGN FIRM: Forsman & Bodenfors Design, Gothenburg
ART DIRECTOR/ DESIGNER: Anders Kornestedt
PHOTOGRAPHER: Lasse Lindqvist

36 POSTER FOR AN EXHIBITION OF THE WORK OF TEXTILE
DESIGNER LOUISE SASS
DESIGN FIRM: Forsman & Bodenfors Design, Gothenburg
ART DIRECTOR/ DESIGNER: Anders Kornestedt
CLIENT: Röhsska Museet

37 PACKAGING FOR FLAVOURED MILK
DESIGN FIRM: Forsman & Bodenfors Design, Gothenburg
ART DIRECTOR/ DESIGNER: Anders Kornestedt
ILLUSTRATOR: Moses Voigt
CLIENT: Arla Mjölk

38, 39 ADVERTISEMENTS FOR FENDER GUITARS
AGENCY: Jerlov & Company, Gothenburg
ART DIRECTOR: Magnus Tengby

40 POSTER FOR "MAIJAZZ 1999", A FESTIVAL IN NORWAY
ILLUSTRATOR: Lasse Skarbovik, Stockholm
AGENCY: Melvar & Lien
ART DIRECTOR/ DESIGNER: Kjell Ramsdal

41-43 NORDSJÖ COMPANY PRESENTATION FOR A PAINT MANUFACTURER
DESIGN FIRM: Ahlqvist & Co. Reklambyrå, Malmö
ART DIRECTOR: Christer Strandberg
COPY DIRECTOR: Klas Tjebbes
PHOTOGRAPHER: Gerry Johansson
CLIENT: Akzo Nobel Decorative Coatings AB

44, 45 EXHIBITION CATALOGUE SHOWING WORK OF SWEDISH DESIGNER SIGRARD BERNADOTTE
DESIGN FIRM: Forsman & Bodenfors Design, Gothenburg
ART DIRECTOR/ DESIGNER: Anders Kornestedt
PHOTOGRAPHER: Per Magnus Persson
CLIENT: Nationalmuseum

46 PACKAGING FOR A LINE OF SAUCES AND MARINADES
DESIGN FIRM: Tennis, Anyone?, Gothenburg
ART DIRECTOR: Fredrik Ganslandt
PHOTOGRAPHER: Christer Ehrling
CLIENT: Ridderheims Delikatesser AB

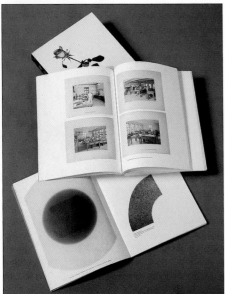

47 ILLUSTRATIONS FOR THE NORWEGIAN OIL MUSEUM
ILLUSTRATOR: Lasse Skarbovik, Stockholm
AGENCY: Melvar & Lien
DESIGNER: Mona Havgland

48 BOXED SET OF BOOKS CELEBRATING 150 YEARS OF THE GOTHENBURG SCHOOL OF ARTS AND CRAFTS
DESIGN FIRM: Forsman & Bodenfors Design, Gothenburg
ART DIRECTORS/ DESIGNERS: Anders Kornestedt, Andreas Kittel
DESIGNER: Catharina Starby
CLIENT: Göteborgs Slöjdförening

49 COVER OF 1998 ANNUAL REPORT FOR AN OWNER OF APARTMENT HOUSES
DESIGNER/ ILLUSTRATOR: Lasse Skarbovik, Stockholm
CLIENT: HSB

50 POSTER FOR THE 1999 ECEEE BI-ANNUAL CONFERENCE
DESIGN FIRM: Björkman & Mitchell AB, Stockholm
DESIGNER: Klas Björkman
CLIENT: European Council for an Energy Efficient Economy

51 SPREAD FROM THE MEDIA SUPPLEMENT "PRINT. DEAD OR ALIVE?" FOR THE NEWSPAPER "SVENSKA DAGBLADET"
DESIGN FIRM: Graceland Sthlm/ Tank, Stockholm
ART DIRECTOR: Jakob Westman
CLIENT: Daniel Collin

SWITZERLAND: COUNTRY FILE

HOTELS

HOTEL DU CLOS DE SADEX, 131, ROUTE DE LAUSANNE, NYON. T (+41) 22 61 28 31 Modestly-sized, quiet, reasonably-priced hotel, where good cuisine is matched by friendly staff. Established fifty years ago in a large, old house facing Lake Geneva surrounded by a large garden. Relaxed and conservative. Breakfast is served on a balcony overlooking Lake Geneva – a memorable sight in itself in summer and autumn. Good wine list. (Paul Hogarth, Painter & Illustrator, Hidcote Bartrim)

HOTEL WIDDER, RENNWEG 7, ZÜRICH. A small luxury hotel with individually designed rooms. Live jazz lives on in the Widder Bar and there are four in-house restaurants. (André Schneiter, Partner and Graphic Designer, Zürich)

RESTAURANTS, CAFÉS & BARS

CHEZ DONATI, ST JOHANNS-VORSTADT 48, BASEL. T (+41) 61 322 0913 Delightful Art Deco restaurant overlooking the Rhine with lots of atmosphere and a spectacular Italian-style family cuisine. (Georg Staehelin, Designer, Zürich)

WIRTSCHAFT ZUM WIESENGRUND, KLEINDORFSTRASSE 61, UETIKON. T (+41) 1 920 6360 Beautiful restaurant – an old farmhouse masterfully converted by architect Hans Draher into a very modern, top-quality country inn. Swiss food, simple and tasty. Thirty minutes from downtown Zürich, the road follows the lake …. not an unpleasant ride …. (Fritz Gottschalk, Designer, Zürich)

TERRASSE RESTAURANT, LIMMATQUAI 3, ZÜRICH. The 'in' place: beautiful architecture and interior design.

KAUFLEUTEN RESTAURANT AND CLUB, PELIKANSTRASSE 18, ZÜRICH. Another 'in' place for clubbing or chilling out, in an old and beautiful theatre. (André Schneiter, Partner and Graphic Designer, Zürich)

RESTAURANT EIERBRECHT, WASERSTRASSE, 36, ZÜRICH. Run by the daughter of Walter Herdeg, the founder editor of "Graphis" magazine. The food with a bias towards vegetarian and organic. About fifteen minutes by bus from the city centre, high up with views over the Alps. (Pat Schleger, Designer, London)

RESTAURANT BLAUE ENTE, SEEFELDSTRASSE 223, ZÜRICH. T (+41) 1 55 77 06 Located in a converted mill which has become the centre of art and design. The restaurant is a 'must' in Zürich, where the beautiful people and the avant garde meet. The food is creative and interesting, and the desserts are recommended. Good selection of Swiss wines. (Ursula Hiestand, Designer, Zürich)

WÜRSTLI BAR, BELLEVUEPLATZ, ZÜRICH. Small bar (short on comfort, long on ambiance) selling one of the best würstli (sausage) in Zürich. Afterwards, wash your hands in "Switzerland's most beautiful wash basin" around the corner. (Suan Tung Brooks & Bob Brooks, Film Directors, London)

MUSEUMS & GALLERIES

SAMMLUNG KARIKATUREN & CARTOONS (CARICATURE & CARTOON COLLECTION), ST ALBAN-VORSTADT 9, BASEL. T (+41) 61 22 13 36 Situated in the centre of Basel, you will find a unique museum housing a rare collection of international caricatures and cartoons. Open Wednesday-Saturday & Sundays. (Verner Panton†, Designer, Basel)

MUSEO CANTONALE D'ARTE, LUGANO (TICINO). Newly-renovated building in the pedestrian centre. Interesting scheduled installations. The museum's signage and stunning posters are by Bruno Monguzzi. (Helen & Gene Federico, Illustrator/Designer, New York)

THE FONDATION BEYELERS, RIEHEN (outside Basel). Breathtaking collection, ranging from Cézanne to Pollock, Stella and Rothko. The best Picassos and Kandinsky we've ever seen. A beautiful building by Renzo Piano (Pompidou) all in glass with meadows and cows outside. Classic music hours in different rooms. Our highlight of the year. (Olle Eksell, Designer, Stockholm)

GALLERY HAUSER + WIRTH, GRÜNBERGSTRASSE 7, ST. GALLEN. The most trendy art gallery in Switzerland …. (André Schneiter, Partner and Graphic Designer, Zürich)

MUSEUM FÜR GESTALTUNG ZÜRICH, AUSSTELLUNGSSTRASSE 60, ZÜRICH. T (+41) 1 446 22 11 The gallery of the Hochschule für Gestaltung und Kunst puts on challenging exhibitions of superior quality from art, graphic design and industrial design to interior design and architecture. Nice catalogues and books for sale. Closed Mondays. (Heinz Wild, Designer, Zürich)

PLACES OF INTEREST

DESIGN CENTRE D'S AG, MÜHLE, LANGENTHAL. T (+41) 62 923 03 33 Organisers of the Swiss Design Prize and Designer's Saturdays

EIGENTÜMERVERWALTUNG BAD VALS, KURZENTRUM, VALS. T (+41) 81 935 14 81 (Jacqueline Jeanmaire, Art Director, Bern)

THERME VALS, VALS. T (+41) 81 920 70 70 This spa by architect Peter Zumthor is a gorgeous minimal space set in the middle of rugged mountains (and you can swim from the inside out). There are different pools, a steam bath and an acoustic pool, where you sit in the water playing to your own echo. (Stefan Sagmeister, Designer, New York)

BOOKSHOPS & SHOPPING

KRAUTHAMMER, ROBERT, BUCHHANDLUNG FÜR ARCHITEKTUR UND KUNST, OBERE ZÄUNE 24, ZÜRICH. T (+41) 1 251 20 10 Very nice bookstore with a great selection of books on design and architecture. Wide range of international publications. A wonderful place to spend some time discovering new finds in the world of design and architecture. Closed Saturdays. (Heinz Wild, Designer, Zürich)

Area | 1,000 km2	041.3	Capital City	Bern	Monetary Unit	Swiss franken, franc, franco	
Population | 1,000	7,260	Capital City Population | 1,000	129,400			
Design Population | 1,000	001.5	Languages	German, French, Italian	GDP per Capita (US $)	23,800	
				International Dialling Code	+41	

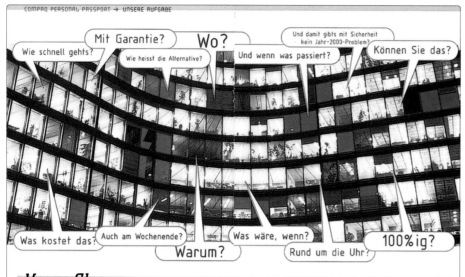

1, 2 IDENTITY BOOKLETS FOR COMPAQ COMPUTER EMPLOYEES
DESIGN FIRM: Jeanmaire & Michel, Bern
ART DIRECTORS: Stephan Michel, Jacqueline Jeanmaire
DESIGNER: Regula Doebeli

3 COVER OF ANNUAL REPORT FOR AN ENVIRONMENTAL
PROTECTION FOUNDATION
DESIGN FIRM: Wild & Frey, Zürich
ART DIRECTORS: Lucia Frey, Heinz Wild
DESIGNER: Lucia Frey
PHOTOGRAPHER: Pascal Wüest
CLIENT: Stiftung Umwelt-Einsatz Schweiz

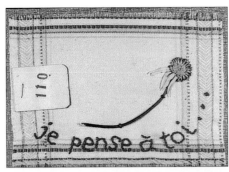

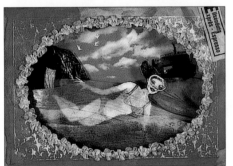

4-9 POSTCARD SERIES BASED ON A LOVE STORY
ILLUSTRATOR: Florance Plojoux, Geneva
CLIENT: Masani's Cards for Free

10 "HEIDI IN FRANKFURT", A BOOKLET CREATED FOR THE
FRANKFURT BOOK FAIR
DESIGN FIRM: Jeanmaire & Michel, Bern
ART DIRECTORS: Stephan Michel, Jacqueline Jeanmaire
DESIGNER: Regula Doebeli
CLIENT: Swiss Books Publishers Association

»smart solution 002: Kaufen Sie sich ein grosses Auto.

«In der Stadt soll man den Verkehr einschränken», sagen Puristen. «In der Stadt ist der smart genau so viel Auto, wie der Mensch braucht», meinen wir. Aussen: 2,50 m lang und somit zirka einen Meter kürzer als die meisten Kleinwagen. Innen: mehr Bewegungsfreiheit für zwei Personen als in mancher Mittelklasse-limousine. Und rundum: dank der TRIDION-Sicherheitszelle aus Stahl ebenso sicher.

Damit ist der smart in jeder Hinsicht so gross, dass andere sich daran messen müssen. Dass es noch mehr Spass macht, den smart zu fahren, als ihn zu parken, finden Sie bei Ihrer ersten Stadtrundfahrt am besten selber raus. Bitte vereinbaren Sie einen Termin für Ihre Probefahrt. Wir freuen uns auf Ihren Besuch: **smart Center Zürich/Wallisellen, Husacherstrasse 1 (neben Einkaufszentrum Glatt), 01/877 66 66.**

»smart solution 012: Einladung zum Probeparken.

»smart solution 003: Horizont erweiterung.

»smart solution 007: Das schnellste Auto der Welt.

«Farbe ist Ausdruck der Persönlichkeit», sagen Psychologen. «Mit dem smart können Sie schneller neu Farbe bekennen als mit jedem anderen Auto», sagen wir: von Gelb auf Rot in 60 Minuten. Möglich macht's ein Umdenkprozess im Automobilbau. Mit dem ersten serienmässigen Bodypanel-System bleiben Sie flexibel und Ihr smart in vogue. Und wenn Sie die Bodypanels mal auswechseln,

kostet das nicht mehr als die Neulackierung des Kotflügels bei manch anderen Autos. Wir zeigen Ihnen, wie schnell und preisgünstig der Service rund ums Auto sein kann. Möchten Sie den smart mal probefahren? Bitte vereinbaren Sie einen Termin. Wir freuen uns auf Ihren Besuch: **smart Center Zürich/Wallisellen, Husacherstrasse 1 (neben Einkaufszentrum Glatt), 01/877 66 66.**

11-14 ADVERTISING CAMPAIGN FOR SMART CARS
AGENCY: Weber, Hodel, Schmid, Zürich
CREATIVE DIRECTOR: Liliane Lerch
ART DIRECTORS: Michel Girardin, Thomas von Ah, Patricia Zaugg
DESIGNERS: Oliver Brunschwiler, Christian Bircher
PHOTOGRAPHER: Liz Collins
CLIENT: MCC Micro Compact Car smart GmbH

15 COLOUR BOARD FOR SMART CARS
AGENCY: Weber, Hodel, Schmid, Zürich
CREATIVE DIRECTOR: Liliane Lerch
ART DIRECTOR: Oliver Brunschwiler
PHOTOGRAPHY: Roth & Schmid, Zürich
CLIENT: MCC Micro Compact Car smart GmbH

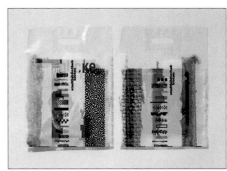

Ist das Leben kurz? Es gibt lange und kurze Tage. Minuten, die sich wie Stunden hinziehen. Oder Stunden, die wie Sekunden verfliegen. Für uns Menschen scheint es keine neutrale Zeitmessung zu geben. Wir empfinden die Zeit als kurz oder lang. Das Leben ist lang. Das Leben ist kurz. Das eine stimmt wie das andere.

Die ASPECTA Lebensversicherung ist offen für das verschiedene Empfinden der Menschen. Offen für die verschiedensten Lebensweisen. Offen für Neues. Wenn Anfang des nächsten Jahrtausends Europa, und damit auch Menschen und Sprachen, noch näher zusammenrücken, ist die ASPECTA Lebensversicherung für noch mehr Menschen der verläßliche Spezialist im Management für Lebensrisiken. Zusammen packen wir die kurzen und langen Momente im Leben erfolgreich an.

Sicherheit und individuelles Asset Management

Innovationen zur optimalen Abdeckung von Versorgungsrisiken

16 1998-1999 BROCHURE FOR SMARTWARE, THE SMART CARS CLOTHING AND ACCESSORIES LINE
AGENCY: Weber, Hodel, Schmid, Zürich
CREATIVE DIRECTOR: Liliane Lerch
ART DIRECTORS: Thomas von Ah, Oliver Brunschwiler
PHOTOGRAPHERS: Serge Hoeltschi, Thomas Eugster
CLIENT: MCC Micro Compact Car smart GmbH

17 SPREAD FROM 1998 ANNUAL REPORT FOR AN INSURANCE COMPANY
DESIGN FIRM: Külling & Partners Identity, Zürich
ART DIRECTOR: André Schneiter
DESIGNER: Yvonne Kupper
CLIENT: Aspecta Lebensversicherung ag

18 SHOPPING BAG DESIGN FOR A BOOKSTORE
DESIGN FIRM: Bildinfarkt GmbH für Visuelle Gestaltung, Kloten
DESIGNERS: Thomas Knöri, André Seiffert
CLIENT: Stadtbibliothek Kloten

19 SPREAD FROM SELF-PROMOTIONAL BOOK
DESIGN FIRM: Advertising, Art & Ideas Ltd, Zürich
ART DIRECTOR: Stefan Winzenried
DESIGNER: Oliver Haefeli

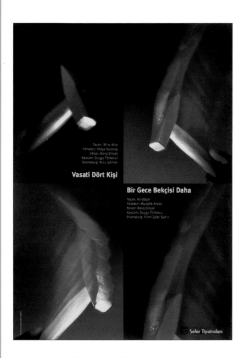

TURKEY: COUNTRY FILE

HOTELS

KARABEY APARTMENT HOTEL, BODRUM Beautiful view, flowers everywhere, beautiful architecture. (Olle Eksell, Designer, Stockholm)

KADIR'S, OLYMPUS, ANTALYA. T (+90) 242 892 1250 If you are the more adventurous type and travelling on a budget, why not try the tree houses at Kadir's? They have a selection of accommodation, and the most expensive with toilet and shower en suite (fully plumbed) will cost around £5.50 per person with breakfast and dinner included. (Julia Wyatt, Co-Editor, Feedback, London)

RESTAURANTS, CAFÉS & BARS

PANDELI'S RESTAURANT, MISIR CARSIST (THE SPICE BAZAAR), HAMIDIYE CADDESI, ISTANBUL. In the domed rooms above the entrance gateway of the Spice Bazaar facing the Galata Bridge is this excellent restaurant. Views over the Golden Horn (and an exotic approach if you wander through the market from the opposite entrance). The building lies behind the Yeni Cami — the New Mosque. (Spencer de Grey, Architect, London)

HACI ABDULLA, 17 SAKIZAGA CADESI, BEYOGLU, ISTANBUL. T (+90) 212 293 8561 The thing that strikes you first about this famous old restaurant (established 1957) is the huge number of glass jars ranged round the entrance, full of preserved fruits and compotes in jewelled colours. This simple, friendly restaurant is one of the best for Ottoman cuisine. Many and varied dishes, including the well-known Hünkar Begendi ('Sultan's Delight') — eggplant purée with lamb stew. Not expensive. Open 13.30-10.30pm. (Zafer Baran, Photographer, Richmond, Surrey)

SÜHEYIA, KALYONCU KULLUK CAD. 45, BAHKPAZARI BEYOGLU, ISTANBUL. T (+90) 212 251 83 47 A friendly Turkish restaurant serving home-made appetizers, olive oil and meat dishes. Turkish music later in the evening. Open 19.00-02.00. Closed Sundays. (Yesim Demir, Creative Director, Istanbul)

PLACES OF INTEREST

SULTAN AHMET CAMI (BLUE MOSQUE), SULTANAHMET MEYD, ISTANBUL. With its shimmering blue tiles, 260 stained-glass windows and six minarets, this mosque is a beautiful monument to Islam. Built in the early 17th-century. There is a carpet and kilim museum in the cellars.

KARIYE CAMII, ISTANBUL. Also known as the Church of St. Saviour in Chora in the Old City between the Golden Horn and Edirne Gate. I was amazed by the freshness and vitality of its Byzantine mosaics and frescoes. The restoration work is of high quality and this relatively unknown museum is well worth a visit. (Zafer Baran, Photographer, Richmond, Surrey)

GALATASARAY FISH MARKET, ISTIKLAL CAD., GALATASARAY-BEYOGLU, ISTANBUL. Daily market selling much more than fish — there is a wonderful variety of produce including hard-to-find items like garden cress, Beluga caviar and creme fraiche poured from a bucket, piles of fresh mushrooms, fresh poultry, regional cheeses, herbs, spices and coffee beans. Fish varieties change with the season: winter brings tuna and swordfish and summer, fresh salmon and trout, all at unbelievable prices. (Yesim Demir, Creative Director, Istanbul)

---

1 POSTER FOR ISTANBUL CITY THEATRES
DESIGN FIRM: RPM/ Radar CDP Europe, Istanbul
DESIGNER: Yesim Demir

2 SPREAD FROM THE BOOK: "NEMRUT: THE MOUNTAIN OF GODS"
DESIGN FIRM: RPM/ Radar CDP Europe, Istanbul
DESIGNER: Yesim Demir
CLIENT: AYGAZ A.S.

Area | 1,000 km2	779.2	Capital City	Ankara	Monetary Unit	Turkish lira
Population | 1,000	64,567	Capital City Population | 1,000	2,900	GDP per Capita (US $)	6,000
Design Population | 1,000	000.5	Languages	Turkish, Kurdish, Arabic	International Dialling Code	+90

UNITED KINGDOM: COUNTRY FILE

HOTELS

SIBBETS HOUSE HOTEL, 26 NORTHUMBERLAND STREET, EDINBURGH. The most romantic hotel with four poster beds and only 5 minutes walk from all the art galleries. (Michael Joseph, Photographer, London)

ONE DEVONSHIRE GARDENS, GLASGOW. T (+44) 141 339 2001 A wonderful conversion of a row of late Georgian houses into an hotel, complete with pre-Raphaelite stained glass windows on the main staircase. Breakfasts are superb, and the rooms are something else. (Ralph Steadman, Illustrator, London)

MILLERS, 111A WESTBOURNE GROVE, LONDON. T (+44) 20 7243 1024 The owner is renowned antiques guru and publisher of the annual antiques bible, "Millers Antiques Guide". The wonderful 7-room hotel is dripping in gold frames, busts, oil paintings, objects and character. (Lize Mifflin Schmid, Illustrator, Zürich)

GARTHMYL HALL, GARTHMYL, MONTGOMERY, POWYS. T (+44) 1686 640 550 This bed and breakfast is run by a very good ex-graphic designer and ex-lighting designer who gave up their original careers for the easy life to run it ! As you might expect, everything is done beautifully. Food, décor and hospitality. (John McConnell, Designer, London)

RESTAURANTS, CAFÉS & BARS

THE WILLOW TEA ROOM, 217 SAUCHIEHALL STREET, GLASGOW. T (+44) 141 332 1521 Enter the tea rooms via a jewellers on the ground floor and sample a delightful traditional tea whilst admiring the 'Glasgow Style' which became an inspiration to artists, designers and architects the world over. (Mervyn Kurlansky, Designer, Copenhagen)

RULES, 35 MAIDEN LANE, LONDON. T (+44) 20 7836 5314 If you are a theatre buff or a literary person, don't miss Rules. It is London's oldest restaurant (about 200 years old) and filled with history. It is like stepping into another period and time. The oak walls are jammed with theatrical and literary memorabilia, playbills, paintings and prints. Charles Dickens was a regular here, as well as Edward VII and Lillie Langtry. The English dishes are a feast for the eyes as well as the palate. Near Covent Garden, just off the Strand. (Helen Marcus, Photographer, New York)

THE HAND & SHEARS, 1 MIDDLE STREET, CLOTH FAIR, LONDON. T (+44) 20 7600 0257 What makes this a typical City of London pub is the roaring fire, Courage Directors beer on the hand pump and crunchy, overcooked sausages. It looks as though nothing has changed for years. Cloth Fair itself is interesting because parts of it escaped the burning and so pre-date the Fire of London. (David Stuart, Designer, London)

BAR ITALIA, GREEK STREET, LONDON. Open 24 hours and serving the best coffee in London. The atmosphere is busy and jostling whether it is 02.00 or 14.00 hours. (Quentin Newark, Designer, London)

LANGAN'S BRASSERIE, STRATTON STREET, LONDON. T (+44) 20 7493 6437 Founded by Peter Langan of Odin's fame. He created a true Parisian-style brasserie, serving excellent food with musical entertainment most evenings. The menu, designed by Hockney, has the dishes written in the traditional French-menu script and printed by a gelatine off-set process. Tastefully decorated with the works of some of Britain's greatest contemporary artists, who can often be seen 'eating off' their works of art. (Arnold Schwartzman, Film-maker/Designer, Los Angeles)

MUSEUMS & GALLERIES

THE GLASGOW SCHOOL OF ART, 167 RENFREW STREET, GLASGOW. T (+44) 141 332 9797 Charles Rennie Mackintosh's building is proudly described by the school itself as "the first important monument to the Modern Movement in Europe" and is as impressive as this claim suggests. Delightful experiences at every turn like Mackintosh's remarkable furniture and the breathtaking library. (Mervyn Kurlansky, Designer, Copenhagen)

THE PACK AGE, THE ALBERT WAREHOUSE, GLOUCESTER DOCKS, GLOUCESTER. T (+44) 1452 32309 A fascinating museum of package design, housed in a 19th-century warehouse is the Robert Opie collection of tins, cartons, packets, display cards, posters, hoardings, boxes and bottles from the 19th-century to the present day. (Arnold Schwartzman, Film-maker & Designer, Los Angeles)

THE GEFFRYE MUSEUM, KINGSLAND ROAD, LONDON. T (+44) 20 7739 9893 This little-known museum in the East End of London is a must for students of the history of domestic design. Located in a row of elegant 18th-century alms houses sensitively converted to house a historical series of sitting room settings, running from Tudor times to the 1990s. A recent extension shows permanent and temporary design exhibitions and a simple restaurant — the fishcakes are delicious. Closed Mondays. (Peter Gorb, Design Management, London)

THE DESIGN MUSEUM, BUTLER'S WHARF, SHAD THAMES, LONDON. T (+44) 20 7407 6261 The first museum dedicated to product design. Its floors contain a number of exhibits, a graphics gallery, films and video, library and a riverside café/bar.

MOMI (MUSEUM OF THE MOVING IMAGE), SOUTH BANK ARTS CENTRE, LONDON. T (+44) 20 7928 3535 A must for visitors. Part of the British Film Institute and nestled beneath Waterloo Bridge, this most comprehensive museum of the cinema takes you through the discovery of motion pictures to the silent movies, animation, newsreel, documentary, special effects, British, foreign and Hollywood films — as well as the history of television. (Arnold Schwartzman, Film-maker/Designer, Los Angeles)

DODO, ADMIRAL VERNON MARKET, 141/149 PORTOBELLO ROAD, LONDON. See Liz Farrow's amazing collection of advertising posters and signs. Specialising from 1900-1910. Very well catalogued for easy viewing. (Jessica Strang, Photographer, London)

PLACES OF INTEREST

THE TYPOGRAPHY WORKSHOP, UNIT 313, 31 CLERKENWELL CLOSE, LONDON. T (+44) 20 7490 4386 A shrine to the true typographic spirit, this small workshop is crammed with the most exquisite of metal types; one of the largest collections of wood letter, and everything to do with letterpress printing, including one of the biggest letterpress proofing presses remaining. (Alan Kitching, Typographer/Printmaker, London)

THE GLOBE THEATRE, BANKSIDE, BEAR GARDENS, LONDON. Guaranteed to be one of the most memorable afternoons of your life. Buy a matinee ticket for £5.00. Stroll into the pit. Buy a delicious piece of quiche or a toffee apple and get as close to the stage as you can. The stage is usually covered with wettened reeds, which fill your nostrils with a musty smell. You've never seen Shakespeare like this .... the intensity of the experience cannot be had in any conventional theatre. You will be deeply moved. (Quentin Newark, Designer, London)

BOOKSHOPS & SHOPPING

ATLANTIS EUROPEAN LTD, 146 BRICK LANE, LONDON. T (+44) 20 7377 8855 Located in a vast ex-brewery in the East End, this cathedral-like space sells paints, brushes, paper and every conceivable tool and material a fine artist could wish for. More artists are living in close proximity in this area of London than any other place in the world. (Roger Law, Caricaturist, London)

THE PRINT ROOM, 37 MUSEUM STREET, LONDON. T (+44) 20 7430 0159 Carries a wonderful selection of antique prints, maps and books. There are early political cartoons, military, botanical and architectural prints — enough for a couple of hours browsing on a rainy afternoon. (Neil Shakery, Designer, San Francisco)

THE REAL POSTER GALLERY, 72 WESTBOURNE GROVE, LONDON. T (+44) 20 7727 4488 Real film posters. Not for the financially faint-hearted. (Alain Fletcher, Designer, London)

CECIL COURT, LONDON Whenever I'm in London, I always steal enough time to visit Cecil Court, a one-block mews filled with the most fantastic array of 'curiosity' shops: old print dealers, theatre memorabilia, cigarette card shops (a must for graphic designers) and a fine book store, Ann Creed Books Ltd, devoted to design. You'll find everything from Eric Gill to Neville Brody here. (Kit Hinrichs, Designer, San Francisco)

Area | 1,000 km2	244.0	Capital City	London	Monetary Unit	Pound sterling (£)	
Population | 1,000	58,200	Capital City Population | 1,000	7,335	GDP per Capita (US $)	18,913	
Design Population | 1,000	006.0	Languages	English, Welsh, Scottish (Gaelic)	International Dialling Code	+44	

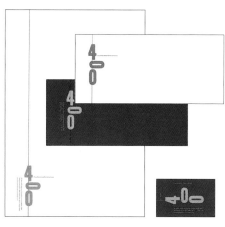

1, 2 SELF-PROMOTIONAL BROCHURE
DESIGN FIRM: Thirst Design + Marketing, Odiham
ART DIRECTOR: Nigel Cattermull
DESIGNER: Caroline Pugh
PHOTOGRAPHER: Paul Venning

3 STATIONERY FOR A FIRM INVOLVED IN FOOD/ COOKING
JOURNALISM AND RESEARCH
DESIGN FIRM: Graham Pritchard Design, London
DESIGNER: Graham Pritchard
CLIENT: FORK

4 STATIONERY FOR FOUR HUNDRED FILMS LTD
DESIGN FIRM: Frost Design, London
ART DIRECTOR: Vince Frost
DESIGNER: Melanie Mues

5 LABEL DESIGN FOR FINCA FLICHMAN ARGENTA WINERY
DESIGN FIRM: Lewis Moberly, London
ART DIRECTOR: Mary Lewis
DESIGNERS: Mary Lewis, Joanne Smith

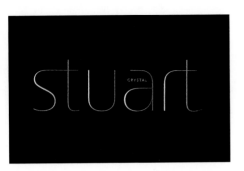

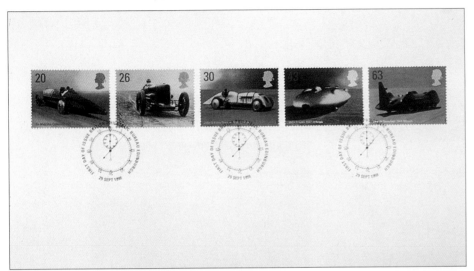

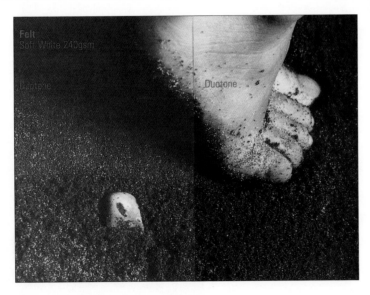

LINKLATERS
& ALLIANCE

The essentials
Construction & Engineering Group

6 STUART CRYSTAL LOGO
DESIGN FIRM: Lewis Moberly, London
ART DIRECTOR: Mary Lewis
DESIGNER: Paul Cilia La Corte
CLIENT: Stuart & Sons Ltd

7 COMMEMORATIVE STAMPS FOR ROYAL MAIL
DESIGN FIRM: Roundel, London
ART DIRECTOR: Michael Denny
DESIGNERS: Jeremy Roots, Stephen Parker
ILLUSTRATOR: Richard Green (Cobb stamp)

8 BROCHURE PROMOTING LANAGRAPHIC PAPER
DESIGN FIRM: Roundel, London
ART DIRECTOR: John Bateson
DESIGNERS: Mark McConnachie, Alec Law
PHOTOGRAPHY: Ben Jennings, Science Photo Library
ILLUSTRATORS: Roger Taylor, Mark McConnachie
CLIENT: Zanders Fine Papers

9 BROCHURE FOR LINKLATERS, A LAW FIRM
DESIGN FIRM: Saatchi & Saatchi Design, London
ART DIRECTOR: Nicola Penny
DESIGNER: Danny Burchell

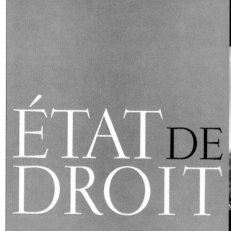

EURoPE
UNDER
A SINGLe
ROOF 1949 1999

EВРОПА
под ОДНоЙ
КРЫШЕЙ
1949–1999

ÉTAT DE DROIT

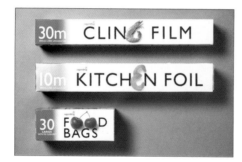

30m CLIN6 FILM

10m KITCH N FOIL

30 F D BAGS

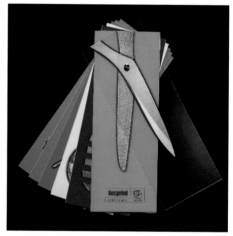

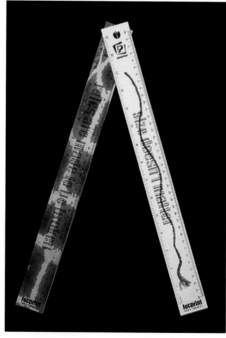

10-12 COVER AND SPREAD FROM BOOK (IN DIFFERENT
LANGUAGE VERSIONS) COMMEMORATING 50TH ANNIVERSARY OF
THE COUNCIL OF EUROPE
DESIGN FIRM: FutureBrand Davies Baron, London
ART DIRECTOR/ DESIGNER: Wladimir Marnich
PHOTOGRAPHY: Magnum Photos

13 FOOD WRAP PACKAGING FOR SUPERDRUG
DESIGN FIRM: Turner Duckworth, London
ART DIRECTORS: Bruce Duckworth, David Turner
DESIGNER: Jonathan Sleeman
PHOTOGRAPHER: Carol Sharp

14, 15 MAILERS FOR LAUNCH OF NEW PVC MATERIAL
DESIGN FIRM: HGV, London
ART DIRECTORS: Jim Sutherland, Pierre Vermeir
DESIGNERS: Jim Sutherland, Stuart Radford
PHOTOGRAPHER: John Edwards
CLIENT: Printall

16-19 WEB SITE FOR PHOTOGRAPHER EDWARD WEBB
(www.edwebb.dircon.co.uk)
DESIGN FIRM: HGV, London
ART DIRECTORS: Jim Sutherland, Pierre Vermeir
DESIGNERS: Stuart Radford, Dominic Edmunds

20 PROMOTIONAL BOOKLET FOR A PAPER COMPANY
DESIGN FIRM: HGV, London
ART DIRECTORS/ DESIGNERS: Pierre Vermeir, Jim Sutherland
PHOTOGRAPHER: Duncan Smith
CLIENT: James McNaughton Paper Group Ltd

21 ONE OF A SERIES OF POSTERS PROMOTING GUITARIST STEVE HACKETT
DESIGN FIRM: Lippa Pearce Design, London
ART DIRECTOR/ DESIGNER: Harry Pearce
CLIENT: Kudos Music

22 PACKAGING FOR ALTITUDE SPRING WATER
DESIGN FIRM: Pearlfisher, London
DESIGNER: Jonathan Ford

23 IDENTITY FOR PRISM RESTAURANT
DESIGN FIRM: Michael Nash Associates, London
ART DIRECTORS: Stephanie Nash, Anthony Michael
DESIGNER: Sandra Curtis
CLIENT: Harvey Nichols

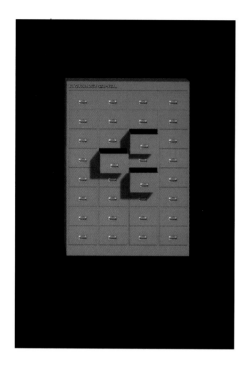

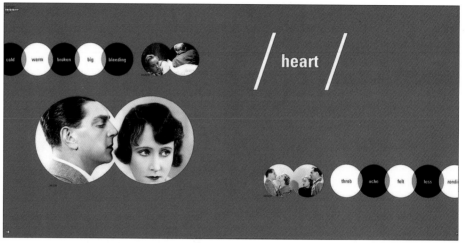

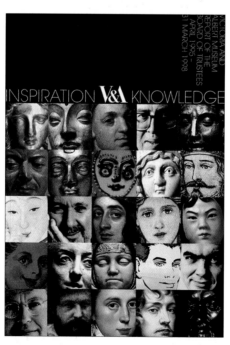

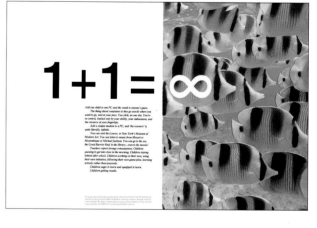

24 ONE OF A SERIES OF TEASER POSTERS FOR AN INTERNATIONAL CONSULTING GROUP
DESIGN FIRM: Mytton Williams, Bath
ART DIRECTOR: Bob Mytton
DESIGNER: Stuart Youngs
PHOTOGRAPHER: John Matchett
CLIENT: Arthur Andersen

25-27 THREE CATALOGUES FOR THE HULTON GETTY PICTURE COLLECTION, A PHOTO ARCHIVE
DESIGN FIRM: Navy Blue Design Consultants, London
ART DIRECTOR: Geoff Nicol
DESIGNERS: Clare Lundy, Gerard Ivall

28 IDENTITY FOR FINCA FLICHMAN ARGENTA WINERY
DESIGN FIRM: Lewis Moberly, London
ART DIRECTOR: Mary Lewis
DESIGNERS: Mary Lewis, Joanne Smith

29 VICTORIA AND ALBERT MUSEUM TRIANNUAL REVIEW
DESIGN FIRM: HGV, London
ART DIRECTOR/ DESIGNER: Pierre Vermeir

30 CORPORATE BROCHURE FOR BRITISH TELECOMMUNICATIONS
DESIGN FIRM: Addison, London
ART DIRECTOR: Peter Chodel
DESIGNERS: Phil Rushdon, Rob Lamb

Marathon Man

Ampersand sent Michael Johnson to Horsham to ask John Gorham, recently made an honorary member of D&AD, about ideas, chocolate bars, planting azaleas and five decades in the design business

31 STATIONERY FOR ARC DANCE COMPANY
DESIGN FIRM: HGV, London
ART DIRECTORS: Jim Sutherland, Pierre Vermeir
DESIGNER: Jim Sutherland
PHOTOGRAPHER: Sheila Rock

32 PACKAGING FOR WAITROSE JUICES
DESIGN FIRM: Lewis Moberly, London
ART DIRECTOR: Mary Lewis
DESIGNERS: Mary Lewis, Ann Marshall, Daniela Nunzi
PHOTOGRAPHER: Juliette Piddington

33 BROCHURE FOR NEIL MYERSON SOLICITORS
DESIGN FIRM: HGV, London
ART DIRECTORS: Jim Sutherland, Pierre Vermeir
DESIGNER: Mark Wheatcroft
PHOTOGRAPHER: Duncan Smith
ILLUSTRATORS: John Geary, Alan Levett

34, 35 "AMPERSAND" MAGAZINE
DESIGN FIRM: Frost Design, London
ART DIRECTOR: Vince Frost
DESIGNERS: Vince Frost, Melanie Mues
PHOTOGRAPHER (cover photo): Paul Tozer
CLIENT: British Design & Art Direction

36 BOOKLET ACCOMPANYING EXHIBITION "SEVEN (UNKNOWN) BELGIANS IN NEW YORK"
DESIGN FIRM: Nick Eagleton Design, London
DESIGNER: Nick Eagleton
ILLUSTRATORS/ PHOTOGRAPHERS: Nick Eagleton, Alexander Gorlizki
CLIENT: Alexander Gorlizki

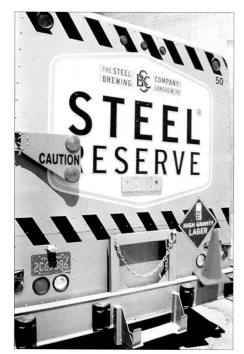

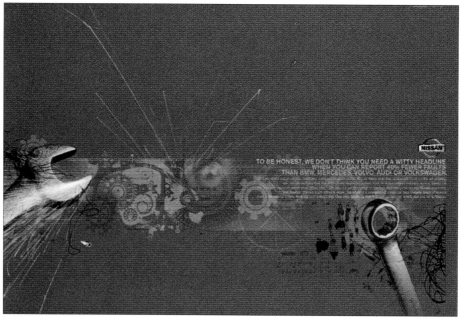

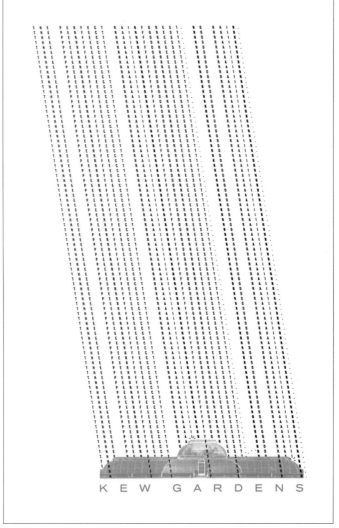

43 1998 ANNUAL REPORT FOR A CONSORTIUM OF ART COLLEGES
DESIGN FIRM: Trickett & Webb, London
DESIGNERS: Lynn Trickett, Brian Webb, Heidi Lightfoot
CLIENT: The London Institute

44 IDENTITY FOR TELEGRAPH COLOUR LIBRARY
DESIGN FIRM: HGV, London
ART DIRECTORS: Pierre Vermeir, Jim Sutherland
DESIGNERS: Pierre Vermeir, Jim Sutherland, Stuart Radford, Dominic Edmunds
PHOTOGRAPHER: John Edwards

45, 46 IDENTITY FOR A BOOKSTORE COFFEE SHOP
DESIGN FIRM: Ergo: Identity Consultants, London
ART DIRECTOR: Simon John
DESIGNER: Richard Haywood
CLIENT: Borders UK

47 RAINFOREST POSTER FOR KEW GARDENS
AGENCY: TBWA, London
ART DIRECTOR/ DESIGNER: Paul Belford

48, 49 SPREADS FROM "LIFE", SUNDAY MAGAZINE OF "THE OBSERVER"
ART DIRECTOR: Wayne Ford, London
PHOTOGRAPHY: Andrew Testa (48), Estate of Francesca Woodman (49)

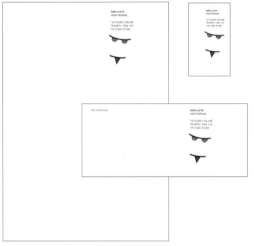

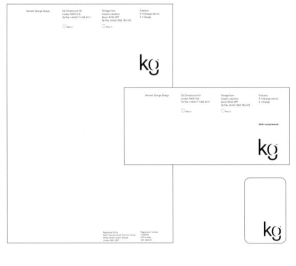

50 SPREAD FROM "LIFE", SUNDAY MAGAZINE OF
"THE OBSERVER"
ART DIRECTOR: Wayne Ford, London
PHOTOGRAPHER: John Reardon

51 CALENDAR BASED ON CLASSIFIED ADS, A JOINT PROMOTION
OF TRICKETT & WEBB AND AUGUSTUS MARTIN, PRINTERS
DESIGN FIRM: Trickett & Webb, London
DESIGNERS: Lynn Trickett, Brian Webb, Heidi Lightfoot

52 PACKAGING FOR AN AROMATHERAPY RANGE
DESIGN FIRM: Lippa Pearce Design, London
ART DIRECTOR: Harry Pearce
DESIGNERS: Harry Pearce, Jenny Allen
CLIENT: Nelson & Russell

53 INVITATION TO AN EXHIBITION INTRODING AN INNOVATIVE
INHALER FOR ASTHMA SUFFERERS
DESIGN FIRM: FOUR IV Design Consultants, London
ART DIRECTOR: Chris Dewar-Dixon
DESIGNER: Louise Edwards (graphics)
CLIENT: Nortons Healthcare

54 STATIONERY FOR SIAN LLOYD, TV WEATHERGIRL, IN WHICH
COLD- AND WARM-FRONT SYMBOLS TAKE ON NEW MEANING
DESIGN FIRM: Thirteen, London
ART DIRECTORS/ DESIGNERS: Aled Phillips, Mark Lester

55 LOGO AND STATIONERY FOR KENNETH GRANGE DESIGN
DESIGN FIRM: Lippa Pearce Design, London
ART DIRECTOR/ DESIGNER: Harry Pearce

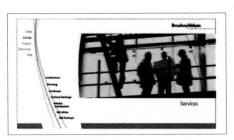

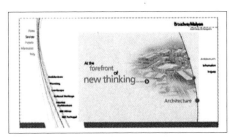

56 BROCHURE FOR RANDOM TECHNOLOGIES
DESIGN FIRM: Struktur Design, London
DESIGNER: Roger Fawcett-Tang
PHOTOGRAPHER: Xavier Young

57-59 WEB SITE FOR AN ARCHITECTURAL PRACTICE
(www.broadwaymalyan.co.uk)
DESIGN FIRM: Paper White Ltd, London
PRODUCER: Andrew Walker
DESIGNER: Paul Fennell
CLIENT: Broadway Malyan

60, 61 POSTCARD (60) AND STAMP (61) MAILERS FOR
PHOTONICA, A PHOTOLIBRARY
DESIGN FIRM: Frost Design, London
ART DIRECTOR: Vince Frost
DESIGNERS: Melanie Mues, Vince Frost

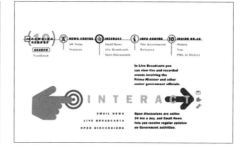

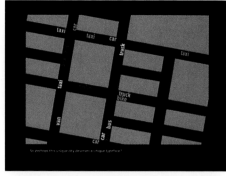

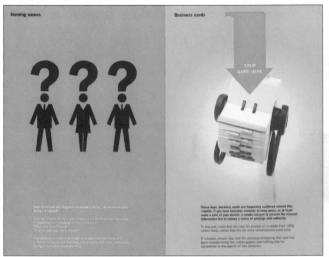

67 POP-UP CALENDAR FOR THE ROYAL SOCIETY OF ARTS
DESIGN FIRM: Trickett & Webb, London
DESIGNERS: Lynn Trickett, Brian Webb, Heidi Lightfoot
ILLUSTRATOR: Corina Fletcher

68-70 SHORT ANIMATION SHOWING POTENTIAL USES OF GLASGOW 1999 TYPEFACE AND IDENTITY
DESIGN FIRM: MetaDesign, London
ART DIRECTOR: Tim Fendley
DESIGNERS: Sam Davy, Frances Jackson, David Eveleigh
CLIENT: Glasgow 1999: UK City of Architecture and Design

71 PACKAGING FOR QUINTA DO PORTAL WINES
(capitalizing on 'portal' name with doorway theme on labels)
DESIGN FIRM: Blackburn's Ltd, London
ART DIRECTOR: John Blackburn
DESIGNER: Roberta Oates
ILLUSTRATOR: Martin Leman

72 "RAGS TO RICHES" BROCHURE PROMOTING CRANE'S CREST FINE PAPER
DESIGN FIRM: Dew Gibbons, London
ART DIRECTORS: Shaun Dew, Steve Gibbons
DESIGNER: Paul Tunnicliffe
PHOTOGRAPHER: John Edwards
CLIENT: ISTD

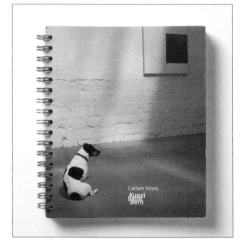

73 SELF-PROMOTIONAL BROCHURE
DESIGN FIRM: Addison, London
ART DIRECTOR: Nick Jones
DESIGNERS: Nick Jones, Steve Parker

74 EXHIBITION CATALOGUE FOR THE ROYAL COLLEGE OF ART ARCHITECTURE DEPARTMENT
DESIGNERS: Esther Mildenberger, Brian Switzer, London
PHOTOGRAPHY: Frank Thurston, Esther Mildenberger, RCA students
CLIENT: Royal College of Art London, Architecture and Interiors

75 ADVERTISEMENT FOR FIRETRAP FASHION OUTLET
DESIGN FIRM: Fold 7, London
ART DIRECTORS: Ryan Newey, Simon Packer
DESIGNER: Simon Packer
ILLUSTRATOR: Henry Obasi
PHOTOGRAPHER: Ryan Newey

76, 77 CATALOGUE FOR CALLUM INNES EXHIBITION HELD AT THE IKON GALLERY IN BIRMINGHAM AND THE KUNSTHALLE IN BERN, SWITZERLAND
DESIGNER: Lucy Richards, Edinburgh

78 COVER OF LONDON PHOTOGRAPHIC AWARDS ANNUAL
DESIGN FIRM: e-fact.limited, London
ART DIRECTOR: Natalie Woolcock
PHOTOGRAPHER (cover photo): Trish Morrissey

Area | 1,000 km2	102.1		Capital City	Belgrade		Monetary Unit	Yugoslavian dinar
Population | 1,000	10,350		Capital City Population | 1,000	1,405		GDP per Capita (US $)	1,487
Design Population | 1,000	000.3		Languages	Serbo-Croatian, Albanian		International Dialling Code	+381

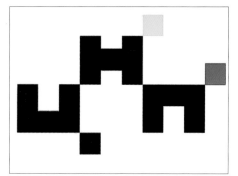

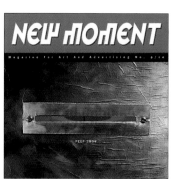

1 POSTER FOR THE YUGOSLAV DRAMA THEATRE
DESIGN FIRM: New Moment Design, Belgrade
ART DIRECTOR/ DESIGNER/ PHOTOGRAPHER: Slavimir Stojanovic

2 LOGO FOR INTERMEDIA, AN INDEPENDENT PUBLISHING HOUSE
DESIGN FIRM: New Moment Design, Belgrade
ART DIRECTOR/ DESIGNER: Slavimir Stojanovic

3 LOGO FOR MONTENEGRO NATIONAL THEATRE
DESIGN FIRM: New Moment Design, Belgrade
ART DIRECTOR/ DESIGNER: Slavimir Stojanovic

4 "FREE PRESS FOR FREE PEOPLE" POSTER
DESIGN FIRM: Focus Communications, Belgrade
(& Celje, Slovenia)
ART DIRECTOR: Igor Avzner
DESIGNER: Marica Kuznjecov
PHOTOGRAPHER: Nenad Kojadinovic
COPYWRITER: Ivana Avzner
CLIENT: Radio B92

5 THEATRE POSTER
ART DIRECTOR/ DESIGNER: Atila Kapitanj
PHOTOGRAPHER: Vladimir Cervenka
CLIENT: Narodno Pozoríste Uzice

6 THEATRE POSTER
ART DIRECTOR/ DESIGNER: Atila Kapitanj
CLIENT: Scena No 1

7-8 COVER AND SPREAD FROM "NEW MOMENT",
A MAGAZINE ABOUT ART AND ADVERTISING
DESIGN FIRM: New Moment Design, Belgrade
ART DIRECTOR/ DESIGNER: Slavimir Stojanovic

FULL TANK

ITALIAN FASHION BRAND DIESEL'S UNFETTERED ATTITUDE FUELS THE IMAGINATION OF CONSUMERS AND ADVERTISERS ALIKE

BY JIM DAVIES

Back in the 1980s, a European advertising campaign for Wrangler jeans used the tag line "Be more than just a number." It was a clear dig at market leader Levi's, whose 501 jeans had seemingly colonized every 14-to-40-year-old butt from Brussels to Berlin. At the same time, it hinted at the eternal contradiction facing all youth marketers: When everyone has become a rebel, no one's a rebel anymore.

The Italian clothing brand Diesel has somehow managed to dodge this issue altogether. With shops in 80 countries, over 1,000 employees, and turnover of $320 million in 1998, you'd think the 20-year-old brand would have passed firmly into shopping mall territory by now. Not a bit of it. Expertly walking a tightrope, Diesel manages to be at once irreverent and aspirational, innovative yet accessible. According to its charismatic founder and president, Renzo Rosso, this is because the company has always studiously ignored the "slavish trend-following" typical of the fashion industry. Over the years, he has consistently encouraged his designers to set their own agendas rather than get cricks in their necks looking over their shoulders for inspiration.

1. "School's Out," spring/summer, 1999

2. "Car crash," autumn, 1994.

3. Logo for 55DSL, 1995.

4. Logo for Diesel StyleLab, 1998.

5. "Christmas Day, 1917," autumn/winter, 1998.

6. "Shopping is the meaning of life," autumn, 1999.

7. "Funeral," spring, 1996.

8. "Pigs," autumn, 1994.

9. "How to be a weather forecaster," spring, 1992.

10. "How to vibrate with happiness," autumn, 1993.

11. "Lucky Beer," autumn, 1997.

12-14. Pages for Diesel's virtual store, UK: www.diesel.co.uk/store/home.html (12), www.diesel.co.uk/store/female/index.html (13,14).

The company's pricing policy certainly has something to do with the exclusivity, and thus the trendiness, of the product. A pair of Diesel jeans doesn't come cheap. They can cost up to $120, a considerable sum when you take into account the supposed decline in the denim market and the cut-price competition. But of course, Diesel isn't just about jeans, it's about attitude, the notion that if you get the Diesel joke, you're somehow part of the Diesel worldwide family. Take Diesel's leading men's jean, Keetar, which is eulogized on Diesel's U.K. Web site and virtual store not for its fit or fabric, but because it allows easy access should you need to re-adjust your testicles.

This kind of droll, near-the-knuckle humour informs virtually all of Diesel's marketing communications. Its prominent "Successful Living" print campaign, formulated collaboratively with the Swedish ad agency Paradiset, explores themes and issues that most companies would shy well away from. Try apartheid, suicide, religion, plastic

surgery, hard drugs, tobacco, lesbianism, communism, car crashes, bestiality, corporate power, advertising, gun laws, bondage, decadence, and bigamy. It's easy to draw parallels with fellow Italian clothing company Benetton's deliberately provocative advertising output, but the difference is that Diesel's is far less po-faced and always executed with a cheeky, knowing wink.

"When we started out with our first worldwide advertising campaign in 1991," says Renzo Rosso, "we hoped to create a dialogue with our customers. We had been watching most of the world's advertising talking in monologues and we wanted to do it the other way round. We wanted people to think, to question, and to react. In order to do that, we had to discard all the accepted assumptions about how to create effective advertising. We tried to come up with advertising that was surprising, thought-provoking, engaging, humorous, and true to ourselves."

For a better understanding of Diesel's unorthodox communications philosophy, it's worth going back to the company's roots, and, more particularly, to those of its Peter Pan-like kingpin. As a child, growing up on his father's modest farm in northern Italy, Rosso had no aspirations whatsoever to become involved in the fashion industry. He helped out on the land and was content enough to live the simple life in Brugine, a small town of about 2,000 people, where there was just one car and one television set. For a time, he tried making a living by breeding rabbits and playing rock guitar. But his father encouraged him to broaden his horizons, and in the early 1970s he enrolled at the Marconi Technical Institute, one of Italy's first fashion schools, for a five-year course in textiles and manufacturing.

1. "School's Out," spring/summer, 1999
2. "Car crash," autumn, 1994.
3. Logo for 55DSL, 1995.
4. Logo for DieselStyleLab, 1998.
5. "Christmas Day, 1917," autumn/winter, 1998.
6. "Shopping is the meaning of life," autumn, 1999.
7. "Funeral," spring, 1996.
8. "Pigs," autumn, 1994.
9. "How to be a weather forecaster," spring, 1992.
10. "How to vibrate with happiness," autumn, 1993.
11. "Lucky Beer," autumn, 1997.
12-14. Pages for Diesel's virtual store, UK: www.diesel.co.uk/store/home.html (12),
www.diesel.co.uk/store/female/index.html (13,14).

1

2

3

4

5

6

7

8

9

10

11

12

13
14

It was an epiphany for Rosso. Outside of college hours, he began making outlandish clothes, first for himself, then for his friends, and began formulating plans for what he called a "style laboratory."

Soon after graduating, Rosso was fortunate enough to meet businessman Adriano Goldschmied, the man who was to have "the single most formative influence on my career." Goldschmied hired him as a production technician for his company, Moltex. By 1978, Rosso had persuaded his boss to join him in a new casual-wear manufacturing venture. Already with an eye to international markets, Rosso called the company Diesel, because the pronunciation was the same in most languages, and people the world over would know more or less what it meant.

Diesel became part of a local collective of casual-wear brands that operated under the name Genius. (Labels so-dubbed that had blazes of fashionability during the 1980s and early 1990s were Replay, Katherine Hamnet Denim, Bo Bo Kaminsky, and Goldie.) Seven years later, Rosso was in a position to buy his partner out and break away from the Genius collective altogether. He brought in a core group of designers and briefed them to experiment under the "unwritten rule that we would manufacture items of clothing that we ourselves would want to wear."

More recently, the original Diesel brand has diversified. It now sells kids' clothing and (under licence) sunglasses and scent. It has also launched an upmarket casual range called Diesel Style Lab, as well as D-Diesel and 55DSL, respectively its denim and sports-wear collections.

The clothes are unquestionably the starting point for Diesel's stand-out aesthetic. The company's oeuvre includes sweaters that are perfectly clean, but look as if they have been covered in dirt; shirts that are made to look permanently crumpled; a pair of pants with reinforced crotch and knee pads based on mapping diagrams found in an obscure military manual. But just as important as the clothing is the buzz Diesel has managed to create around its merchandise. Brian Baderman, the British designer-turned-commercials director who designed 17 outlandish brochures for the company during the early-to-mid-1990s, puts it this way: "[Fashion] products tend to be remarkably similar. The only thing that's different is the label. It's the hype that surrounds a label that gives it force and magic. Until recently, fashion has taken itself with an almost religious seriousness. I was lucky enough to have a client prepared to play with irony and mock itself in public."

He has a point. The pages of "Vogue" and the like may be packed with fashion images by the highest-paid photographers in the world, but switch the ever-so-discreet logos around and you'd be hard-pressed to tell the difference between them. With comparatively limited resources, Diesel was determined to stand out from the fashion pack, and to this end it developed an unusual way of creating its corporate message. "We always try to challenge the competition," claims Maurizio Marchiori, international advertising and communications manager for Diesel. "We aim to achieve an emotional energy in our communications. It's a process. Every day, something changes. Every day, we try to achieve something new, something better. Sometimes we don't succeed, but at least we're trying."

Corporate communications, like the rest of the Diesel output, are masterminded from the so-called "Diesel village" in Molvena, just outside of Venice in north east Italy. Some 350 employees, varying widely in nationality and disciplines, have taken over the once-sleepy town and live an almost commune-like existence, eating, sleeping, and breathing Diesel.

Ask Diesel creative director and head of design Wilbert Das about the philosophy behind the company's visual support material and you get an answer that could be interpreted as vague, evasive even: "I don't really think about it," he says. "It's become so natural now, it's almost a state of mind." The thing is, you can believe him. This Dutchman has been with the company 11 years and seen it mushroom from just 28 people. He joined up as a designer soon after graduating in fashion from the Academy of Fine Arts in Holland, and now heads up a team comprised of seven graphic designers, three interior designers, six fashion designers, two accessories designers, three new media designers, and six assistants. You could say he's grown up with the company. "Not many people leave," says Das,

sounding only slightly sinister. "If they do, it tends to be for personal reasons: boyfriends, girlfriends, that kind of thing. [The Diesel staff] enjoy living in nature, in a nice environment, and they also get a lot of opportunity to travel."

Cross-disciplinary interaction is encouraged and ideas are accepted from wherever they may emanate. (At the end of my interview with Maurizio Marchiori, he mentioned that if I had any unusual ideas for promoting Diesel, he'd be all too ready to listen to them.) This kind of laid-back, democratic approach extends to Diesel's relationship with its outside creative agencies. Marchiori contends that Diesel doesn't hire and brief in the traditional manner; rather, it brings together a small group of individuals who respect each other and communicate effectively. "It doesn't matter where the idea originates, from the agency or in-house. We treat the people from the agency as if they belong to our company." In addition, agency and photographer are rarely credited for their contribution, because this is seen only as part of the overall process. "Diesel is always the hero of the advertising," says Marchiori, "not any individual."

Unusual for the television-centric world of advertising, it's been Diesel's print campaigns that have established its personality and voice. The "Successful Living" campaign – a sideways take on American 1950s domestic appliance advertising – has been going nearly ten years and achieved remarkably high visibility considering the medium. Deliberately low-rent commercials, many directed with aplomb by the voguish Swedish collective Traktor, have made ripples, but generally haven't had enough exposure to create an impression internationally. "We're not a giant company," says Marchiori. "We don't have a super budget to show our commercials worldwide, but we trust magazines and they seem to work for the brand." This relative impecuniousness didn't stop Diesel being named Advertiser of the Year at the Cannes International Advertising Festival in 1998.

It's telling that the garish photographic tableau approach pioneered by Diesel is becoming more popular with other advertisers (the recently launched Boo.com Internet shopping service has adopted it, for example). It will be interesting to see if Diesel will change direction or continue ploughing the same furrow. So far, it has stocked the advertising world with some memorable images: midget basketball players, smooching sailors, a boardroom table populated by blow-up sex dolls, generals in diapers, caged women in fur coats, naked office workers. Often featuring multitudes of characters, the setups in the ads are immaculately staged, and the clothes are typically modelled in a throwaway, almost incidental way – sometimes you have to look twice to figure out who's wearing them. The framing and furniture of the ads, however, remains remarkably consistent: a bold red rectangle in the top left-hand corner, with the word "Diesel" in prominent white sans caps, and the sub-line underneath reading either "Successful Living" or "Jeans and Workwear."

The invitation to doubletake is the very crux of the company's communication strategy, if any concept so formal exists in the laid-back world of Diesel. Where minimal text appears, it reads just a little strangely, as if it has been poorly translated. A press ad featuring a gallery of men apparently looking for love under the banner "Diesel Lonely Hearts Club" carries typical small ad copy for each. One of them reads: "Lonely? No-one to hugg [sic]. Kiss? XXX? No problemas. Non-religious Hispanic bodybuilder gives you tender love and care. You can also contact me for any type of poetic conversations."

It's just off-kilter enough to make you read it again. This oddball-English effect might be inevitable, given that it's the result of an Italian-Swedish collaboration. But then, even the words on Diesel jeans labels are curious. "Diesel Industry Denim Division. Registered trademark. Type RR55. Superior Quality Jeans. Ideal for work and pleasure. Regulated." Are they serious or spoofing? Clearly "Type RR55" is nothing more than a reference to Renzo Rosso and his year of birth, 1955. Yet the more descriptive words also hint at heavy-duty, no-nonsense industrial production. And do they mean "work and leisure" rather than "work and pleasure?" Who can tell? Diesel has managed to hold our attention and get us asking questions again.

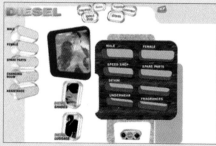

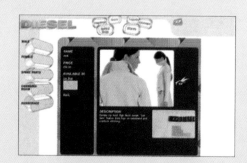

The same tongue-in-cheek aesthetic has been seamlessly transferred to the Internet, a medium that Diesel has embraced wholeheartedly. "Every day you have to drink water," says Marchiori, "the same way you have to be interested in the Internet. But we do it the Diesel way. We need to invest more, study more."

As well as sites devoted to individual collections, virtual stores have been established in Switzerland, Finland, and the U.K.

Significantly behind the jokey facade, they work. A few months ago, I ordered a pair of jeans, which duly arrived the next day. I was able to track them as they were transferred from van to train to van, right up to my front door. What's more, they are supremely comfortable. Well, you know what they say about Keetars.

Jim Davies is a writer and editor. He has contributed to, among others, "Eye", "Design", and "Campaign" magazines and "The Independent", "The Guardian", and "The Sunday Times" newspapers.

MOVIE STILLS
THE POSTERS OF CZECH ILLUSTRATOR ALES NAJBRT HAVE HELPED MAKE THE TOWN OF KARLOVY VARY A HOUSEHOLD NAME TO FILM BUFFS WORLDWIDE

BY DANA BARTELT

The Czech spa town Karlovy Vary, near the German border, is celebrated for its elegant, opulent 19th-century architecture, still visible today in the numerous hotels, villas, bathhouses, and colonnades lining each side of the Teplá River that runs through the centre of town. Since time immemorial, kings and emperors, politicians and financiers, artists and musicians have flocked to Karlovy Vary (or Carlsbad, in German) to cure their ills by drinking and bathing in the local springs' hot, sulphurous water. (Johann Wolfgang Goethe purportedly visited the place at the age of 70 to take a "cure" with the 17-year-old daughter of a neighbouring spa owner.)

Last summer, I arrived in Karlovy Vary with a group of graphic design students on the last weekend of its International Film Festival, perhaps the town's greatest claim to fame beyond its architectural treasures. I'd arranged this weekend excursion to the famous spa town as director of the North Carolina State University Summer Study in Prague Programme. Goethe doesn't often stop by anymore, but the 54-year-old film festival attracts its own set of dignitaries: One night I happened upon some of the students at the Grand Hotel Pupp, a wedding cake of a hotel accommodating the celebrities attending the festival, only to learn I was five minutes too late to witness an appearance by Woody Harrelson.

The excitement of the festival is apparent as you approach the town centre, encountering crowds of festival guests and tourists, numerous vendors selling thin round "oplatky" wafers, and banners and oversized posters announcing the festival's offerings along the promenades flanking the Teplá. Last summer, long ribbons flowed from huge orange lips attached to the façade of the Thermal Sanatorium – a modern intrusion, erected in 1977 – that serves as the centre of the festival. Tourists gather for outdoor performances or surround portraitists and caricaturists.

1. Poster for 31st International Film Festival Karlovy Vary, 1996. Design firm: Studio Najbrt & Lev, Prague; designer: Ales Najbrt; photographer: Tono Stano; client: Film Festival Karlovy Vary Foundation.

2. Banner for 32nd International Film Festival Karlovy Vary, 1997. Design firm: Studio Najbrt & Lev, Prague; designer: Ales Najbrt; photographer: Tono Stano; client: Film Festival Karlovy Vary Foundation.

3. Poster for 33rd International Film Festival Karlovy Vary, 1998. Design firm: Studio Najbrt & Lev, Prague; designer: Ales Najbrt; photographer: Tono Stano; client: Film Festival Karlovy Vary Foundation.

I've made this annual excursion with students for almost ten years, and midway through that period, I noticed a change in the "look" of the festival, which I attributed to a young Prague-based graphic designer, Ales Najbrt (AL-esh NAY-bert). I was familiar with Najbrt's design, having included some of it in two exhibitions I curated. I first saw his work when he was a student of Jan Solpera, professor of type design at Prague's Academy of Applied Arts, who is known internationally for posters with expressive typography and who taught type design at the NCSU summer programme in 1991.

Najbrt is recognized for his original typeface design, the trademark of all his work. For the 1997 Karlovy Vary International Film Festival, he borrowed a black-cat-and-spotlight symbol from a scene in a film by Czech director Jan Svěrak. "The animated typography evokes the impression of a freeze-frame moment," wrote Iva Janaková, curator at the Museum of Decorative Arts in Prague, in a 1998 issue of "Baseline" magazine. "In addition, it recalls the photographic experiments of László Moholy-Nagy and of Karel Teige in Czechoslovakia. The '30s are further evoked through the spatial effect achieved by the use of diagonals."

Najbrt graduated a year before the upheaval that ended Communist rule in 1989 and he was ready for the Czech Republic to become a capitalist society. The old regime had published movie posters and books, providing some work for artists and graphic designers, but Czech designers were now scrambling to keep pace with foreign ad agencies moving into Prague after the job market became competitive.

Energetic and versatile, Najbrt initiated several projects including the avant-garde magazine "Raut". Maria Rogal, a graphic design professor at the University of Florida, explains that "Raut" unites Czech art, literature, and poetry with obscure history and societal commentary. Najbrt's design work is informed by his experience as an actor in the Sklep Theatre and as a musician in the Maly Tanecni (Little Dance) Universal Prague orchestra, and by his participation in Prague 5, a partnership of artists, actors, musicians, and the art group Tvrdohlavi (The Stubborn Ones). For three years he was art director of the weekly "Reflex", a magazine covering underground culture, drugs, sex, and other formerly taboo subjects – as well as politics. In 1994, Najbrt teamed up with partner Pavel Lev to found Najbrt & Lev Studio.

Collaboration is also at the heart of his relationship with the Karlovy Vary festival. Czech actor Jiří Bartoška, the festival's president, invited Najbrt, photographer Tono Stano, choreographer Michal Caban, and scenographer/architect Simon Caban to create all promotional and informational materials: standard and oversized posters, billboards, banners, advertisements, catalogues, programmes, tickets, invitations, and, starting this year, the trophy. "We influence each other," says Najbrt, "and we are given a lot of freedom."

Each year, Karlovy Vary's organizers use a different theme. "I want to create a design that will be a surprise for each year's festival guests," Najbrt says. "This is the most prestigious film event in Central Europe, so it is important that the concept reflects its energy and position among such events."

In 1995, the first year the team designed the festival's materials, they used a seductive photograph of a young girl that evoked Czech director Gustav Machat's famous '30s film "Ecstasy". In 1999, the 100th anniversary of the birth of the well-loved Czech film actor Oldrich Novy, "We used a photograph [of Novy] found by a collector that set the style for this year's festival, in its traditional character typical of the old Czech films," says Najbrt. "The important thing is to communicate the theme in simple design terms. Personal style is secondary."

In 1997, the festival was raised to Category-A film-festival status, ranking it with the festivals in Cannes, Venice, and Berlin. Last year it drew 128,000 visitors – good news for a country playing capitalist catch-up after years of Communist rule.

Dana Bartelt teaches graphic design at Loyola University in New Orleans and is working on a 75-year history of Czech posters.

1. Poster for 31st International Film Festival Karlovy Vary, 1996. Design firm: Studio Najbrt & Lev, Prague; designer: Ales Najbrt; photographer: Tono Stano; client: Film Festival Karlovy Vary Foundation.
2. Banner for 32nd International Film Festival Karlovy Vary, 1997. Design firm: Studio Najbrt & Lev, Prague; designer: Ales Najbrt; photographer: Tono Stano; client: Film Festival Karlovy Vary Foundation.
3. Poster for 33rd International Film Festival Karlovy Vary, 1998. Design firm: Studio Najbrt & Lev, Prague; designer: Ales Najbrt; photographer: Tono Stano; client: Film Festival Karlovy Vary Foundation.

THE WRITING ON THE WALL
NORTHERN IRELAND'S TURBULENT HISTORY IS POWERFULLY DOCUMENTED IN OUTDOOR MURALS PAINTED BY UNTRAINED ARTISTS FROM BOTH REPUBLICAN AND UNIONIST CAMPS

TEXT AND PHOTOS BY BILL ROLSTON

When most people think of murals, what comes to mind is Mexico in the 1920s, when "los tres grandes" – David Siquieros, Diego Rivera, and José Orozco – already established painters, began creating monumental murals supporting the revolution. People usually don't consider Northern Ireland in this context, but the tradition of political murals was already more than a decade old in Ireland when it became a celebrated art form in Mexico.

In 1908, a shipyard worker named John McLean painted a mural on a wall in East Belfast, depicting the Battle of the Boyne in 1690, when Protestant Prince William of Orange defeated Catholic King James IV in the struggle for the English throne. In the last decades of the 19th century, the Battle of the Boyne had been depicted on cloth banners displayed in commemorations each July, but McLean's innovation launched a trend that quickly became widespread in Protestant communities.

1. Whiterock Road, West Belfast, 1994. This light-hearted mural, painted in the lead-up to the IRA cease-fire of 1994, depicts British soldiers being carried by doves back to England from Ireland.
2. Ardoyne Avenue, South Belfast, 1999. Human rights lawyer Rosemary Nelson was killed by Loyalists in 1999, ten years after the death of another human rights lawyer, Pat Finucane. The mural calls for an international investigation into allegations of police collusion in the deaths, and demands the disbandment of the RUC (Royal Ulster Constabulary, the local 90-percent-Protestant police force).
3. Finbank Gardens, South Belfast, 1998. Loyalist prisoners are depicted on the prison walls, along with names of local Loyalist prisoners, emblems of the Ulster Defence Association (UDA) and Ulster Freedom Fighters (UFF), and the letters "POW," for prisoners of war.
4. Lenadoon Avenue, West Belfast, 1996. This mural depicts the mythological Celtic northern warrior, Cuchulain. Alongside and above are the names and portraits of Irish Republican Army volunteers from the local area who have died in combat. Below are the crests of the four provinces of Ireland, and the word "Saoirse" (freedom).

5. Beechmount Grove, West Belfast, 1997. Sinn Fein president Gerry Adams won the seat for the constituency of West Belfast in 1983, lost it later to the Social Democratic and Labour Party, but won it back in 1997. A roving mural of Adams in the lead-up to the 1997 election is shown in the foreground, as another mural, depicting the similarity between the political struggles in the North of Ireland and the Basque country/Euskadi (in Spain) is unveiled in the background.
6. United South Link, West Belfast, 1998. This mural was painted for the bicentenary of the United Irishmen (Na hÉireannaigh Aontaithe), a revolutionary Republican organization. The slogan – "It is new strung and shall be heard" – refers to the harp as a symbol of the United Irishmen's struggle.
7. Shiels Street, West Belfast, 1998. Painted as part of the West Belfast Festival, and unveiled by the Cuban ambassador to the European Union, the mural depicts Che Guevara, scenes from Cuba, and Republican prisoners in the 1970s reading from Guevara's works.
8. Dromara Street, West Belfast, 1999. The Good Friday Agreement of 1997 promised, among other things, "freedom from sectarian harassment." This mural reproduces (left) the cover of the Agreement document, sent to every household, and counterposes the reality of continuing attacks on Catholics and their property.

9. Newtownards Road, East Belfast, 1999. Memorial mural to the 36th Ulster Division, formally the Ulster Volunteer Force, which was decimated at the Battle of the Somme in July, 1916.
10. Lenadoon Avenue, West Belfast, 1998. This memorial to Joe McDonnell, the fifth hunger-striker to die during the Republican hunger strike of 1981, contains the names of all ten strikers, as well as a quotation from McDonnell.
11. Mersey Street, East Belfast, 1996. Members of the Ulster Volunteer Force (UVF, another Loyalist paramilitary group) are shown in action. Above the main picture is the emblem of the UVF, the Red Hand of Ulster, a traditional Loyalist symbol, and the slogan "For God and Ulster."
12. Mersey Street, East Belfast, 1997. UFF members pose with weapons, along with the motto of the UFF's parent organization, UDA, "Quis separabit" (Who will separate), and the clenched Red Hand of Ulster. The letters "UYM" above refer to the Ulster Youth Movement, youth wing of the UDA.
13. Essex Street, South Belfast, 1998. In recent years, residents of the Nationalist Lower Ormeau Road community have protested the Orange Order marches through their area. The mural depicts a drummer from the nearby Ballynafeigh Loyal Orange Lodge (LOL), whose claim to a "right to march" leads to the imprisonment of local Nationalists.

14. Iverna Street, South Belfast, 1998. Joe Bratty, leader of the UFF in South Belfast, was killed by the IRA shortly before the 1994 cease-fire.

15. Bonds Street, Derry, 1997. In this UDA mural, an avenging death figure moves among the bodies of dead Nationalists, with the war-ravaged Republican Bogside area of Derry in the background. The slogan above reads in part: "We determine the guilty, we decide the punishment." The image was adapted from an Iron Maiden album cover.

16. Ballymena, County Antrim, 1998. "King Billy" (William III) crosses the Boyne in 1690, during one of the battles which secured him the English crown. This was the predominant image in Loyalist murals in the first half of the 20th century.

In prior decades, a protracted struggle for Irish home rule had raged in the British Parliament, which passed three Home Rule bills that failed to materialize. The unsuccessful Easter Rising of 1916, an attempt to establish an independent Irish Republic, lit a spark that flamed up during the 1918 British parliamentary elections, when Sinn Fein, the pro-independence party, took 80 percent of the Irish seats and established its own parliament. A war with England from 1919 to 1921 led to Ireland's partition into an independent Republic in the south and the British-controlled Northern Ireland, with its own government and police force. (Its Protestant population opposed Home Rule, favoured the union with Britain, and established a government-in-waiting poised to assume rule.)

In working-class Protestant, or Unionist, areas, murals articulated and confirmed the public's collective identity. Before partition, murals indicated the working class's opposition to Home Rule and its support of a union with Britain; in the violence following partition, they lent a reassuring focus amidst the turmoil. And when Northern Ireland's institutions were fully rooted, the murals became a symbolic daily reminder of the new order: a celebration of what one Unionist prime minister called "a Protestant parliament for a Protestant people."

Unionist murals were highly ritualistic in form and content. The vast majority depicted King William III (formerly William of Orange) crossing the River Boyne on a white horse, and were painted or repainted annually to celebrate the anniversary of the July 12 victory. The murals bore no complex political statements, no representations of the new parliament or police force, no witty cartoons deriding Irish Nationalists or Republicans. The simple repetition of the image became an anchor for the identity of Ulster, as Unionists still refer to Northern Ireland.

The Nationalists and Republicans had no such anchor. Having fought to establish an independent Ireland, they were now a minority in a state whose existence they loathed, as countless new laws and daily practices reminded them constantly. The very streets belonged to the Unionists, who marched through town centres each July 12. For the Unionist working class, painting murals amounted to a civic right and duty, but no such privileges were conferred on the minority. Of course, the Nationalists rebelled throughout the 20th century, with military campaigns staged by the illegal Irish Republican Army (IRA) as well as with nonviolent protest. But by the late 1960s, the lid could not be kept on this boiling political cauldron. A civil rights campaign was beaten off the streets, first by the Royal Ulster Constabulary (RUC), and later by the British Army. The last big civil rights march, on January 30, 1972, resulted in 14 deaths inflicted by British soldiers in an event now known as Bloody Sunday. Meanwhile, the IRA grew in numbers and military capability.

Many IRA activists served long prison sentences, initially under a "political status" that was withdrawn in 1976, when the activists, refusing to wear prison uniforms, began wearing towels and blankets. Denied visitation rights (and bathroom access) in such garb, the Republican prisoners eventually undertook a hunger strike in 1981 to regain their political status, and ten died. Outside the prison walls, young Republicans began to draw support by painting slogans and murals in Nationalist areas. Where there had never been murals, there were now hundreds.

1. Whiterock Road, West Belfast, 1994. This light-hearted mural, painted in the lead-up to the IRA cease-fire of 1994, depicts British soldiers being carried by doves back to England from Ireland.
2. Ardoyne Avenue, South Belfast, 1999. Human rights lawyer Rosemary Nelson was killed by Loyalists in 1999, ten years after the death of another human rights lawyer, Pat Finucane. The mural calls for an international investigation into allegations of police collusion in the deaths, and demands the disbandment of the RUC (Royal Ulster Constabulary, the local 90-percent-Protestant police force).
3. Finbank Gardens, South Belfast, 1998. Loyalist prisoners are depicted on the prison walls, along with names of local Loyalist prisoners, emblems of the Ulster Defence Association (UDA) and Ulster Freedom Fighters (UFF), and the letters "POW," for prisoners of war.
4. Lenadoon Avenue, West Belfast, 1996. This mural depicts the mythological Celtic northern warrior, Cuchulain. Alongside and above are the names and portraits of Irish Republican Army volunteers from the local area who have died in combat. Below are the crests of the four provinces of Ireland, and the word "Saoirse" (freedom).

5. Beechmount Grove, West Belfast, 1997. Sinn Fein president Gerry Adams won the seat for the constituency of West Belfast in 1983, lost it later to the Social Democratic and Labour Party, but won it back in 1997. A roving mural of Adams in the lead-up to the 1997 election is shown in the foreground, as another mural, depicting the similarity between the political struggles in the North of Ireland and the Basque country/Euskadi (in Spain) is unveiled in the background.
6. United South Link, West Belfast, 1998. This mural was painted for the bicentenary of the United Irishmen (Na hÉireannaigh Aontaithe), a revolutionary Republican organization. The slogan — "It is new strung and shall be heard" — refers to the harp as a symbol of the United Irishmen's struggle.
7. Shiels Street, West Belfast, 1998. Painted as part of the West Belfast Festival, and unveiled by the Cuban ambassador to the European Union, the mural depicts Che Guevara, scenes from Cuba, and Republican prisoners in the 1970s reading from Guevara's works.
8. Dromara Street, 1999. The Good Friday Agreement of 1997 promised, among other things, "freedom from sectarian harassment." This mural reproduces (left) the cover of the Agreement document, sent to every household, and counterposes the reality of continuing attacks on Catholics and their property.

9. Newtownards Road, East Belfast, 1999. Memorial mural to the 36th Ulster Division, formally the Ulster Volunteer Force, which was decimated at the Battle of the Somme in July, 1916.
10. Lenadoon Avenue, West Belfast, 1998. This memorial to Joe McDonnell, the fifth hunger-striker to die during the Republican hunger strike of 1981, contains the names of all ten strikers, as well as a quotation from McDonnell.
11. Mersey Street, East Belfast, 1996. Members of the Ulster Volunteer Force (UVF, another Loyalist paramilitary group) are shown in action. Above the main picture is the emblem of the UVF, the Red Hand of Ulster, a traditional Loyalist symbol, and the slogan "For God and Ulster."
12. Mersey Street, East Belfast, 1997. UFF members pose with weapons, along with the motto of the UFF's parent organization, UDA, "Quis separabit" (Who will separate), and the clenched Red Hand of Ulster. The letters "UYM" above refer to the Ulster Youth Movement, youth wing of the UDA.
13. Essex Street, South Belfast, 1998. In recent years, residents of the Nationalist Lower Ormeau Road community have protested the Orange Order marches through their area. The mural depicts a drummer from the nearby Ballynafeigh Loyal Orange Lodge (LOL), whose claim to a "right to march" leads to the imprisonment of local Nationalists.

14. Iverna Street, South Belfast, 1998. Joe Bratty, leader of the UFF in South Belfast, was killed by the IRA shortly before the 1994 cease-fire.

15. Bonds Street, Derry, 1997. In this UDA mural, an avenging death figure moves among the bodies of dead Nationalists, with the war-ravaged Republican Bogside area of Derry in the background. The slogan above reads in part: "We determine the guilty, we decide the punishment." The image was adapted from an Iron Maiden album cover.

16. Ballymena, County Antrim, 1998. "King Billy" (William III) crosses the Boyne in 1690, during one of the battles which secured him the English crown. This was the predominant image in Loyalist murals in the first half of the 20th century.

1	2	3	4	5	6

7	8	9	10	11	12

13	14	15	16

After the hunger strike – ultimately, political status was returned to the prisoners – new murals kept appearing with a wide range of themes, including the military campaign of the IRA, and the promotion of Sinn Fein's newfound electoral strategy, encouraging the public to vote instead of the abstentionist protest that had prevailed. Other murals railed at the government's "security" measures, such as the use of plastic bullets, and still others alluded to political struggles in other parts of the world.

At the same time, the Loyalist tradition of mural painting continued, but only as a shadow of its original force – as though its confidence level was inversely proportional to the growth of Nationalist and Republican conviction. In the 1970s, fewer Loyalist murals of "King Billy" appeared, in deference to the more common depiction of flags, symbols, and heraldic devices. Their graphic execution was competent, but, significantly, they contained no representations of people. It was a telling revelation of Unionism's identity crisis: Once dominant and unassailable, the movement no longer knew how it fit into the political picture.

From the mid-1980s, Loyalist militants stepped up their military campaign, and the walls dutifully reflected the changes: By the 1990s, the vast majority of Loyalist murals depicted armed paramilitary members. But then the political landscape changed rapidly, when the British military and the IRA began negotiating a peace process resulting in an IRA cease-fire in 1994, which still holds despite 17 months of war in the interim. Nationalist murals immediately reflected the new political climate. Many depicted Republican aspirations – the release of IRA prisoners, the disbandment of the RUC, the withdrawal of the British Army – and stopped depicting IRA members and activities.

Although some recent Loyalist murals have depicted political demands (particularly the release of Loyalist prisoners) and the Battle of the Somme, most still include paramilitary figures. Some are relatively unthreatening memorials to fallen comrades, but many are chilling and menacing. Such murals may reassure these communities amidst massive political change, like the possibility of Sinn Fein-elected representatives to a new parliament, and the radical restructuring of the RUC, once little more than the Unionists' armed wing. In these circumstances, the Loyalists seek to remind their followers of their vigilance and continued protection.

Still, the traditional means of protection has been sustained terrorism against the Nationalists, who find little comfort in the content of the murals. Paradoxically, the most bloodthirsty murals exist in areas where small parties linked to the Loyalist paramilitary groups enjoy the most political support, but the Loyalist progressive stances on human rights and social inclusion are not depicted in these murals.

1. Whiterock Road, West Belfast, 1994. This light-hearted mural, painted in the lead-up to the IRA cease-fire of 1994, depicts British soldiers being carried by doves back to England from Ireland.
2. Ardoyne Avenue, South Belfast, 1999. Human rights lawyer Rosemary Nelson was killed by Loyalists in 1999, ten years after the death of another human rights lawyer, Pat Finucane. The mural calls for an international investigation into allegations of police collusion in the deaths, and demands the disbandment of the RUC (Royal Ulster Constabulary, the local 90-percent-Protestant police force).
3. Finbank Gardens, South Belfast, 1998. Loyalist prisoners are depicted on the prison walls, along with names of local Loyalist prisoners, emblems of the Ulster Defence Association (UDA) and Ulster Freedom Fighters (UFF), and the letters "POW," for prisoners of war.
4. Lenadoon Avenue, West Belfast, 1996. This mural depicts the mythological Celtic northern warrior, Cuchulain. Alongside and above are the names and portraits of Irish Republican Army volunteers from the local area who have died in combat. Below are the crests of the four provinces of Ireland, and the word "Saoirse" (freedom).

5. Beechmount Grove, West Belfast, 1997. Sinn Fein president Gerry Adams won the seat for the constituency of West Belfast in 1983, lost it later to the Social Democratic and Labour Party, but won it back in 1997. A roving mural of Adams in the lead-up to the 1997 election is shown in the foreground, as another mural, depicting the similarity between the political struggles in the North of Ireland and the Basque country/Euskadi (in Spain) is unveiled in the background.
6. United South Link, West Belfast, 1998. This mural was painted for the bicentenary of the United Irishmen (Na hÉireannaigh Aontaithe), a revolutionary Republican organization. The slogan – "It is new strung and shall be heard" – refers to the harp as a symbol of the United Irishmen's struggle.
7. Shiels Street, West Belfast, 1998. Painted as part of the West Belfast Festival, the mural depicts Che Guevara, scenes from Cuba, and Republican prisoners in the 1970s reading from Guevara's works.
8. Dromara Street, 1999. The Good Friday Agreement of 1997 promised, among other things, "freedom from sectarian harassment." This mural reproduces (left) the cover of the Agreement document, sent to every household, and counterposes the reality of continuing attacks on Catholics and their property.

9. Newtownards Road, East Belfast, 1999. Memorial mural to the 36th Ulster Division, formally the Ulster Volunteer Force, which was decimated at the Battle of the Somme in July, 1916.
10. Lenadoon Avenue, West Belfast, 1998. This memorial to Joe McDonnell, the fifth hunger-striker to die during the Republican hunger strike of 1981, contains the names of all ten strikers, as well as a quotation from McDonnell.
11. Mersey Street, East Belfast, 1996. Members of the Ulster Volunteer Force (UVF, another Loyalist paramilitary group) are shown in action. Above the main picture is the emblem of the UVF, the Red Hand of Ulster, a traditional Loyalist symbol, and the slogan "For God and Ulster."
12. Mersey Street, East Belfast, 1997. UFF members pose with weapons, along with the motto of the UFF's parent organization, UDA, "Quis separabit" (Who will separate), and the clenched Red Hand of Ulster. The letters "UYM" above refer to the Ulster Youth Movement, youth wing of the UDA.
13. Essex Street, South Belfast, 1998. In recent years, residents of the Nationalist Lower Ormeau Road community have protested the Orange Order marches through their area. The mural depicts a drummer from the nearby Ballynafeigh Loyal Orange Lodge (LOL), whose claim to a "right to march" leads to the imprisonment of local Nationalists.

THE **AGREEMENT**
"THE RIGHT TO FREEDOM FROM SECTARIAN HARASSMENT."

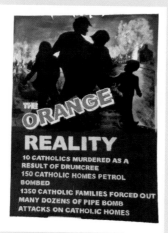

THE **ORANGE REALITY**
10 CATHOLICS MURDERED AS A RESULT OF DRUMCREE
150 CATHOLIC HOMES PETROL BOMBED
1350 CATHOLIC FAMILIES FORCED OUT
MANY DOZENS OF PIPE BOMB ATTACKS ON CATHOLIC HOMES

36TH ULSTER DIVISION
1916 1ST JULY
BATTLE OF THE SOMME.

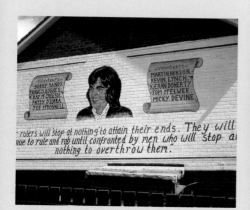

14. Iverna Street, South Belfast, 1998. Joe Bratty, leader of the UFF in South Belfast, was killed by the IRA shortly before the 1994 cease-fire.

15. Bonds Street, Derry, 1997. In this UDA mural, an avenging death figure moves among the bodies of dead Nationalists, with the war-ravaged Republican Bogside area of Derry in the background. The slogan above reads in part: "We determine the guilty, we decide the punishment." The image was adapted from an Iron Maiden album cover.

16. Ballymena, County Antrim, 1998. "King Billy" (William III) crosses the Boyne in 1690, during one of the battles which secured him the English crown. This was the predominant image in Loyalist murals in the first half of the 20th century.

1	2	3	4	5	6
7	8	9	10	11	12
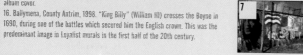					
13	14	15	16		

In this sense, the younger Republican mural tradition appears sturdier, more likely to survive the political transition than the Loyalists'. On both sides of the political debate, murals are painted by untrained artists, mostly men and boys, and often by ex-prisoners. If the murals are any measure, the Republicans seem to have embraced the peace process with greater gusto, though they're still quick to point out the shortcomings: Numerous murals depict the failure to establish a cross-community government, as well as the unfulfilled promise of the 1997 Good Friday Agreement – that everyone should live free of sectarian harassment.

Despite such criticism, it is in some sense easier for the Republicans to be expansive than the Loyalists. Starting as the underdogs, they now have everything to gain from radical political change, while the Loyalists and Unionists fear they have everything to lose. This relentless reciprocity continues to be voiced loud and clear on the walls of Northern Ireland.

Bill Rolston is a professor of sociology at the University of Ulster in Jordanstown, Northern Ireland. He is author of "Drawing Support: Murals in the North of Ireland" and "Drawing Support 2: Murals of War and Peace" (Beyond the Pale Publications, Belfast, 1992 and 1995). For information on these books, see Beyond the Pale Web site: www.btpale.ie

A POSTCARD FROM THE EDGE
Having a wonderful time! How was your summer?

1. Whiterock Road, West Belfast, 1994. This light-hearted mural, painted in the lead-up to the IRA cease-fire of 1994, depicts British soldiers being carried by doves back to England from Ireland.
2. Ardoyne Avenue, South Belfast, 1999. Human rights lawyer Rosemary Nelson was killed by Loyalists in 1999, ten years after the death of another human rights lawyer, Pat Finucane. The mural calls for an international investigation into allegations of police collusion in the deaths, and demands the disbandment of the RUC (Royal Ulster Constabulary, the local 90-percent-Protestant police force).
3. Finbank Gardens, South Belfast, 1998. Loyalist prisoners are depicted on the prison walls, along with names of local Loyalist prisoners, emblems of the Ulster Defence Association (UDA) and Ulster Freedom Fighters (UFF), and the letters "POW," for prisoners of war.
4. Lenadoon Avenue, West Belfast, 1996. This mural depicts the mythological Celtic northern warrior, Cuchulain. Alongside and above are the names and portraits of Irish Republican Army volunteers from the local area who have died in combat. Below are the crests of the four provinces of Ireland, and the word "Saoirse" (freedom).

5. Beechmount Grove, West Belfast, 1997. Sinn Fein president Gerry Adams won the seat for the constituency of West Belfast in 1983, lost it later to the Social Democratic and Labour Party, but won it back in 1997. A roving mural of Adams in the lead-up to the 1997 election is shown in the foreground, as another mural, depicting the similarity between the political struggles in the North of Ireland and the Basque country/Euskadi (in Spain) is unveiled in the background.
6. United South Link, West Belfast, 1998. This mural was painted for the bicentenary of the United Irishmen (Na hÉireannaigh Aontaithe), a revolutionary Republican organization. The slogan – "It is new strung and shall be heard" – refers to the harp as a symbol of the United Irishmen's struggle.
7. Shiels Street, West Belfast, 1998. Painted as part of the West Belfast Festival, and unveiled by the Cuban ambassador to the European Union, the mural depicts Che Guevara, scenes from Cuba, and Republican prisoners in the 1970s reading from Guevara's works.
8. Dromara Street, 1999. The Good Friday Agreement of 1997 promised, among other things, "freedom from sectarian harassment." This mural reproduces (left) the cover of the Agreement document, sent to every household, and counterposes the reality of continuing attacks on Catholics and their property.

9. Newtownards Road, East Belfast, 1999. Memorial mural to the 36th Ulster Division, formally the Ulster Volunteer Force, which was decimated at the Battle of the Somme in July, 1916.
10. Lenadoon Avenue, West Belfast, 1998. This memorial to Joe McDonnell, the fifth hunger-striker to die during the Republican hunger strike of 1981, contains the names of all ten strikers, as well as a quotation from McDonnell.
11. Mersey Street, East Belfast, 1996. Members of the Ulster Volunteer Force (UVF, another Loyalist paramilitary group) are shown in action. Above the main picture is the emblem of the UVF, the Red Hand of Ulster, a traditional Loyalist symbol, and the slogan "For God and Ulster."
12. Mersey Street, East Belfast, 1997. UFF members pose with weapons, along with the motto of the UFF's parent organization, UDA, "Quis separabit" (Who will separate), and the clenched Red Hand of Ulster. The letters "UYM" above refer to the Ulster Youth Movement, youth wing of the UDA.
13. Essex Street, South Belfast, 1998. In recent years, residents of the Nationalist Lower Ormeau Road community have protested the Orange Order marches through their area. The mural depicts a drummer from the nearby Ballynafeigh Loyal Orange Lodge (LOL), whose claim to a "right to march" leads to the imprisonment of local Nationalists.

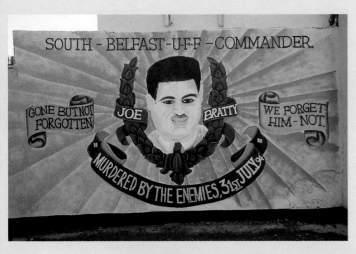

14. Iverna Street, South Belfast, 1998. Joe Bratty, leader of the UFF in South Belfast, was killed by the IRA shortly before the 1994 cease-fire.
15. Bonds Street, Derry, 1997. In this UDA mural, an avenging death figure moves among the bodies of dead Nationalists, with the war-ravaged Republican Bogside area of Derry in the background. The slogan above reads in part: "We determine the guilty, we decide the punishment." The image was adapted from an Iron Maiden album cover.
16. Ballymena, County Antrim, 1998. "King Billy" (William III) crosses the Boyne in 1690, during one of the battles which secured him the English crown. This was the predominant image in Loyalist murals in the first half of the 20th century.

1	2	3	4	5	6
7	8	9	10	11	12

13	14	15	16

JAZZ COMPOSITIONS
SWISS DESIGNER NIKLAUS TROXLER'S MUSIC FESTIVAL POSTERS UNLEASH A SILENT TORRENT OF GRAPHIC SOUNDS

BY TIM RICH

Our eyes lock. Her long, dark lashes open wide as she surveys me. My train has drifted to a halt and I sit here, motionless, separated from her by a thin sheet of glass. In the distance, a chainsaw gnaws at something hard. The wind gently ruffles her thick brown hair. She tosses her head back and a bell clangs out across the muddy, trodden field. The train hisses, scrapes, then edges onward. She eyes the wheels and lets out a phlegmy "moo."

I've arrived in the Luzerner Hinterland, central Switzerland, home to farming, logging, and one of Europe's most consistently excellent poster designers, Niklaus Troxler. This isn't chocolate-box country; this is real, working Switzerland.

I get to Troxler's handsome chalet-style property in Willisau (population 7,000). He greets me with a broad smile and ushers me into the house that serves as home for his family (his wife and three daughters) and his studio (one assistant and one trainee).

Troxler, 53, was born and raised here in Willisau, the second eldest of five brothers and sisters and the son of a car paint-sprayer. "I think the paint-spraying was the first influence of colour on me," he says. "I always liked to watch how my father mixed up the colours and I liked the smell, too. It's just like the smell when I'm silk-screening colours now."

As a boy, Troxler wanted to become a car designer, but an apprenticeship as a typesetter diverted his energies into typography and printing. He completed his training and in 1967 took up a place at the design school (Schule für Gestaltung) in Luzern. He found debate and inspiration there, with the dominant Josef Müller-Brockmann-inspired culture of rationality, simplicity, and typography enduring a bombardment by the charismatic colourings and eccentricities of the outside world. To a young Troxler, pop art was more exciting than Akzidenz Grotesk, so, despite the strictures of his tutors, he was soon employing everything from hand lettering and Cooper Black to that spawn of the devil, felt-tip pens. "It was important for me not to be a Swiss designer," he says. And how.

Typography guru Hans-Rudolf Lutz arrived at the college in 1969 and encouraged his students to explore and experiment, but an even greater influence was already at work on Troxler. Having organized concerts in Willisau since 1966, he was now immersed in the world of free-form jazz. Time spent working in Paris after college gave him close contact not only with clients (including book publisher CLA Editions and "Revue Psychologique") but with jazz musicians, and when he returned home a year later he found it a fertile place to cultivate both relationships.

By 1975, Troxler's concerts had turned into a major festival. Every year since then, he has created posters for the event itself and for the individual performances. The result: a body of work stretching over 25 years that is remarkable not just because Troxler is effectively designer, client, and customer/jazz aficionado all at once; and not just because it is so rare for one designer to produce work for one event for such a long period of time – but also because the character of the work created is so varied in concept and style.

I ask him whether the multiple client-designer-aficionado personality he brings to the drawing board helps or hinders the creative process. "It helps," he says, in eloquent, considered tones. "It all works together in my head. I simply

Photo: Emanuel Ammon

think to myself, 'What is this event that is coming to me here?'"

He never consults the musicians involved, so his greatest challenge is not to appeal to the sensibilities of a "client" but to ensure that his own approach is fresh. "The greatest pressure is everything that you've already done. You have to free your head so you're like a child."

He has more than met the challenge. Look through the recent book on his work, "Jazz Blvd" (Lars Müller Publishers, 1999), and you see the evolution of an extraordinary graphic language. Early on, there are the scribblings and scrawlings of the young maverick, with all sorts of influences at large: pop art, Magritte, Milton Glaser, Heinz Edelmann's "Yellow Submarine". But you can also trace an assured, almost classicist handling of typography and the first flowerings of more idiosyncratic illustrative styles and devices. For example, the European

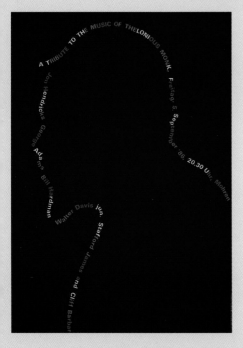

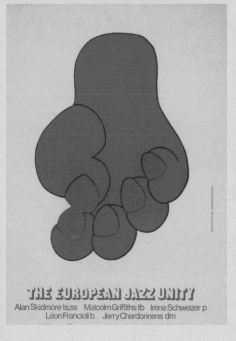

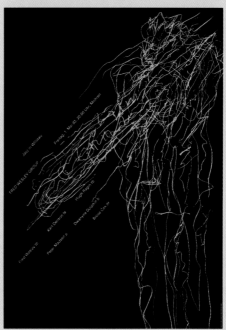

1. Poster for "A Tribute to the Music of Thelonious Monk," 1986. Client: Jazz in Willisau.
2. Poster for jazz trio Bassdrumbone, 1999. Client: Jazz in Willisau.
3. Poster for Cecil Taylor solo performance, 1989. Client: Jazz in Willisau.
4. Poster for The European Jazz Unity, 1972. Client: Jazz in Willisau.
5. "Dead Trees," personal work, 1992.
6. Poster for the Fred Wesley Group, 1992. Client: Jazz in Willisau.
7. Poster for a performance of Italian musicians Gianluigi Trovesi and Gianni Coscia, 1999. Client: Jazz in Willisau.
8. Poster for the McCoy Tyner Sextet, 1980. Client: Jazz in Willisau.
9. Poster for performance of "Jazz Meets India," 1983. Client: Jazz in Willisau.
10. 1998 New Year's poster for Siebdruck Bosch, a silk-screen printer.
11. Poster for saxophonist Tim Berne, 1998. Client: Jazz in Willisau.
12. Poster for Ned Rothenberg's Sync, 1999. Client: Jazz in Willisau.
13. Poster for Jamaaladeen Tacuma's Brotherzone, 1998. Client: Jazz in Willisau.
14. 1999 New Year's poster for silk-screen printer Siebdruck Bosch.
15. Poster for the 1998 Jazz in Willisau Festival. Client: Jazz in Willisau.
16. Poster for Werner Ludi Sunnymoon and the Vienna Art Orchestra. Client: Jazz in Willisau.
17. Poster for the 1999 Jazz in Willisau Festival. Client: Jazz in Willisau.

1	2	3	4	5	6
7	8	9	10	11	12
13	14	15	16	17	

Jazz Unity poster (Fig. 4) of 1972 gives the first outing to a pared-down approach that is subsequently evolved in numerous works, including "Cecil Taylor Solo" (Fig. 3) in 1989 and "Dead Trees" (Fig. 5) in 1992. Then there's his coloured line drawing, seen first in 1977 with a joint Dewey Redman Quartet and Marion Brown Quartet poster and developed until it reaches a frenetic climax in 1992 with posters for the Fred Wesley Group (Fig. 6) and the main festival.

And just when you might be starting to form a theory that Troxler is most interesting for the diversity and elasticity of his illustration, you come across two pieces of typographic mastery: "McCoy Tyner Sextet" (Fig. 8, 1980) and a typographic portrait of Thelonious Monk (Fig. 1, 1986). Countless other stylistic and technical devices can be seen entering the Troxler range and later enjoying delightful reincarnation. Geometric shapes, dense line drawings, visual puns – the breadth is dizzying, as is his dexterity with symbols, not least his handling of that key jazz icon, the saxophone. Troxler's saxes come at you as snakes, a gin bottle, a telephone, a skyscraper – always with relevance to the artist or event promoted. "Jazz Blvd" is also a wilderness where beasts tread. Alligators, fish, pigs, birds, and black panthers all appear in its pages. Each symbol has relevance to the concert, but they also convey something of the wild and instinctive nature of great jazz in general. Even his cows seem to want to syncopate the tinkling of their bells.

It is tempting to employ musical metaphors when describing Troxler's art, but one should be wary of loose parallels. You could say he is the jazz musician of the poster – extemporizing, personal, expressive. Well, yes, his work can be spontaneous, he does offer a personal response, and his posters are certainly expressive. But there are limitations. The nature of his chosen form and that of a musician have important differences and have different relationships to time. The jazz-poster designer talks to people about an upcoming performance – the future. The musician performs to an audience there to experience the moment – the present.

The jazz poster is silent and still; jazz music sounds and flows. They are different arts. And yet a great poster can break beyond its conventional role. It can delight and entertain. "All art constantly aspires towards the condition of music," declared 19th-century critic and academic Walter Pater. At its best, when it performs in the present and delights the viewer, Troxler's art achieves something close to that condition.

There is also kinship between the initial stage of Troxler's design process and the act of performing music. "The best thing is when I think, not 'Oh, I want to do a poster,' but when I just like to play," he says, warming to the subject. "I don't think in a format, I think about the subject. It's about playing with what's in my head. Then I get more concrete and I start to figure out an idea."

Getting more concrete means acting less like a performer and more like a composer. He crafts the graphic language of the medium – the patterns, shapes, textures, and colours – just as the writer of music orders the composition. "I learn a lot from music," says Troxler. "The structure, the rhythm, the order, the interaction – there's always something different."

His use of colour is the most spectacular example of this musicality. In "A Tribute to the Music of Thelonious Monk," for example, the colours selected for each letter don't denote the beginning and end of each word but instead create an easy flow that hints at the feel of Monk's music. Similarly, his poster for the Lake, Hopkins and Cyrille trio in 1992 places lines of red, yellow, and green among many lines of blue, suggesting three elements playing within a system.

I ask him if he ever created a poster and subsequently thought it was better than the concert it was for. He smiles: "Yes . . . but the opposite, too – the poster hasn't been good enough for the concert. But I don't feel I have to explain the music on the poster. It has to be a poster, it has to announce, it has to interest people in the music, but I don't need to explain. It's like the elephant in "Jazz Meets India" (Fig. 9, 1983) – it can be enough for someone to see the poster without seeing the elephant. It's a little game with the audience. First, of course, I have to get them to

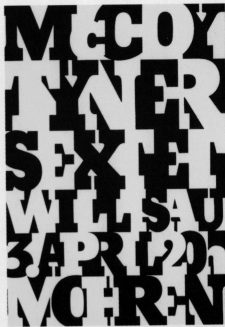

Ein farbiges Jahr bei Bösch Siebdruck AG Stans/Luzern

1. Poster for "A Tribute to the Music of Thelonious Monk," 1986. Client: Jazz in Willisau.
2. Poster for jazz trio Bassdrumbone, 1999. Client: Jazz in Willisau.
3. Poster for Cecil Taylor solo performance, 1989. Client: Jazz in Willisau.
4. Poster for The European Jazz Unity, 1972. Client: Jazz in Willisau.
5. "Dead Trees," personal work, 1992.
6. Poster for the Fred Wesley Group, 1992. Client: Jazz in Willisau.
7. Poster for a performance of Italian musicians Gianluigi Trovesi and Gianni Coscia, 1999. Client: Jazz in Willisau.
8. Poster for the McCoy Tyner Sextet, 1980. Client: Jazz in Willisau.
9. Poster for performance of "Jazz Meets India," 1983. Client: Jazz in Willisau.
10. 1998 New Year's poster for Siebdruck Bosch, a silk-screen printer.
11. Poster for saxophonist Tim Berne, 1998. Client: Jazz in Willisau.
12. Poster for Ned Rothenberg's Sync, 1999. Client: Jazz in Willisau.
13. Poster for Jamaaladeen Tacuma's Brotherzone, 1998. Client: Jazz in Willisau.
14. 1999 New Year's poster for silk-screen printer Siebdruck Bosch.
15. Poster for the 1998 Jazz in Willisau Festival. Client: Jazz in Willisau.
16. Poster for Werner Ludi Sunnymoon and the Vienna Art Orchestra. Client: Jazz in Willisau.
17. Poster for the 1999 Jazz in Willisau Festival. Client: Jazz in Willisau.

1	2	3	4	5	6
7	8	9	10	11	12
13	14	15	16	17	

look at the poster and that's never easy. No one goes into the street to see a poster. But then we can play."

Troxler doesn't just do jazz. He's produced a best-selling watch for Swatch, packaging for luxury-goods companies, and numerous large-scale illustrative works on buildings. He's also created posters on political and social subjects, from child protection to debates about Switzerland and the European Union, as well as "Dead Trees." While these maintain the excellence of his jazz works, his occasional forays into other arts do not.

I remark that his theatre posters lack the engagement and charisma of his musical work. "You're right, in the music I feel freer," he responds. "I know more, I am more involved. I am always very pleased when I do a good piece that is not a jazz poster because it is more difficult for me. Sometimes it's not so easy with clients, especially theatres. You have to sell it to many people. Sometimes there is a compromise."

The technically minded might be interested to learn that Troxler continues to use all sorts of methods, from scribbling to mousing, and it's impossible to work out what is done on computer and what is not. He takes delight in showing me a poster with a whiff of the Mac about it, then says "Not this!" Next, he points out a crazed illustration that looks like it came direct from the soul. "This is done on the computer!" he laughs.

But more interesting than the how of his craft is the why of his format. I ask if he ever feels limited by posters. "I paint as well, but it's not that important to me. I think the greatest work is to do a poster." I ponder aloud that it's strange how few great artists make great posters (Miró, for one), and how few great poster designers make great paintings. "I don't have a problem with that," he says. "For me, my painting is a private thing. Galleries invite me to exhibit my paintings and sometimes I say, 'Well, okay, but I would like my posters here, too.' I love posters!"

Recently, Troxler has been experimenting with triple-width formats ("very expensive") and, partly as a result of his 18 months as professor of communication design and illustration at the Academy of Fine Arts in Stuttgart, Germany, he has been developing a more immediate approach, too. "I think the students have helped me because they criticize my work – I learn from them. When I look at posters out there in the world, I think they have so much technique. I want more directness. I want it to be like an action, a graffiti."

Interview over, Troxler takes me on a brief tour of Willisau. It's the pretty side of pleasant: a market town with nice medieval bits surrounded by steep meadowy hills. Troxler's signature is everywhere, from the town sign to the bright illustrations on school buildings; a poster on a billboard site that is his to use freely, and the hall and field where his festival takes place. Little wonder that he was made an Honorary Citizen here in 1994.

"I've always had contact with musicians and other designers," he says, waving to a friend in the street, "so I don't think it's so important where you work, I think it's more important to be open." Indeed, it's amazing where openness can take you.

All work shown was designed and illustrated by Niklaus Troxler.

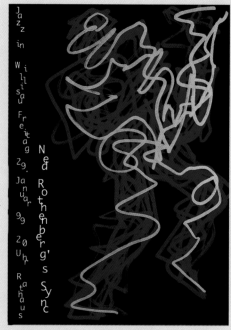

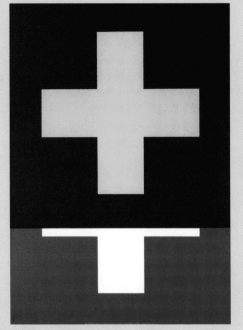

1. Poster for "A Tribute to the Music of Thelonious Monk," 1986. Client: Jazz in Willisau.

2. Poster for jazz trio Bassdrumbone, 1999. Client: Jazz in Willisau.

3. Poster for Cecil Taylor solo performance, 1989. Client: Jazz in Willisau.

4. Poster for The European Jazz Unity, 1972. Client: Jazz in Willisau.

5. "Dead Trees," personal work, 1992.

6. Poster for the Fred Wesley Group, 1992. Client: Jazz in Willisau.

7. Poster for a performance of Italian musicians Gianluigi Trovesi and Gianni Coscia, 1999. Client: Jazz in Willisau.

8. Poster for the McCoy Tyner Sextet, 1980. Client: Jazz in Willisau.

9. Poster for performance of "Jazz Meets India," 1983. Client: Jazz in Willisau.

10. 1998 New Year's poster for Siebdruck Bosch, a silk-screen printer.

11. Poster for saxophonist Tim Berne, 1998. Client: Jazz in Willisau.

12. Poster for Ned Rothenberg's Sync, 1999. Client: Jazz in Willisau.

13. Poster for Jamaaladeen Tacuma's Brotherzone, 1998. Client: Jazz in Willisau.

14. 1999 New Year's poster for silk-screen printer Siebdruck Bosch.

15. Poster for the 1998 Jazz in Willisau Festival. Client: Jazz in Willisau.

16. Poster for Werner Ludi Sunnymoon and the Vienna Art Orchestra. Client: Jazz in Willisau.

17. Poster for the 1999 Jazz in Willisau Festival. Client: Jazz in Willisau.

1	2	3	4	5	6
7	8	9	10	11	12
13	14	15	16	17	

EUROTONGUE
AS CLOSER INTEGRATION OF THE EUROPEAN UNION CONTINUES, IS THERE A NEED FOR A SINGLE EUROPEAN LANGUAGE? HOW MIGHT DESIGNERS CONTRIBUTE?

BY QUENTIN NEWARK

In January 2000, the first notes and coins of the Euro, the single European currency, appeared. One of the most cherished dreams of all those who had wanted a united Europe became real. Next, tax rates will gradually become uniform and a single European army is under discussion. We already have one flag, one Parliament, one overarching set of laws: How soon can it be before we have one language, and with it, a new alphabet, or new typography?

Of course, in reality, "local" languages – English, Spanish, German, French, Italian, Dutch, and so on – will probably always remain. After all, there are still strong bands of Catalan and Breton speakers, outnumbered in their own countries by Spanish and French speakers, respectively.

But we will need some common way to discuss and describe the things that we will soon share, including many of the artifacts for which designers are responsible: packaging, advertising, signage, TV graphics, and official documents.

The obvious language, one might think, is English; surely, most Europeans speak some English already? Not according to one survey (Van der Sandt, 1989), which found that only six percent of the total population had a "truly correct comprehension of the English language [in Western Europe]," which "falls noticeably beneath our most pessimistic expectations."

Anyway, the problem is more complex than merely picking a language from the selection on offer: "Closer integration" sounds smooth and natural, but the countries are not like a newly married couple, eager to coil together, full of understanding and generosity. The reality is that the nations are more like prisoners forced into the same cell: suspicious, territorial, with any sign of backing down seen as a weakness that will bring terrible retribution in the showers. Traditional animosities still simmer under the surface; the countries of Europe may have decided to make a go of it together, but to the extent of officially adopting another's language? Never.

Efforts to select a common language have already met with failure more than once. In 1946, at a conference of World War II allies to discuss the economic rebuilding of Europe, the U.S. and Britain proposed that English be the accepted common language at the meeting. Charles de Gaulle insisted that French, as the traditional language of international diplomacy, should be the language used. Britain's Prime Minister Clement Attlee agreed that, yes, French was a wonderful language – for menus. The conference was held in English, but the remark did nothing for relations between Britain and France.

One might think that, today, the countries would be a little less precious than in that tense, postwar atmosphere. But during Finland's recent presidency of the European Union, Germany insisted that if Finnish was going to be recognized as an official language for the length of the presidency, alongside French and English, so should German be. If it wasn't, they said, they would stay away from a critical summit. A thorny issue indeed, but how best to resolve it?

If we can't use English, could we use BASIC (British, American, Scientific, International, Commercial) English? C.K. Ogden's 1929 language is a subset of English containing just 850 words (the average college student has a vocabulary of 12,000 words). The language consists of words describing operations, things, and qualities, and according to its creator, could be learned in 40 hours by anyone who spoke a Germanic or Romance European language. While perhaps not appropriate for poetry, it should be more than adequate for signage and packaging – even some technical literature. Alas, it is still English, which might make it unacceptable in the current political climate.

With it go other "reduced" languages such as Simplified English and the Caterpillar Tractor Company's 1971 language, Caterpillar Fundamental English. Everyone understands road signs and airport pictograms, so perhaps these point the way forward. After all, hieroglyphs were used by ancient cultures successfully for thousands of years, and arguably the longest-lasting language in the world – Chinese – has a pictographic alphabet.

Could all Europeans learn a set of pictographic building blocks through which simple ideas could be expressed? Probably, but the inhibiting problem with visual alphabets is expressing even slightly sophisticated ideas. Icons are fine for expressing ideas that are physical. The icon matches something we can see in the physical world; it is in effect a drawing, an image; man, woman. But the problem begins when you try to show ideas that are not physical; how do you show "marriage" rather than just "relationship," or "older Spanish man, from a tacky rock band, and younger, wealthy Slavic woman?"

It is the ability of words to describe subtlety and nuance, in such a short space and so quickly, that makes them such efficient carriers of information. Picture languages need far more room and time to do the same job; whereas our alphabet uses just 26 letters combined to make different words, the Chinese pictographic alphabet has 3,000 characters, and even they are combined to make more complex words. And there were some 5,000 ancient Egyptian hieroglyphs.

While it is diverting to think about new kinds of alphabet, the first step toward some sort of common European language has actually been taken, and it has been driven by soup and chocolate. As the Union expands – potentially to more than 20 countries in the next three years – the list of languages grows: Czech, Polish, Romanian, Hungarian, Slovakian. Soft-drink cans and packs of batteries, with their already long strips of translated ingredients on the back, will not get any bigger. There will be more and more text, and less and less space, for branding and pictures of the product; we will be in danger of entirely typographic packaging (which, however good that sounds to designers, will probably harm sales in the long run). In an effort to deal with this, all of the most common ingredients listed on packs will be spelled out in one language – Latin. So "milk", "mælk", "milch", "latte", "lait" all turn into the Latin word – "lac". Of course, this is fine if you were once invaded by the Romans and they left you their linguistic legacy, but for the Poles and Finns, Latin might as well be double Dutch. Latin is unlikely to find wider currency outside the little 6-point world of packaging, if only because it has so much cultural baggage. The Germans resisted Latin culture fiercely for 2,000 years, inventing Gothic architecture and Protestantism in the process. So rather than reaching back to a mother tongue, perhaps we could go further to join languages and make a daughter tongue.

Kuragon, Esperanto! Invented in 1887 by a polyglot Jewish Pole called Ludwig Lazarus Zamenhoff, Esperanto means "hope". It consists of a lot of root words, which are combined or changed with suffixes and prefixes. It is part French, part Latin, German, and Slavic. In case you thought it was confined to the margins of history as a slightly risible experiment, Bill Auld, a Scottish poet who writes exclusively in Esperanto, was recently shortlisted for the Nobel Prize for Literature. An estimated 15 million people speak this language without a country. Quite amazingly, as a sign of how successfully it works, in 1966 a petition with a million signatures proposing Esperanto as the official language for the whole world was put to a vote at the United Nations. It was only barely defeated.

ANYONE FOR ESPERANTO?

Nobel-nominated Scottish poet Bill Auld writes in Esperanto. Here is an extract in Esperanto and with a translation in English from Auld's most highly regarded work, cited by the Nobel Prize committee, "La Infana Raso" (The Infant Race). Exploring ideas about the brotherhood of man and utopias, it could be seen as a comment on European Union. It's called "Links."

Kuragon, homofratog de ciu hautkoloro
la tempmirago, kiu dialgis nin damninde
nin fine rekunigoa!
Kag dume, palpe, blinde,
ni venas, iras, eroj en ceno kies finon,
ne formas ni nek vidos, Kuragon kaj obstinon!

Courage, my brothers of every hue,
the time mirage that scattered us unkindly will reunite us!
Meanwhile, feebly, blindly,
we come and go, links in a chain whose end,
we are not and shall not see, take heart, be strong!

Esperanto aside, I firmly believe there will eventually be a single European language, if we wait long enough. It will be a creole, an alloy, a salad. Indeed, this article is written in a language that is a perfect example of how this will work. English is a blend of two languages, Teutonic Anglo-Saxon and Latinate Norman French, with notable words and phrases from Norse, Celtic, modern French, Urdu, and Chinese. The biggest transition took about 300 years, from 1066 when the Normans invaded Anglo-Saxon England to around 1300 when a language that was recognizably English was first spoken. While this might seem like a vast time span, it is only five times the period from World War II to the present.

NOT SPOKEN HERE

Although there are currently 15 member states in the European Union, there are only 11 official languages. This is because several countries share a main language; Germany and Austria both speak German, for example. The Union has a harshly reductive impulse when it comes to language. The term "expansion" refers to more countries joining in order to expand the single marketplace: Their languages will not be welcome. Rather than expand our linguistic culture, the official desire is to abbreviate it. The "language" of each country is taken very literally to be the majority language: All the other languages, spoken by millions of Europeans, are excluded. So no Basque or Catalan, no Gaelic or Breton, no Yiddish or Romany.

Perhaps it is best to see language less as the protected possession of a nation state and more as the currency of a cultural and economic area that ignores national boundaries. English is the language most spoken throughout Europe, and indeed the world. Estimates vary, but about a billion people will be speaking English this year; that is utility that is impossible to resist.

The next most important language in European terms is German. Germany is the true heart of Europe, both geographically and in terms of financial and political influence. German is spoken by 100 million people, and it forms the root of several other European languages – Dutch, Flemish, Danish, and Swedish. It is the European language most favoured and used by a further 20 million – Czechs, Poles, Romanians, Hungarians, and Russians. Any new tongue will almost certainly use English as its base, combined with German. The other prominent nations, France and Italy, will find their vocabulary used as colour to describe the fine things in life like food and art, supplementing the new practical and guttural verbal currency. Every expensive restaurant in England already prints its menu in French. These delicious words will simply increase the quantity of Latinate words already present in English. Greek had its input, 2,500 years ago, and I can confidently predict that the Slavic languages, Finnish, Basque, and Latvian, will have no influence on the new tongue whatsoever. Oh, and by the way, all Americans will speak this new creole. How can they not? The slow development and the pressure of economics will ensure it.

It might be a little way off, but designers will be dragged into this new world along with everyone else. They will not only need to speak the new language, whatever it turns out to be, but also use its typefaces and understand its eccentricities. The words and names of everything they know now will change; they might well have to go to the Rathaus to pay their local tax, vote on their komputer, swim in the local piscine.

So the new language the designers of the 21st century will be attempting to develop typographic rules for will be recognizably English with logical and predictable German-style grammar and lots of Latinate words. What might we call such a language, using the usual endings: Eurish, Euroea, Europese, Europan, or given the cultural aggressiveness of the French, Eurench perhaps? My favorite possibility is the shortest and simplest, if not the most auspicious: Eurin.

UNIVERSAL UNIVERSAL

How will we write our new single European language? How many letters will it have, and what will they look like? Most of the much-reported developments in typeface design of the last few years are changes or modifications at a surface level: changes to minor aspects of how the letters are drawn (drawn like chrome or frankensteined from two fonts), or drawing them so that they are barely recognizable, or replacing them with other shapes like photographs or fingers (much like the infamous Mr. Bear, the Letraset alphabet of the 1970s that was made up of polar bears).

Almost no one recently has repeated or taken further the thinking of the early modernists like Herbert Bayer and Jan Tschichold, who saw that a substantial redesign depended on understanding the big historical developments that lie inside the alphabet. Both of their most successful alphabets were called Universal. And they both felt that the curious doubling of the alphabet into "lower" and "uppercase" could

be challenged and reversed – after all, Bayer argued, speech does not use capital letters. This allowed them to reduce the quantity of letters and settle on a simple set of forms. Bayer used only lowercase for his font (1); Tschichold selected one case by choosing from both cases (2). The simplification of the forms was not a stylistic choice, but deeply felt. They believed in rational thinking. Rational as in dispassionate, mathematical, pure. Le Corbusier pointed at the influence most clearly when he said, "The engineer, inspired by the law of economy and governed by mathematical calculation, puts us in accord with universal law."

Two other notable new editions of the alphabet are those by the Pole Wladyslav Strzeminski and the Dutchman Wim Crouwel. Rather than reinvent or reselect letters, both these typefaces involve editing the existing letterforms. Strzeminski's letters rely on each other to supply the visual information we need to read them. You can see how, in the illustration shown (3), the back of the lowercase "a" is supplied by the "n." Crouwel's decision-making is similar, although less radical and therefore more legible (4). The geometry is as far as it can be from the hand-drawn pen shapes of the alphabet we are used to; this is typography made with the ethos of machines.

NO ACCENTS, PLEASE

The next time someone tries to be clever and says that Chinese is the world's most-spoken language, laugh. It is not. There are eight spoken forms in Chinese, some completely unintelligible to large numbers of Chinese: A native of Guangdong has no idea what someone from Beijing is saying. What is powerful and unique is that there is only one alphabet. A book in Chinese can be read by a billion people.

If we are going to develop one tongue, like the Chinese we will need one uniform alphabet. We are close: The Latin alphabet is used throughout Europe, although its form is modified from country to country with accents (and a few additional letters for the Slavic and Greek alphabets). But are these features, which make foreign languages appear so intimidating, really necessary? After all, there are no accents in Braille for the blind, understood by millions. In fact, could Braille be a candidate for the new universal font? It has the advantage of looking quite fantastic, way more radical than even Wim Crouwel's best efforts; it has no accents, only one case – no division into upper- and lower-), and it is fast to learn and wonderfully easy to reproduce.

WELL, IT LOOKS SIMPLE

Otto Neurath, a Viennese social scientist, devised a picture system in the 1920s. It started as a fancy way of drawing charts in dry, heavy sociological textbooks, a laudable aim. Neurath had grand ambitions: He believed that pictures are objective – no cultural or regional differences – and could therefore be understood by anyone. (Things were simple in 1920s Austria; he obviously never tried to find a toilet in a Saudi airport, where the icon of a man is dressed in a long dish-dash.) He called his protolanguage ISOTYPE, which he explained as an acronym of "International System of Typographic Picture Education." But this is thinking backwards – the real origin is etymological: The Greek word "isos" means equal and "typos" means form. His work never developed far beyond a theory, although the geometric simplicity of the drawing style, and the assertions about universality, were to influence the development of later symbol systems, such as Otl Aicher's 1972 Munich Olympics signs and the bland, sexless silhouette figures peopling every airport.

GUESSING GAME

In 1966, two Swedes, Jan Oloo Stundstrom and Sunniva Kellquist, won a competition to design an international ideogrammatic alphabet. The graphic resolution of the icons is very successful and handsome: Each emblem is a ring with very elementary shapes inside it. The thinking by the two designers at first seems clear. "Port," for example, shows a boat-like shape entering a harbour-like curve. And "money" is clever-two equal bars. This exactly parallels the idea of money as an exchange system, the value of labour, or a service or a product having an equivalent money value. But in important areas, the combined imagination of the two designers lets us down. Why is the icon for "women" two dots? Are they nipples? Ovaries? Pig's nostrils? In the end, the scheme fails in the way that all picture-based writing systems fail: It is unable to sustain its own simple logic as the concepts it tries to depict become more complex or more ambiguous.

Quentin Newark is a partner in the design company Atelier Works. He has written for "Graphics International" and "Circular", the journal of the Typographic Circle.

1. Herbert Bayer's Universal typeface.
2. Jan Tschichold's Universal typeface.
3. Wladyslav Strzeminski's circles and straight lines typeface.
4. Wim Crouwel's square New typeface.
5. Braille for "European Union."
6. The elementary principles of ISOTYPE: a shoe, a factory, a shoe factory.
7. Otto Neurath looked at life from a Viennese café, before the collapse of European imperialism. In his system, Europeans are depicted as wearing smart Homburg hats, South Americans sport sombreros, Africans have sculpted hair, Indians all wear turbans, and the rice-planting Chinese are identified by straw "coolie" sun hats.
8. What kind of ideograms would Neurath devise to depict the complex ideas of today's Europe? Here are some possible interpretations of mad-cow disease, the French and English intellectuals' disapproval of American cultural imperialism, and Eastern European refugees.
9. Icons for a port, money, and women.

    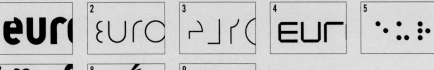

JANUARY 2000
£4.25 UK/$10.95 US
A CENTAUR PUBLICATION

CREATIVE REVIEW IS A VALUABLE RESOURCE IN AN INDUSTRY IN CONSTANT EVOLUTION. IT'S THE BEST SOURCE.
NEVILLE BRODY, RESEARCH STUDIOS

YOU CAN'T LOOK AT DESIGN IN A VACUUM, YOU NEED A BALANCED PERSPECTIVE WHICH IS WHAT CREATIVE REVIEW OFFERS. REFRESHING AND INFORMATIVE.
BILL CAHAN, CAHAN AND ASSOCIATES

AN ESSENTIAL READ FOR ANY OPEN MINDED PERSON IN THE CREATIVE INDUSTRY.
VINCE FROST, FROST DESIGN

BE INSPIRED

For 20 years Creative Review has kept the world's creative community up to date on the developments that matter - the best new work, the people to watch, the latest tools, technologies and industry trends.

Spanning commercials, graphic design, new media, photography, film, typography, animation and music, our editorial focus is unique. You can be sure Creative Review will track the innovations you want to know about.

Every month subscribers receive a full colour magazine featuring over 100 images, access to our website at www.creative-review.co.uk plus our highly acclaimed CD-Rom.

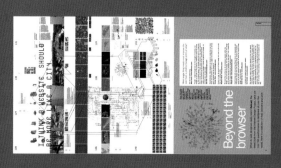

We are offering special subscription rates to European Design Annual readers. Claim 10% off the standard rates by quoting reference CREDA2000.

To subscribe: telephone +44 (0) 171 292 3703.
Fax +44 (0) 171 970 4099. Email crcirc@centaur.co.uk.
Mail Creative Review, 50 Poland Street, London W1V 4AX.

GOLDEN DRUM MAGAZINE — MAY 1999 · No.11

GOLDEN DRUM · OFFICIAL MAGAZINE OF THE NEW EUROPEAN ADVERTISING FESTIVAL, SLOVENIA · IMPRIME · SLOVENIA TAXE PERÇUE · ISSN · 1408 · 7818

Portorož – Port of Roses   Piran

The New Rhythms of the Golden Drum

Golden Drum '99
6th Advertising Festival of the New Europe
October, 4 – 8, 1999, Portorož – Port of Roses

GOLDEN DRUM MAGAZINE — NOVEMBER 1999 · No.15

GOLDEN DRUM · OFFICIAL MAGAZINE OF THE NEW EUROPEAN ADVERTISING FESTIVAL, SLOVENIA · IMPRIME · SLOVENIA TAXE PERÇUE · ISSN · 1408 · 7818

Golden Drum 1999
The New European Advertising – Ever More West of it's Past

Golden Drum for TV Ads and Leo Burnett Agency, Warsaw

Polish Agencies are the Absolute Winners

Golden Drum Magazine

The magazine of the marketing, advertising and design heroes of the New Europe.

The magazine of the best print ads, TV spots, advertising publications and posters from the New Europe.

The magazine of the members of the elite creative directors' club who have been awarded the Golden TAG Heuer Watches for the best advertising campaigns of the New Europe.

The Golden Drum Magazine is the official publication of **Golden Drum Advertising Festival of the New Europe.** The Golden Drum 2000, the 7th Advertising Festival of the New Europe will again take place in Portorož, Slovenia in October 2000.

It's motto, »An excellent education,
a fierce competition,
a wild party and
a tough challenge,«
will be as true as ever.

The Golden Drum features competitions in the following groups:
- TV ads
- Print ads
- Radio ads
- Web sites
- Social and charity advertising
- Advertising campaigns

If you are interested in all this and want to be in touch with the advertising and design scene of the New Europe give us a call or send us your mailing address.

You will join the 13,000 recipients of the Golden Drum Magazine who receive the publication 4 times per year free of charge!

Please contact Ms Petra Garin,
Executive Director of the Golden Drum Festival
Tel.: (+386-61) 139-6050
Fax: (+386-61) 133-9470
E-mail: info@goldendrum.com
http:www.goldendrum.com

i-jusi
Südafrikas Straxxdesign

Tapiro
Design aus der Lagunenstadt

Atelier Beinert
Feine Typografie-Lösungen

novum **VERPACKUNGSDESIGN**

05 / 99

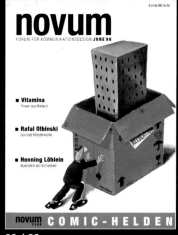

Vitamina
Power aus Mailand

Rafal Olbinski
Surreale Meisterwerke

Henning Löhlein
Illustration als Hochschulfach

novum **COMIC-HELDEN**

06 / 99

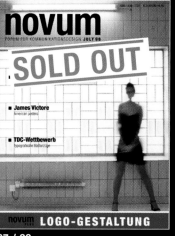

SOLD OUT

James Victore
American posters

TDC-Wettbewerb
typografische Maßarbeit

novum **LOGO-GESTALTUNG**

07 / 99

GGK Lo
Werbehighlights

Sonnoli
Italienischer Typo-Akrobat

SOLD OUT

Interbrand Newell & Sorrell
Londons Markenmacher

novum **BIER-WERBUNG**

08 / 99

Dadara
Illustrationen für Party-People

LCD Graphics
Konzepte fürs Web

Gregor Schuster
Fotografien für Trendprodukte

novum **ZIGARETTEN-WERBUNG**

09 / 99

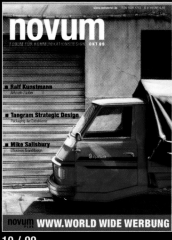

Ralf Kunstmann
Airbrush-Zauber

Tangram Strategic Design
Packaging der Extraklasse

Mike Salisbury
Effektives Brandthinking

novum **WWW.WORLD WIDE WERBUNG**

10 / 99

Anton Atzenhofer
Storyboards & Co.

[bis]
Innovative Typo-Werkstatt

Rex Design
Kreative Ideen aus Brasilien

novum **DESIGN FÜR AUDIO-CD�S**

11 / 99

Alexander Gnädinger
Digitale Schönheiten

Sign Design Award
Zeigen, wo es lang geht

häfelinger & wagner
Präzise Kommunikation

novum **KULTURELLE PLAKATE**

12 / 99

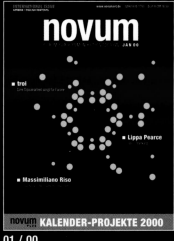

troi
Eine Opernarbeit sorgt für Furore

Lippa Pearce

Massimiliano Riso

novum **KALENDER-PROJEKTE 2000**

01 / 00

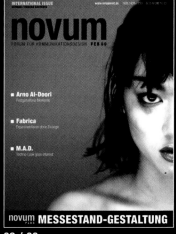

Arno Al-Doori
Festgehaltene Momente

Fabrica
Experimentieren ohne Zwänge

M.A.D.
Techno-Look goes internet

novum **MESSESTAND-GESTALTUNG**

02 / 00

Chris Menke
Kreatives Multitalent

RSKA
Photodesign by Newcomers

Thirteen
Designpower aus Bristol

novum **EDITORIAL DESIGN**

03 / 00

novum
FORUM FÜR KOMMUNIKATIONSDESIGN

Don´t miss out on your subscription!

www.novumnet.de

Lineagrafica is a historical Italian graphic design magazine. Since fifty years the periodical has observed, with a critical eye, the development of the sector of graphic design. In recent years Lineagrafica has followed the digital revolution: an international observation of the new instruments of planning and design of new supports and new media, of the debate on the profession and its new languages.

Lineagrafica
towards new graphic design

NEW MOMENT

Magazine for Art & Advertising

NEW EUROPE - NEW CREATIVITY

New Moment Magazine for Art and Advertising in New Europe (ECE) is published twice a year, in English, in full colour on 150 pages.

The magazine presents an overview of the new creativity in advertising in the New Europe (ECE), new ideas from the fields of art and the visual arts, philosophical

considerations of the ideas coming from societies in transition and its own projects in the fields of art and advertising.

NEW MOMENT MAGAZINE, No.12, 150 pages, price 30 DM.

New Moment, Bežigrad 10, 1000 Ljubljana, Slovenia.

www.newmoment-ideascampus.com

Telephone and fax numbers are listed with their international dialing codes. If dialing within a country, omit the international code and insert a zero ("0") before the number.

Studio Anselmi, Naples
tel: +39 081 200 663
fax: +39 081 552 8176
fig. 49 (p. 68)

Studio Falavigna, Milan
tel: +39 02 70638 475
fax: +39 02 706 00186
e-mail: cirofalavigna@public.it
figs. 15, 16 (p. 64); 51, 52 (p. 69)

Studio FM, Milan
tel: +39 02 655 2063
fax: +39 02 655 2673
e-mail: sergio.menichelli@iol.it
figs. 10-13 (p. 63); 22-24 (p. 65)

Studio Grafico Fausta Orecchio, Rome
tel: +33 06 320 1042
fax: +39 06 326 09088
e-mail: f.orecchio@tiscalinet.it
figs. 4, 6, 7 (p. 62); 18 (p. 64); 25, 26 (p. 65); 35 (p. 67)

Studio Magni, Ferrara
tel/fax: +39 0532 766 897
e-mail: studiomagnife@libero.it
lauramagnife@libero.it
fig. 30 (p. 66)

Studio Tam, Venezia
tel/fax: +39 041 522 6974
e-mail: camre@tin.it
figs. 42-44 (p. 68)

Studiotto, Rome
tel: +39 06 6848 909
fax: +39 06 841 7245
e-mail: c.otto@flashnet.it
fig. 54 (p. 69)

Vertigo Design, Rome
see under Ruggieri, Albert

Winkler & Noah, Rome
tel: +39 0347 0730559
fax: +39 06 51 60 29 64
e-mail: mariniraffaelli@libero.it
fig. 47 (p. 68)

LITHUANIA
jsc "LIEPA", Kaunas
tel/fax: +370 7 205294
e-mail: ausra.lisauskiene@org.ktu.lt
fig. 3 (p. 70)

RIC Ltd, Vilnius
tel: +370 2 685 314
fax: +370 2 685 317
e-mail: infos@ric.lt
figs. 1, 2 (p. 70)

The NETHERLANDS
Anker X Strybos, Utrecht
tel: +31 30 231 8288
+31 30 236 9159
e-mail: info@ankerxs.nl
figs. 16 (p. 76); 23 (p. 77)

Denkbeeld, Utrecht
tel: +31 30 231 7279
fax: +31 30 231 7307
e-mail: mail@denkbeeld.nl
fig. 1 (p. 74)

Fabrique, Delft
tel: +31 15 219 5610
fax: +31 15 219 5601
e-mail: marc@fabrique.nl
figs. 17-19 (p. 77)

Gervais, François, Amsterdam
tel: +31 20 623 7114
fax: +31 20 638 8892
fig. 16 (p. 76)

IRISK, Rotterdam
tel: +31 10 477 4707
e-mail: irisk@freeler.nl
internet: www.artconnection.nl
fig. 3 (p. 74)

KDSP Design bv, Amsterdam
tel: +31 20 530 8000
fax: +31 20 530 8080
e-mail: ksdp@ksdpdesign.nl
figs. 21, 22 (p. 77)

Limage Dangereuse, Rotterdam
tel: +31 10 476 4800
fax: +31 10 476 4880
e-mail: info@limage-dangereuse.nl
figs. 4, 5 (p. 74); 11, 12 (p. 75)

Mattmo Concept + Design, Amsterdam
tel: +31 20 420 6773
fax: +31 20 639 0005
internet: www.mattmo.nl
figs. 6-9 (p. 75)

Shape bv, Amsterdam
tel: +31 20 622 0606
fax: +31 20 622 5355
figs. 2 (p. 74); 20 (p. 77)

Total Design Amsterdam bv, Amsterdam
tel: +31 20 578 9638
fax: +31 20 578 9621
e-mail: hpb@totaldesign.nl
fig. 10 (p. 75)

Uittenhout Design Studio, Wijk en Aalburg
tel: +31 416 692 507
fax: +31 416 692 857
e-mail: uittenhout@uittenhout.nl
internet: www.uittenhout.nl
figs. 13, 14 (p. 76)

NORWAY
Bryce Bennett Communications, Sofiemyr
tel: +47 66 80 0410
fax: +47 66 80 0411
e-mail: bryce@bryce.no
fig. 5 (p. 81)

Griffin, Aina, Oslo
tel: +47 22 80 5470
fax: +47 22 80 5471
e-mail: aina.griffin@orgdot.com
figs. 1-4 (p. 80); 6, 7 (p. 81)

POLAND
Adamczyk, Miroslaw, Poznan
email:
miroslaw.adamczyk@paleta.asp.poznan.pl
figs. 1, 2 (p. 84)

Ammirati Puris Lintas Warsaw, Warsaw
tel: +48 22 848 3131
fax: +48 22 848 8155
e-mail: aplB@mail.pol.pl
figs. 3-5 (p. 84)

Atelier Tadeusz Piechura, Lodz
tel: +48 42 6544 633
fax: +48 42 6544 633
figs. 12, 13 (p. 85)

Corporate Profiles DDB, Warsaw
tel: +48 22 560 3400
fax: +48 22 560 3401
e-mail: cpddb@cpddb.it.pl
figs. 16-20 (p. 86)

Definition Design Sp. zo.o, Warsaw
tel/fax: +48 22 616 0614/ 616 0615
e-mail: defdes@imac.use.pl
figs. 32, 33 (p. 87)

Drukarnia "Modena", Gdynia
tel: +48 58 621 4412
fax: +48 58 621 4414 ext. 112
e-mail: modena@key.net.pl
fig. 10 (p. 85)

KOREK Studio, Warsaw
tel: +48 22 817 0160
fax: +48 22 817 0294
e-mail: korek@atcom.net.pl
figs. 11 (p. 85); 21 (p. 86)

Leo Burnett Sp. zo.o, Warsaw
tel: +48 22 860 9800
fax: +48 22 860 9801
e-mail: lbw@leoburnett.com.pl
figs. 6-8 (p. 84)

Moby Dick Group, Szczecin
tel/fax: +48 91 423 3742
e-mail: mobydick@mobydick.com.pl
fig. 28 (p. 87)

Studio PK, Lodz
tel: +48 42 630 4172
e-mail: studiopk@asp.lodz.pl
fig. 29 (p. 87)

Studio Pro, Torun
tel: +48 56 654 9229
fax: +48 56 661 6921
e-mail: studiopro@studiopro.com.pl
figs. 14, 15 (p. 85)

VFP Communications, Warsaw
tel: +48 22 848 39 22
fax: +48 22 849 7808
e-mail: mpsales@media.com.pl
figs. 23-27 (p. 86); 30, 31 (p. 87)

Zdanowicz & Pawrowski, Poznan
tel: +48 61 855 7347
fax: +48 61 855 7384
e-mail: z-i-p@post.pl
fig. 86 (p. 22)

PORTUGAL
Alves, Nuno, Lisbon
VIEW
tel: +351 21 351 1930
fax: +351 21 351 1934
e-mail: nuno.alves@view.pt
figs. 18 (p. 92); 20, 23 (p. 93)

A&L Criatividade é Comunicação,
S. João Estoril
tel: +351 21 466 7180
fax: +351 21 466 7189
e-mail: a.l@mail.telepac.pt
figs. 7, 8 (p. 91)

Artlandia Design, Lisbon
tel: +351 21 387 1163
fax: +351 21 387 1652
e-mail: artlandia@mail.telepac.pt
fig. 19 (p. 92)

HPP Comunicação, Lisbon
tel: +351 21 385 6610
fax: +351 21 385 6660
e-mail: hppcom@mail.telepac.pt
fig. 4 (p. 90)

João Machado Design, Lda, Oporto
tel: +351 22 610 3772
fax: +351 22 610 3773
e-mail:
jmachado.design@mail.telepac.pt
figs. 22 (p. 93); 24-29 (p. 94)

Novodesign-SA, Lisbon
tel: +351 21 392 3000
fax: +351 21 395 3849
e-mail: novodesign@novodesign.pt
figs. 5, 6 (p. 91)

Pink Design, Vila Nova de Gaia
tel: +351 22 379 2295
figs. 12-16 (p. 92)

R2 Design, Matosinhos
tel: +351 22 938 6865
fax: +351 22 938 9482
e-mail: r2design@mail.telepac.pt
internet: www.rdois.com
figs. 10, 11 (p. 91)

Ricardo Mealha Atelier, Lisbon
tel: +351 21 382 5340
fax: +351 21 385 6274
e-mail: centra@esoterica.pt
figs. 3 (p. 90); 17 (p. 92); 21 (p. 93)

Setezeroum Design, Oporto
tel: +351 22 508 9601
fax: +351 22 550 687
e-mail: setezeroum@mail.telepac.pt
figs. 1, 2 (p. 90); 9 (p. 91)

RUSSIA
Kusnetzov, Denis & Melnikova, Gelena,
Moscow
tel/fax: +7 95 242 6625
email: info@profdesign.ru
internet: www.profdesign.ru
figs. 1-5 (p. 96)

SLOVENIA
A±B (in Exile), Ljubljana
tel/fax: +386 61 136 8051
e-mail: eduard.cehovin@siol.net
figs. 5-9 (p. 98); 13 (p. 99)

DELO, d.d., Ljubljana
tel: +386 61 173 7579
e-mail: dusan.brajic@delo.si
fig. 3 (p. 98)

Kompas Design, d.d., Ljubljana
tel: +386 61 324 391
fax: +386 61 318 197
e-mail: info@kompas-design.si
fig. 4 (p. 98)

Kraft & Werk, Maribor
tel: +386 62 229 7560
fax: +386 62 229 7561
e-mail: kraft-werk@siol.net
fig. 11 (p. 99)

KROG, Ljubljana
tel/fax: +386 61 126 5761
e-mail: edi.berk@krog.si
figs. 10, 12, 14, 15 (p. 99)

"MM" (Marketing Magazine), Ljubljana
tel: +386 61 173 7403
fax: +386 61 173 7407
e-mail: mm@delo.si
figs. 1, 2 (p. 98)

SPAIN
Lamosca, Barcelona
tel: +34 93 441 0100
e-mail: info@lamosca.com
internet: www.lamosca.com
figs. 1-3 (p. 102)

Morera Shining SL, Barcelona
tel: +34 93 303 6990
fax: +34 93 266 0415
e-mail: shining@shiningdesign.com
fig. 7 (p. 103)

Pepe Gimeno - Proyecto Grafico,
Godella (Valencia)
tel: +34 96 390 4074
fax: +34 96 390 4076
e-mail: gimeno@ctv.es
figs. 4-6 (p. 103)

SWEDEN
Ahlqvist & Co Reklambyrå AB, Malmö
tel: +46 40 167 400
fax: +46 40 160 578
e-mail: post@ahlqvist-co.se
figs. 41-43 (p. 110)

Björkman & Mitchell AB, Stockholm
tel: +46 8 702 2367
fax: +46 8 702 2233
e-mail: klas@bjorkman-mitchell.se
fig. 50 (p. 111)

Fenix Reklambyrå AB, Gothenburg
tel: +46 31 131413
fax: +46 31 131010
e-mail: joakim@fenixreklambyra.se
internet: www.fenixreklambyra.se
fig. 7 (p. 106)

Forsman & Bodenfors Design, Gothenburg
tel: +46 31 176 730
fax: +46 31 138 353
e-mail: mail@fb.se
figs. 8, 9 (p. 106); 26 (p. 108); 35-37 (p. 109); 44, 45 (p. 110); 48 (p. 111)

Graceland Sthlm, Stockholm
tel: +46 8 545 152 39
fax: +46 8 545 152 31
e-mail: henrik@graceland-sthlm.com
fig. 51 (p. 111)

Jerlov & Company, Gothenburg
tel: +46 31 774 4300
fax: +46 31 774 4320
e-mail:
camilla.braberg@jerlov-company.se
figs. 28-30 (p. 108); 38, 39 (p. 109)

Kurppa Design, Stockholm
tel: +46 8 669 4994
fax: +46 8 669 4666
email: kurppa@algonet.se
fig. 27 (p. 108)

LOG Kommunikation, Stockholm
tel: +46 8 653 7777
fax: +46 8 653 0737
e-mail: anna.markevarn@log.se
figs. 19, 20 (p. 107)

Rehnberg, Lars, Stockholm
tel: +46 8 22 2950
fax: +46 8 545 17115
e-mail: lars@stockholmillustration.com
figs. 1-6, 10 (p. 106); 13-18 (p. 107)

Satama Interactive, Stockholm
tel: +46 8 506 12410
fax: +46 8 506 12439
e-mail: pija.sundin@satama.com
figs. 31, 32 (p. 108)

Skarbovik, Lasse, Stockholm
tel: +46 8 22 2433
fax: +46 8 545 17115
e-mail:
lasse@stockholmillustration.com
figs. 40 (p. 110); 47, 49 (p. 111)

Sköld Lindau, Annika, Stockholm
tel: +46 8 22 2149
fax: +46 8 545 17115
e-mail:
annika@stockholmillustration.com
figs. 12, 21, 22 (p. 107); 33 (p. 109)

Studio Bubblan AB, Borås
tel: +46 33 414 441
fax: +46 33 132 968
e-mail: kari@bubblan.se
fig. 11 (p. 106)

Tennis, Anyone?, Gothenburg
tel: +46 31 106 060
fax: +46 31 106 070
e-mail: linda@tennisanyone.se
figs. 23-25 (p. 107); 46 (p. 110)

Wognum, Stockholm
tel: +46 8 545 12222
fax: +46 8 545 12233
e-mail: nina@wognum.se
fig. 34 (p. 109)

SWITZERLAND
Advertising, Art & Ideas, Zürich
tel: +41 1 487 4087
fax: +41 1 487 4088
e-mail: info@adart.ch
internet: www.adart.ch
fig. 19 (p. 117)

Bildinfarkt GmbH für Visuelle Gestaltung,
Kloten
tel: +41 1 813 3656
fax: +41 1 813 5196
e-mail: bildinfarkt@swissonline.ch
fig. 18 (p. 117)

Jeanmaire & Michel Kommunikations - und
Werbeagentur AB, Bern
tel: +41 31 327 8080
fax: +41 31 327 8081
e-mail: agentur@agentur.ch
internet: www.agentur.ch
figs. 1, 2 (p. 114); 10 (p. 115)

Külling + Partner Identity, Zürich
tel: +41 1 253 8888
fax: +41 1 253 8899
e-mail: kpi@kpi-identity.ch
fig. 17 (p. 117)

Plojoux, Florance, Geneva
tel: +41 22 345 8760
e-mail: plojoux.flo@span.ch
figs. 4-9 (p. 115)

Weber, Hodel, Schmid AG, Zürich
tel: +41 1 405 4455
fax: +41 1 405 4466
internet: www.whs.ch
figs. 11-14, 15 (p. 116); 16 (p. 117)

Wild & Frey, Agentur für Design, Zürich
tel: +41 1 280 0898
fax: +41 1 280 0899
e-mail: office@wildfrey.ch
fig. 3 (p. 114)

TURKEY
RPM/Radar CDP Europe, Istanbul
tel: +90 212 227 9777
fax: +90 212 227 9757
e-mail: rpmradar@turk.net
figs. 1, 2 (p. 118)

UK
Addison, London
tel: +44 20 7403 7444
fax: +44 20 7403 1243
e-mail: sam.hannam@addison.co.uk
internet: www.addison.co.uk
figs. 30 (p. 126); 73 (p. 134)

Blackburn's Ltd, London
tel: +44 20 7734 7646
fax: +44 20 7437 0017
e-mail: caroline@blackburns.ltd.uk
figs. 39 (p. 128); 71 (p. 133)

Conran Design Group, London
tel: +44 20 7566 4566
fax: +44 20 7566 4555
e-mail: cdg@conrandesigngroup.com
internet: www.conrandesigngroup.com
figs. 40, 41 (p. 128)

Dew Gibbons, London
tel: +44 20 7388 3377
fax: +44 20 7388 1122
e-mail: shaun@dewgibbons.com
figs. 66 (p. 132); 72 (p. 133)

e-fact.limited, London
tel: +44 20 7880 4700
fax: +44 20 7880 4799
e-mail: mail@e-fact.com
fig. 78 (p. 134)

Ergo: Identity Consultants, London
tel: +44 20 7602 6022
fax: +44 20 7603 6333
e-mail: hannah@ergo-id.co.uk
internet: www.ergo-id.co.uk
figs. 45, 46 (p. 129)

Fold 7, London
tel: +44 20 7251 0101
fax: +44 20 7251 0202
e-mail: henry@fold7.co.uk
fig. 75 (p. 134)

Ford, Wayne, London
tel: +44 20 7713 4212
fax: +44 20 7239 9837
e-mail: wayne.ford@observer.co.uk
figs. 48, 49 (p. 129); 50 (p. 130)

FOUR IV Design Consultants Ltd, London
tel: +44 20 7837 8659
fax: +44 20 7837 8679
e-mail: design@fouriv.com
fig. 53 (p. 130)

Frost Design Ltd, London
tel: +44 20 7490 7994
fax: +44 20 7490 7995
e-mail: info@frostdesign.demon.co.uk
internet: www.frostdesign.co.uk
fig. 4 (p. 120); 34, 35 (p. 127); 60, 61 (p. 131)

Futurebrand Davies Baron, London
tel: +44 20 7556 9800
fax: +44 20 7734 0291
e-mail: cchallis@futurebrand.com
figs. 10-12 (p. 124)

Gowdy, Caroline, London
tel: +44 20 7731 5380
fig. 63 (p. 132)

Graham Pritchard Design, London
tel: +44 20 8766 8922
e-mail: graham@geevee.demon.co.uk
fig. 3 (p. 122)

HGV, London
tel: +44 20 7278 4449
fax: +44 20 7837 4666
internet: www.hgv.co.uk (under construction)
figs. 14, 15 (p. 124); 16-19, 20 (p. 125); 29 (p. 126); 31, 33 (p. 127); 44 (p. 129)

Lewis Moberly, London
tel: +44 20 7580 9252
fax: +44 20 7255 1671
e-mail: lewismoberly@enterprise.net
fig. 5 (p. 122); 6 (p. 123); 28 (p. 126); 32 (p. 127)

Lippa Pearce Design Ltd, Twickenham
tel: +44 20 8744 2100
fax: +44 20 8744 2770
e-mail:
abi.overd@lippapearcedesign.com
figs. 21 (p. 125); 52 (p. 130); 55 (p. 130)

MetaDesign London, London
tel: +44 20 7520 1000
fax: +44 20 7520 1099
e-mail: ljones@metadesign.co.uk
internet: www.metadesign.co.uk
figs. 68-70 (p. 133)

Michael Nash Associates, London
tel: +44 20 7631 3370
fax: +44 20 7637 9629
e-mail: wendy@michaelnash.co.uk
fig. 23 (p. 125)

Mildenberger, Esther, London / Bühl
tel/fax: +44 20 7923 1546 / +49 7223 999 095
e-mail: emildenberger@hotmail.com
fig. 74 (p. 134)

Mytton Williams, Bath
tel: +44 1225 442634
fax: +44 1225 442639
e-mail: design@myttonwilliams.co.uk
internet: www.myttonwilliams.co.uk
fig. 24 (p. 126)

Navy Blue Design Consultants, London
tel: +44 20 7253 0316
fax: +44 20 7553 9409
e-mail: geoff@navyblue.com
internet: www.navyblue
figs. 25-27 (p. 126)

Nick Eagleton Design, London
tel: +44 20 7700 0235
fax: +44 20 7700 3542
e-mail: ne@eagleton.netkonect.co.uk
fig. 36 (p. 127)

Oyster Partners Ltd, London
tel: +44 20 7446 7500
fax: +44 20 7446 7555
e-mail: start@oyster.co.uk
internet: www.oyster.co.uk
figs. 64, 65 (p. 132)

Paper White Ltd, London
tel: +44 20 7401 8358
fax: +44 20 7401 8357
e-mail: post@paperwhite.co.uk
internet: www.paperwhite.co.uk
figs. 57-59 (p. 131)

Pearlfisher, London
tel: +44 20 7603 8666
fax: +44 20 7603 1208
e-mail: jonathan@pearlfisher.co.uk
fig. 22 (p. 125)

Richards, Lucy, Edinburgh
tel/fax: +44 131 555 5400
e-mail: person@easynet.co.uk
figs. 76, 77 (p. 134)

Roundel, London
tel: +44 20 7221 1951
fax: +44 20 7221 1843
e-mail: info@roundel.com
internet: www.roundel.com
figs. 7, 8 (p. 123)

Saatchi & Saatchi Design, London
tel: +44 20 7307 5327
fax: +44 20 7307 5238
e-mail: saatchi@saatchi-design.com
fig. 9 (p. 123)

Struktur Design, London
tel: +44 20 7833 5626
fax: +44 20 7833 5636
e-mail: struktur@easynet.co.uk
fig. 56 (p. 131)

TBWA, London
tel: +44 20 7573 7147
fax: +44 20 7637 5504
e-mail: paul.belford@tbwa-europe.com
figs. 42 (p. 128); 47 (p. 129)

Thirst Design + Marketing, Odiham
tel: +44 1256 701 401
fax: +44 1256 701 331
e-mail: thirst@odiham.netkonect.co.uk
internet: www.thirst-design.co.uk
www.thirst-e.com
figs. 1, 2 (p. 123)

Thirteen, Isleworth
tel/fax: +44 029 2025 3767
fig. 54 (p. 130)

Trickett & Webb Ltd, London
tel: +44 20 7388 5832
fax: +44 20 7387 4287
e-mail: lynn@tricketts.co.uk
internet: www.tricketts.co.uk
www.tricketts.co.uk/calendar/index.html
figs. 43 (p. 129); 51 (p. 130); 62 (p. 132); 67 (p. 133)

Turner Duckworth, London
tel: +44 20 8994 7190
fax: +44 20 8994 7192
e-mail: bruce@turnerduckworth.co.uk
www.turnerduckworth.com
figs. 13 (p. 124); 37, 38 (p. 128)

YUGOSLAVIA
Focus Communications, Belgrade
(also Celje, Slovenia)
e-mail: igorfocus@yahoo.com
fig. 4 (p. 136)

Kapitanj, Atila, Novi Sad
tel: +381 21 332 058
e-mail: postoic@eunet.yu
fig. 5 (p. 136)

New Moment Design - Ideas Campus,
Belgrade
tel: +381 11 322 9992
fax: +381 11 620 560
e-mail: info@sd-newmoment.si
figs. 1-3, 7, 8 (p. 136)